WELLS, FARGO DETECTIVE

WELLS, FARGO
DETECTIVE

The Biography of James B. Hume

by RICHARD DILLON

New Foreword by
Roger D. McGrath

RENO : UNIVERSITY OF NEVADA PRESS : 1986

VINTAGE WEST SERIES EDITOR

ROBERT E. BLESSE

Wells, Fargo Detective: The Biography of James B. Hume, by Richard Dillon, was originally published in 1969 by Coward-McCann, Inc., of New York. The present volume reproduces the original edition except for the following changes: the front matter has been modified to reflect the new publisher, and a foreword to the new edition, by Roger D. McGrath, has been added. The cover art is reproduced from an oil painting, "Staging in California," by J. Gutzon Borglum, courtesy of the Joslyn Art Museum, Omaha, Nebraska.

Library of Congress Cataloging-in-Publication Data

Dillon, Richard H.
  Wells, Fargo detective.

  (Vintage West series)
  Reprint. Originally published: New York :
Coward-McCann, 1969
  Bibliography: p.
  Includes index.
  1. Hume, James B., 1827–1904. 2. Detectives—
United States—Biography. 3. Wells, Fargo & Company.
I. Title. II. Series.
HV7911.H8D5 1986   363.2'89'0924 [B]   86–11304
ISBN 0-87417-113-X (pbk. : alk. paper)

The paper used in this book meets the requirements of American National Standard for Information Sciences—Permanence of Paper for Printed Library Materials, ANSI Z39.48-1984. The binding is sewn for strength and durability.

UNIVERSITY OF NEVADA PRESS, RENO, NEVADA 89557 USA
COPYRIGHT © RICHARD DILLON 1986. ALL RIGHTS RESERVED
COVER DESIGN BY DAVE COMSTOCK
PRINTED IN THE UNITED STATES OF AMERICA

For

RALPH MOODY

FOREWORD TO THE NEW EDITION

RICHARD DILLON is a historian who writes often and writes well. He has authored more than fifteen books and has garnered several literary honors including the James D. Phelan Award, the Gold Medal of the Commonwealth Club of California, and the Spur Award of the Western Writers of America. The first and foremost job of any historian is to tell a good story and to tell that story without sacrificing accuracy. Dillon does just that. His works are always readable, fast-paced, and lively. Moreover, his research skills are invariably evident: much of his work is based on primary sources. But then he knows his way around a library and he knows how to pick his way through a manuscript collection. For nearly thirty years he was librarian of the Sutro Library in San Francisco.

How anyone could be both a head librarian and, at the same time, such a prolific author of serious, well-researched nonfiction (as well as being a husband and the father of three sons) is a mystery that perhaps he will reveal in his memoirs. Technology is not the answer. Neither the computer nor the typewriter is his servant. He does all his work in longhand. The answer may lie in his heritage. All of his grandparents were Irish immigrants, and perhaps he has the blood of a *seanachie* flowing in his veins. From the time of Finn MacCool and before, the *seanachie* or historian was one of the most revered figures in Gaelic Ireland.

When *Wells, Fargo Detective* was first published in 1969, it was one of only a handful of books that dealt with the detective in the Old West. It still is. William Collier's *Dave Cook of the Rockies,* David J. Cook's *Hands Up: Twenty Years of Detective Life in the Mountains and on the Plains,* Fred Dodge's *Undercover for Wells, Fargo: The Unvarnished Recollections of Fred Dodge,* Thomas Furlong's *Fifty Years a Detective,* James D. Horan's *The Pinkerton Story,* and Charles Siringo's *Two Evil Isms: Pinkertonism and Anarchism* are the only other works that focus on the detective of the frontier. Moreover, it should be noted that except for the books by Collier and Horan, these works are literature of reminiscence—the personal recollections of the authors—rather than scholarly studies.

Why so little has been written about the detective, a fascinating and important figure in western law enforcement, is another mystery. As late as 1983 Richard Maxwell Brown, the author of *Strain of Violence: Historical Studies of American Violence and Vigilantism,* said that a "dimension of legal law enforcement in the West that cries out for scholarly investigation is the activities of the private detective agencies." Richard Dillon is one of the few who have done such an investigation. Furthermore, he is the only one to have looked at James B. Hume, probably the most important of the detectives operating in the West and certainly the foremost detective that the Wells, Fargo Company ever employed.

Born in New York and raised on an Indiana farm, Jim Hume rebelled against his dour and unbending Scots Presbyterian father and headed overland to California in 1850. He was soon prospecting in the Mother Lode country and would continue to do so for ten years, although he never had more than moderate success. After serving briefly as a deputy sheriff and as a tax collector in El Dorado County, Hume was appointed city marshal of Placerville, the county seat, in 1862. The job mostly saw Hume collecting license fees, supervising street cleaning, and having dogs tagged; the county sheriff handled the important cases. Nonetheless, at the age of thirty-five Hume had finally found a career.

In 1864 Hume became the under sheriff of El Dorado County and experienced his first gun battle when he and his deputies attempted to capture the Ike McCollum gang. Shortly after that incident one of his deputies surprised a group of Confederate sympathizers who had robbed a stage at Bullion Bend and was killed in an exchange of gunfire. The loss, as a contemporary report said, left Hume "frantic with grief and rage." It also left him virtually obsessed, determined to bring the culprits to justice. Like the legendary Mountie of the Royal Canadian Mounted Police, Hume always got his man.

Not until 1873, after he had solved several important criminal cases and had served as the deputy warden of the Nevada State Prison, did Hume become Wells, Fargo's chief detective. He was forty-six years old at the time but would serve the company for thirty years. Although younger detectives took over much of his case load during his last year or two of service, he continued to be actively involved in criminal investigation until a few months before his death in 1904 at the age of seventy-seven. Throughout his career Hume was known as a square-shooter by both lawmen and outlaws. Several outlaws looked upon Hume not as an enemy but as an adversary. Hume often humorously noted that nowhere was his personal standing higher than among residents of the San Quentin and Folsom prisons.

Hume's years with Wells, Fargo—during which he encountered such highwaymen as Milton Sharp, Dick Fellows, and Black Bart and helped make criminal investigation a science—as well as his years as a prospector and those as a sheriff are vividly and intimately recounted by Richard Dillon. The vividness of description comes from Dillon's talent as a writer, and the personal quality is a result of Dillon's use of Hume's own manuscript collection, which is housed in the History Room of the Wells Fargo Bank in San Francisco. Hume evidently intended to write an autobiography one day and, in preparation for such an undertaking, he neatly filed all his own letters and telegrams and filled scrapbooks with newspaper clippings of his achievements and photographs of his favorite highwaymen. Even Hume's clumsy letters to his bride-to-be, a young schoolmarm nearly thirty years his junior, are in the collection.

Dillon's important contribution to the history of the Old West and to the history of western lawmen and detectives has aged well. It is still must reading for scholars and buffs alike.

UNIVERSITY OF CALIFORNIA,   ROGER D. McGRATH
LOS ANGELES

ACKNOWLEDGMENTS

M Y particular gratitude goes to Irene Simpson, director of the History Room of the Wells, Fargo Bank in San Francisco, for her splendid research help, and to her aides Elaine Gilleran, Merrilee Gwerder, and Ann Redl. Thanks are also due to others, mainly: Hubert and Nathaniel Wyckoff, Joe Rosa, Dr. William N. Davis, Beverly L. Levenson, J. L. McPheeters, Dr. Ben F. Gilbert, John Porter Bloom, R. Coke Wood, Allan R. Ottley, Robert Klassen, Miriam Meyer Pike, Clyde Arbuckle, Dorothy Firebaugh, Sibley S. Morrill, E. B. (Pete) Long, Stuart Nixon, Nita Spangler, Carlo M. DeFerrari, Robert Greenwood, Newton Baird, Dr. Oscar Winther, C. E. Dornsbusch, Roger Rees, George D. Gavin, Bruce M. King, Daniel D. Holt, George D. Gavin, Thomas H. Peterson, Frederick C. Gale, Waddell Smith, Marion Welliver, Myrtle Myles, Donald Bowers, Donald T. Clark, Nancy Bowers, Rita Berner, James Abajian, Maude K. Swingle, Thelma J. Rowlison, Harold Hamill, Dr. Leo Stanley, Stewart Mitchell, Howard Davidson, Caroline Dunn, Corlee Deal, Lillian Countryman, Helen McTaggart, Charlotte Tufts, Gladys Ladu, William Ramirez, Gladys Hansen, John D. Gilchriese, James J. Heslin, Frances B. McDonald, William G. Tyrell, and my fellow authors Ralph Moody, Robert West Howard, Ferol Egan, and David Myrick.

9

CONTENTS

11

INTRODUCTION

THE express business was founded in the United States by William F. Harnden and the brothers B. D. and L. B. Earle, all operating between New York and Boston *circa* 1835. Later Harnden's Albany agent was Henry Wells, born in Thetford, Vermont, who won a kind of regional fame by expressing in Buffalo's first fresh oysters. The whole world would eventually be his particular oyster.

In 1850 he joined with William G. Fargo of Onondaga County, New York, to form the American Express Company. Two years later, the partners sat down, and like Spain and Portugal at the Treaty of Tordesillas, carving the world up between them, Wells and Fargo boldly divided the United States into two spheres of express hegemony. American Express, the parent company, was to take all business in the East; its newborn scion, Wells, Fargo & Company, was to handle all express from the Missouri and Mississippi rivers to the Pacific shore.

To catch up with well-established Adams & Company in San Francisco, Wells, Fargo cut New York-California express rates via Panama from 75 cents a pound (minimum weight) on packages up to 15 pounds to 40 cents. (A small daguerreotype—until Wells, Fargo arrived on the scene—might cost $3 to send to California from the East Coast, and it was said that an ordinary-size novel could run to as much as $12 in express charges.) Wells,

Fargo in 1852, however, was small potatoes, indeed, when compared to Adams & Company, whose gold shipment East that year was $600,000; Wells, Fargo's (its first), $21,000.

A little more than two and a half years after Wells, Fargo opened its headquarters (July 1, 1852) in Sam Brannan's fireproof brick building on Montgomery Street, San Francisco, a financial panic struck the city. The Ohio and Mississippi Railroad failure knocked down—domino fashion—the St. Louis banking house of Page & Bacon, its subsidiary, Page, Bacon & Company of San Francisco, and the latter's associate in banking and express, Adams & Company. Though the parent firm continued in the East and Midwest as the Adams Express Company, the San Francisco firm failed completely. Wells, Fargo, via skillful management of its resources, weathered Black Friday—February 23, 1855—although it had temporarily to close its banking departments in San Francisco and Sacramento. It celebrated its surprise victory over its rival by moving to finer quarters, the Parrott Building, constructed by Chinese masons of stone blocks quarried in China. Wells, Fargo replaced as a tenant none other than Adams & Company.

The young firm quickly demonstrated its solvency to the business community and earned such tributes as the following from the Shasta *Courier:* "Wells, Fargo & Company stood the shock without exhibiting the least quivering. They have, in consequence, the confidence of the entire commercial portion of the state." Wells, Fargo had already bought up such small express firms as Gregory's, Todd's, and Hunter's; now it contracted with the near monopoly in staging, the California Stage Company, and, unlike Adams & Company, began to establish permanent branches on the major trade routes of the Far West. By 1857 Wells, Fargo had 87 express agencies in the West; by 1859 there were 126 between Canada and Mexico. In 1861 the company took over the financially ailing Pony Express. Soon, Wells, Fargo was winning new friends by bringing the first block ice to thirsty Los Angelenos and delivering firkins of reasonably fresh Vermont butter to the miners of the Mother Lode and even to Nevada. Wells, Fargo's "fast-freights" hauled mundane supplies—food, tools, liquor, clothing—while the express shipments took care of what was commonly termed treasure in the nineteenth century—gold dust and nuggets, currency, drafts and notes, coin, and gold and silver bullion. The company used Concord stages, railroad cars, Sacramento River steamboats, clipper ships, and ocean steamers. Wells, Fargo was flourishing with fast-freight rates between San Francisco and Nevada of 7 cents a pound and express rates of 12 cents a pound in 1867. Between San Francisco and Salt Lake City these rose to 50 cents and 60 cents respectively.

It is commonly said that Nevada silver and California gold saved the Union. It was Wells, Fargo that guarded and delivered the precious metals. According to Wells, Fargo historian Lucius Beebe, the company earned some $12,000,000 in Nevada freight charges alone in the year 1864.

In the West, Wells, Fargo replaced the expressman's carpetbag or trunk with a sturdy, green-painted, wooden box bound with strap iron and sealed with a hasp and a lock—the chest that has come to be almost a trademark for Wells, Fargo & Company. Only company agents at each end of a stage run had keys to the chest; no drivers or shotgun guards were given keys, so road agents had to shoot, chisel, ax, or dynamite the lock off to get at the strongbox's contents. A waybill, or book of waybills, was enclosed with the valuables in the box. If a bandit robbed a stage and made off with the box, without discarding the waybill, the sender agent would make up a duplicate of this invoice or bill of lading for the intended recipient agent, which Wells, Fargo detectives would copy in order to forward their investigations. It was a simple system of control, but it worked. Later, as bandits became more familiar with the system, Wells, Fargo replaced the wooden boxes with iron ones bolted to the stagecoaches. Dynamite then became a must for a successful holdup.

The growth of Wells, Fargo was continuous. Its 156 agencies of 1863 became 573 by 1880 and 2,830 by 1892. Its policy was to make good to shippers, instantly, all losses in transit and to trust to its detective force not only to catch the culprit but to recover enough of the loot to get the books to balance. And it succeeded. Wells, Fargo paid dividends which made other joint-stock companies turn jade green with envy—never less than 6 percent between 1872 and 1902, often 8, 10 or 12 percent, and, once, in 1860, an incredible 18-percent return. From 1852 on, Wells, Fargo competed with the United States government in delivering the mails in the West, even erecting its own private mailboxes on San Francisco street corners and establishing a fast intracity mail, for messages and small parcels, by a pony express. Its West-wide mail service was better than the Post Office's even before the Wells, Fargo general agent for California, Louis McLane, pioneered the use of franked (prepaid) mail instead of following the old custom of the recipient's paying, on delivery, for his letters. Within a decade the sale of Wells, Fargo envelopes was netting an income of $5,000 a month. In 1864 the company bought 125,000 3-cent stamps and 2,250,000 3-cent-stamped envelopes from the U.S. government to sell to individuals after adding its own frank and marking up the price to 10 cents, thus guaranteeing speedy delivery. So successful was Wells, Fargo as mailman that when the U.S. government investigated the company in 1879 on charges of seeking a mail monopoly in the West, all the charges were quashed because of the angry outcry from satisfied businessmen.

When Wells, Fargo bought Holladay's Overland Mail and Express Company (1866) from the "Stagecoach King," Ben Holladay, for $1,500,000 in cash and $300,000 in Wells, Fargo stock, it acquired control of all passenger and express forwarding avenues worthy of the name west of the Missouri. Wells, Fargo gambled. With the completion of the Central Pacific-Union Pacific railroad line only three years later, it appeared that Wells, Fargo had lost on its gamble; its stock plummeted from $100 a share to $13. Next, the company was subjected to what has been called "the biggest holdup of them all," which took place not on some lonely Sierra stage road but in Omaha, Nebraska, on October 4, 1869. The Big Four—nabobs of the Central Pacific—blandly informed Wells, Fargo that they had contracted with their stooge

16

company, Darius O. Mills' and Lloyd Tevis' Pacific Union Express (of whose stock Central Pacific owned three-fifths) to have exclusive express rights on the overland railroad. This complot, leaving Wells, Fargo only the dwindling stagecoach feeder lines, would have ruined the company. Wells, Fargo gave in to the hijacking, managed to increase its capital from $10,000,000 to $15,000,000 and handed over $5,000,000 to buy out Pacific Union Express, largely a fancy letterhead. By these strenuous efforts, Wells, Fargo managed to stay alive and survive the rapacity of the Big Four, but by 1872 Lloyd Tevis was president of the express company (remaining so for twenty years), and the board included such financial banditti as Leland Stanford and skinflint C. P. Huntington.

Still, Wells, Fargo *did* survive, and it continued to grow until its chief of detectives had a beat that extended as far as Chicago, on the Santa Fe Railroad, and New Orleans, on the Southern Pacific. Eventually, when it absorbed the Erie Express Company in 1888, Wells, Fargo reached New York and became the first true transcontinental express company. By 1875 *Harper's* was suggesting that the express business in the United States had created fifty millionaires. Wells, Fargo was preeminent in the West from 1855 until 1917, when the government took over the operation of the nation's express companies, as well as of its railroads. Today Wells, Fargo confines itself to banking from its old San Francisco headquarters, but the ambience of its many flourishing branches suggests the express offices of yesteryear.

Because Wells, Fargo was handling such immense sums—shipping, for example, 15 tons of gold out of the Sonora, California, office between 1858 and 1861, and a *single* shipment of 900 pounds, worth $90,000, in 1879, and moving $14,907,894 in bullion from Nevada to San Francisco in the one year of 1866—it early attracted bandits, whose cry, "Throw down the box!" was the New World echo of Dick Turpin's classic "Stand and deliver!" Express rates on treasure soared as stage robbers increased until, in 1864 for example, Wells, Fargo charged 4½ percent to carry $1,000 or more in gold from Boise, Idaho Territory, to San Fran-

17

cisco, and 5½ percent for sums under $1,000. Pegging the cost of express shipments did nothing to deter bandits, of course, but the company took care of that matter, too.

In 1873, Wells, Fargo engaged one of the best lawmen in California, James B. Hume, ex-sheriff of El Dorado County, to head its detective bureau. He was its chief special officer from 1873 until his death in 1904. Although Hume was courageous enough and tough as a treenail, he differed mainly from his star-bearing colleagues in that he was a thoroughly professional law officer who sought the orderly arrest, trial and conviction of a guilty party rather than a shoot-out in a dusty street. It was no case of "set a thief to catch a thief" as in some of the Kansas cow towns. Diligently and patiently, he trained himself in the infant science of crime detection, as opposed to the mere apprehension of criminals, and pioneered that science in the early West. Lucius Beebe recalled that Hume, in digging buckshot out of a dead stage horse after the September, 1878, robbery of the down coach on the Yreka-Redding run, was an early practitioner of ballistics. Hume compared the pellets with those he took from a suspected highwayman and sent the fellow up. And Hume's efforts were amply rewarded as he put desperado after desperado behind bars in this fashion, among them the notorious Black Bart.

In the 1880's, while involved in a quarrel with his onetime chief William H. Rogers, whom Jim had served as under sheriff of El Dorado County, Hume understated, considerably, the confidence in which he was held by the company's management. He modestly ventured that his work since 1873 had been "presumably, to their entire satisfaction, as my salary has been increased from time to time, without any importunities by me, until it is now decidedly liberal. I have reason to believe that I enjoy the entire confidence of the Company, for they require no bonds and I am yearly entrusted with hundreds of thousands of dollars of their money."

Hume was, in fact, a highly successful detective. One reason for this was that he could enjoy the luxury of single-mindedness in his investigations, at least until the whole continent became his "beat" and his workload became overwhelming. Where a sheriff would have to give up on a case in order to attend to pressing new business, the more selective Hume could pursue tenaciously every trail and every clue, like a bulldog crossed with a bloodhound. Moreover, he could roam at will throughout the state—and beyond—because of his special status. He enjoyed the close cooperation of all law enforcement men (except a few who were jealous of his fame). The sheriff of Sacramento County could not make an arrest, normally, in Yolo County unless in hot pursuit of criminals, but Hume was not hindered by county lines. He was something like the FBI agent of today; he always kept local officers informed and worked in conjunction with them. California local politics often made rivals of adjoining county seats and their officials, but not in Jim Hume's relationships with sheriffs and district attorneys. He was probably sworn in as a deputy when working in a particular county, to make it easier to secure warrants from a magistrate, serve them, and make arrests. He usually let a local officer make the arrest and always, if possible, was accompanied by a local officer when a search or arrest was anticipated.

Between 1870 and 1900 the entire climate of law enforcement was very different—especially in the Far West—from today's. A suspect was then considered guilty until proved innocent, and peace officers had much more leeway in their actions than today, because of a lack of civil rights legislation to protect citizens from the abuse, real or potential, of police authority. We cannot judge the past by the standards of the present. But if we were to do so, we would probably accuse James B. Hume of forcible entry and illegal search and arrest, though not of police brutality. Policemen's powers were so liberally interpreted in Victorian times that a suspect, guilty or innocent, would usually comply meekly with the orders of a lawman.

Besides the climate of the times, Wells, Fargo's great influence and prestige, and its association with the all-powerful Central Pacific and Southern Pacific railroads, Hume had legal authority to act as he did. Although he was, technically, only a private detective, he could (even if not deputized in a given county) investigate, interrogate, search, disarm, arrest, detain and transport suspects. In short, he could perform virtually all the duties of a county sheriff except booking a prisoner into jail. But—by custom, not law—all such arrests had to be concerned with criminal acts against Wells, Fargo. (Today Wells, Fargo's special policemen can make an arrest outside San Francisco County, where they are deputized, provided the arrest is in connection with a bank matter and they have cleared with the officers of the proper jurisdiction. They cannot make arrests for traffic violations any more than Hume could meddle in non-Wells, Fargo cases, unless in the advisory capacity of a concerned citizen.)

Hume could always take a man into custody, even without a warrant, by means of California's citizen's arrest, codified in 1872 by Sections 834 ff. of the Criminal Code, which state flatly: "An arrest may be made by a peace officer or by a private person." Whether he happened to be deputized or not, Jim Hume could make his pinch as long as he had "reasonable cause" to suspect his man of guilt in a felony and as long as he brought him before a magistrate without unnecessary delay.

Jim Hume was no Sherlock Holmes, but he was the equal of such American detectives as Allan Pinkerton, Isaiah Lees, Harry Morse, and William J. Burns. During his long career in law enforcement—forty-two years—all but eleven of which were in Wells, Fargo employ, he investigated hundreds of fascinating cases. These included the bizarre Bullion Bend double holdup of stagecoaches by California's Confederate guerrillas; the cases of Black Bart, Milton Sharp and Tom Fellows; and the Southern Pacific war, which involved a small army of train robbers, the Dalton brothers, and the almost legendary Sontag and Evans. Hume's dogged efforts in behalf of outlaws whom he knew to have been framed and railroaded for crimes they had not committed are little known and illustrate his deep integrity. To Jim Hume's everlasting credit, he was not hungry for convictions; he fought as hard to keep innocent men out of prison as he did to put the guilty into San Quentin.

RICHARD DILLON

Mill Valley, California
October 10, 1968

20

The bandit grins like it's a joke
He stops the stage and lifts your poke
You want to scrap but, man alive,
That badman totes a forty-five.

OLD CALIFORNIA DOGGEREL

CHAPTER I

———◆———

HOOSIER

BLACK BART declared war on Wells, Fargo & Company on July 26, 1875. His field headquarters was a boulder alongside a dusty road four miles east of the California mining town of Copperopolis. His army was himself, alone; his artillery a double-barreled shotgun—unloaded and propped against the large lichen-covered rock. But the G-2 of this one-man force was impressive —a cunning mind unhampered by morality or cowardice. Thanks to his coolness and savvy, the stagecoach Bart awaited that hot day was to be just the first of many coaches he eventually plundered. West Coast historians still bicker about whether he held up twenty-eight or twenty-nine coaches during his career as a highwayman.

As the creaking, squealing coach crested a rise and rocked around a curve, pursued by a cloud of fine dust, Bart blocked its path. The flour sack masking his head and shoulders made him a bizarre sight—like some ignoble wizard of the Ku Klux Klan. Only piercing blue eyes showed through the jagged cuts in the sacking as Bart, in a deep and hollow voice, delivered his curiously polite ultimatum: "Please throw down the box!" He emphasized his words, however, by outlining a lazy little circle

23

in the air with the muzzle of his shotgun. Hardly had the driver braked his team to a halt than he sent the strongbox thudding to the ground. He was not about to argue with a scatter-gun. Hell, it wasn't his money, anyhow.

Black Bart's success, that warm summer's day, established the style and method from which he seldom deviated. Since he repeated the operation nearly thirty times and was about as careful at covering his tracks as a letter carrier, he should soon have been apprehended. But Bart, who saw life as a kind of devil-may-care poker game, could lose any pursuer in the rugged country he always chose for his getaways. He had no fear at all of not being able to give lawmen the slip, and he was past master at the art of lying low. Choosing the locale and time of his holdups with special care, he spaced his robberies over eight years and four months and ranged over hundreds of miles of spectacular California terrain. And he possessed patience, as well as stamina and cunning.

Bart won all his battles with Wells, Fargo—but the company won the war. It did so, in a sense, on the day it appointed James B. Hume to head its new detective bureau. Any of a half-dozen California peace officers might have pursued Bart as determinedly as did Jim Hume, but none had Hume's expertise in the infant science of criminology. When Wells, Fargo hired Hume, a skilled or trained detective out West was as rare as a sober lawyer. It engaged him in the belief that he was the man most likely to outguess the elusive highwayman, and Wells, Fargo was right.

The man upon whom the West's largest express firm came to depend for the safe arrival of most of its shipments of specie and the recovery of the rest from the hands of raiders was a New York-born Hoosier who had migrated to California during the gold rush. James B. Hume was born on January 23, 1827, in Stamford township, Delaware County, New York. The county seat, Delhi, settled by Scotsmen and Connecticuters, lay 60 miles southwest of Albany, and Hume's actual birthplace, a farm to the east of the village of South Kortright, was still farther to the southwest. The boy grew up in the heart of a tumbled disarray

24

of detached, flat-topped mountains called Oneora (Sky Mountains) by the Indians but renamed the Catskills, after Kaäterskill (Wildcat) Cove, the Dutch name for a creek in one of the water gaps. Delaware County is broken country, rugged by Eastern standards, with a barely 2-mile-wide divide separating the Delaware River at Stamford from the headwaters of the Susquehanna that flow from Lake Otsego. The county, formed in 1797 from parts of older Ulster and Otsego counties, was the Catskill Mountains in miniature, some 1,470 square miles of up and down. It was great country for a youngster to be born to but backwearying and heartbreaking for the adult who was trying to wrest a living from it. There were arable, even fertile, stream valleys and scattered meadows and hillsides suitable for grazing, yet much of the hilly terrain spelled hardscrabble to farmers like Jim Hume's father. The land fought the harvester as it fought the plow; too poor for wheat, it yielded only rye, oats and buckwheat. But the pasturage and hay were good enough for the local milch cows, and the county's firkins of butter became as famous in the market towns of Catskill and Kingston as its applejack or rye whiskey.

Too young to be concerned with crops and prices, Jim Hume gloried in a countryside that, in its loftier hillsides, hid red deer, foxes, woodchucks, even elk and black bear. Wily black bass and brook trout lurked in the streams, and shad made great annual runs in the river. Overhead, shading the sun at times, flew flocks of passenger pigeons. And a boy could always dream of bringing down a predatory wolf or mountain lion (which New Yorkers called panthers, or painters) and collecting the magnificent sum of $15 in bounty.

Dominating the 60 square miles of Stamford township were Mount Utsayantha, highest point in the western Catskills, and its neighbors Mount Churchill and Mount McGregor. Jim Hume learned that Utsayantha was named for a Mohawk princess who, forbidden to marry her Sioux lover, committed suicide by leaping into a nearby lake. Her sorrowing father buried her on the 3,213-foot summit, where, presumably, her ghost still sleeps.

Home and family dominated Jim's childhood. His mother, Catherine Rose Hume, was proud that the county had honored her ancestors by naming Rose's Brook, a Delaware tributary, for them. Her clansmen were devout and strict in their Protestantism.

In Robert Hume, Jr., Catherine Rose found a soul mate. Jim Hume's father was as dour a Scots Presbyterian as ever left Caledonia for America. A militant Christian, Robert Hume was one of those ultraserious men with no time for "nonsense"—a term he applied to almost all manifestations of joy and imagination. He was a stern patriarch, a zealot whose uncompromising, Puritanical regime rested on family worship according to the Shorter Catechism. Mandatory prayers and churchgoing not only provided Jim with a lifetime supply of Biblical quotations, but put the fear of God into him as well. Unfortunately, this damaged the youngster's psyche, for Jim's nature was quite different from his father's. Although as an adult he adhered to a strict code of ethics, he relied on honesty and good judgment rather than religious dogma to guide him. The boy did not fear his father, who loved him in his way, but was completely awed and dominated by him. And it was years before Jim dared stray from the paths of traditional thought and conduct outlined by his father and followed by his older brothers. If the severe plainness of the churches of the Scots Seceders and the prohibition of instrumental music struck the boy as cold and barren, he said nothing.

Although Jim was the second youngest of the ten Hume children, he took his share of family responsibility. Chores were passed down to him like his clothing, and like his brothers and sisters, he was obliged to follow his father's Spartan regime—a life of rising early, working long hours, and going early to bed after prayers. As Jim grew older, he realized that he could not accept his father's Fundamentalism, but fearing to cause dissension, he went through the motions of worship, repressing his true feelings and growing resentment.

In the little free time he had, Jim roamed the brooding hills and trudged up the steep little valleys alongside rushing streams and cataracts. Across pastures brightened in summer with the pesky yellow hankweed, he walked to the open slopes, where ruminating cows stared stupidly at him as he made for the densely oaked summits of the mountains. There, in a patchwork wilderness of ash and birch, beech, spruce, balsam and pine, he indulged in daydreaming—time-wasting and sinful his father would call it. Sometimes he imagined he could see the men busy with maple sugaring or collecting hemlock bark for the tanneries that once had prospered in the county. Before his eyes was the product of their ruthlessness—thousands of skeleton trees, killed by girdling and left to feed the forest fires of summer. Jim's thoughts turned also to the time of the border wars and the American Revolution, when these mountainsides had been dark and bloodied ground. Delaware County, isolated from the Hudson by the Catskills, had been exposed to marauding Indians, and the guerrilla warfare of the eighteenth century had so brutalized the settlers that they, too, had taken scalps freely. Thus the seasons passed for Jim until he reached the age of nine.

During the Age of Jackson, a decade before the gold madness of California, the East experienced a devastating fever— land lust. The Western horizon beckoned to farmers and would-be farmers alike. Free land, or very cheap land, became their lodestar, and even prosaic, no-nonsense Robert Hume was not immune. His dreams were more modest than most, for he looked not to California or even to the Rockies or the Great Plains, but to the unsettled remnants of the old Northwest Territory, where he thought to exchange the Catskill red rock, the logging and stump-burning necessary to clear the fields, and the thin crops of hay for the light, rich, silty loam of Indiana's limestone drift. There he could become a real farmer, raising wheat and corn. His map-roving eye fell on the northwesternmost corner of the state —that gentle, almost woodless, prairie should surely yield him and his eleven dependents a better living.

Even before Jim's birth, his father had disposed of some 266 acres of his Whitesborough patent leasehold. Now he broke with New York entirely and resolved to move his family 500 miles to the west, to the fertile plains between Lake Erie and Lake Michigan. In September, 1836, Robert Hume led his family to the railroad terminus at Spraker's Basin on the Mohawk River, the jumping-off place for the drumlin country through which the Erie Canal had been cut eleven years earlier. On his way westward, Jim Hume unknowingly bypassed the hometowns of the two New Yorkers who were later to change his life: Henry Wells' Port Byron and William George Fargo's Pompey. Jim saw his first railroad cars on the trip and thought they looked like a long string of Concord coaches. He also had his first taste of watermelon—certainly the trip's most impressive event. He had never seen one before his cousin treated him to a slice at Buffalo, but he never forgot the first exquisite mouthful—"the first real delight of my life," he called it, "the most delicious diet in the world."

The Humes crossed Lake Erie by steamer to disembark at Monroe, formerly Frenchtown, on the Raisin River in Michigan. The town, 15 miles north of Toledo, was not incorporated until a year after the Humes' arrival, but it had a school, which Jim attended. Meanwhile, Robert Hume prowled the prairies until he found a perfect farm site in the moraine country of northern Indiana. The tract he chose was on the north edge of Pretty Prairie, almost on the Michigan line, in Lagrange County. It was only 25 miles west of Ohio.

The land contrasted favorably with the Catskills. So few trees had to be cleared to prepare it for tilling that Jim's father could not mark his property lines with blazes but had to plow furrows and plant stakes to define his boundaries. No ax or whipsaw was necessary—only a plow—to transform Pretty Prairie from a vast natural grassland into grainfields. A few mills and forges and the home industries of furniture making, spinning, and toolmaking were agriculture's only rivals in four-year-old Lagrange County. In the swamps there was a little bog ore that made tolerable iron, but the local clay produced poor bricks. Distilleries were the county's only other evidence of the Industrial Revolution. Hard times were in the air, but the elder Hume was not worried. He liked the level or gently rolling ground, the rich-enough soil, and the velvety sea of grass that stretched to clustered oaks and maples dyed brilliant hues by the autumn frost. He determined to put down deep and permanent roots, which he had never done while tenanting a hillside farm in the Catskills. Most important, he owned this land—he was done with leasing, once and for all.

Jim Hume reached the new farm site on February 11, 1837. It lay well to the north of the ponds and swamps of the Pigeon River drainage blamed so rightly by many for the agues and fevers that were the principal hazards of prairie pioneering. Jim learned that his father had also bought property in the village of Lima (now Howe), the old Indian settlement of Mongoquinong, or White Squaw, where the trails of the Potawatamies converged on the Pigeon River. As spring came on, Jim was reminded of the Catskills by the apple trees blossoming on the banks of the Pigeon. They were the legacy of the itinerant preacher John Chapman, better known as Johnny Appleseed, who had passed that way.

Because Jim Hume left New York State as a small boy, Lagrange County, Indiana, provided most of his early memories. He knew the tales of Johnny Appleseed, Chief Shipshewana, and the murderous horse thieves called the Blacklegs, who hid in the swamps to the south of Lima, but what marked his childhood most vividly was the depression. The Humes had chosen a bad time to make a move. The financial thunderheads that had been piling up over America broke in 1837 in a storm of hard times. Money vanished from Indiana, and credit seemed intent on following directly after it. In the words of Lagrange historian Weston A. Goodspeed, "Counterfeiters, thieves and others of their ilk overran the county and, soon, honest settlers could not depend upon the integrity of their neighbors." Storekeepers were reduced to operating on the barter system, taking eggs, butter, wheat, and pork—either live, "in the hide," or in the form of bacon and smoked hams—in lieu of cash. Lima, the county seat, which boasted a population of 200 when the Humes arrived, had grown to only 350 souls four years later.

Recession or not, the Humes' regimen remained exactly as it had been in the Catskills. Breakfast at six began the clockwork day of labor. The family lived on rye bread and on cornmeal made into a gruel they called suppone. They considered their neighbors, mainly ex-Ohioans and New Yorkers, terribly vulgar for calling it mush.

To add to the depression woes came outbreaks of ague and fever. Despite a glacial drift of easily 100 feet above bedrock, Lagrange County did not drain well. Water stood on the ground after rains, bogs bred malarial mosquitoes, and disease spread among the population. Summer was called the sickly season, and during that of 1838 many of the township's settlers suffered either death or bankruptcy as a result of depression, disease, and drought. The village of Ontario, just south of the Hume farm, was a disaster area. Only one man in the entire settlement was well enough to work, and he bravely carried water to the fifteen or eighteen households of his neighbors.

Fortunately, Robert Hume was of the stock that weathers depressions, droughts, and the very wrath of God. He had absolute faith in the efficacy as well as the sanctity of manual labor, and he wanted his sons to share that belief. He also believed that children should be seen and not heard. Jim, the most restive of the children, had long borne an unadmitted grudge against his demanding father. In manhood he would recall, "I never had a holiday. It was work, work, work; plowing and grubbing from six o'clock, A.M., until dark. When the ground was too wet to plow, we had to build fences or haul wood, or hull corn, or clean the barn—never an idle moment. When the circus came around, I had to work until there was just barely time to get to the show and when it was over, I had to hurry home and do double duty to make up the lost time."

Jim was almost out of his teens before he mustered the courage to resist his father's Puritanical discipline. At nineteen, he felt himself to be little better than a workhorse. Although he toiled as long as there was daylight, *not once* did his father ever consult him on his opinions, wishes, or feelings. This hurt Jim deeply. It was not that his father did not love him or that he neglected him. What rankled was being treated like a child, a servant, or a field hand. "My opinions were never asked," he later remarked with lingering bitterness, "nor did I even dare to venture one upon any topic whatever, whether in regard to my work or my own personal wishes, or upon anything else."

Sunday was, technically, a day of rest in the Hume household, but it was as tightly organized as any Monday or Thursday. Every member of the family, except the one chosen to stay home to mind the farm, was required to go to church. The only excuse Robert Hume would accept for nonattendance was total incapacitation. And since he was too stubborn to let Indiana's fevers get him down, he tolerated little illness among his children. Jim remembered, "Often, it seemed to me, when Sunday came, that I would give half the rest of my life to be allowed to stay at home and rest and sleep."

One summer Sunday Jim finally rebelled. By then all his older brothers and sisters had left home, and the household consisted only of his parents, his favorite sister Catherine, or Kate, and himself. There was also a hired hand, Stevens, inevitably a staunch United Presbyterian like the Humes. Jim had washed the carriage the night before, a weekly ritual preparatory to Sunday morning's drive of 10 miles to Lagrange Center for communion services. Since the carriage held only four, Stevens rode a horse to the services. He was saddling his mount that Sunday when young Hume advised him that he could take his place in the buggy since he was not going to church. When Stevens reported to Jim's father that he was ready to drive him and the others to town, the head of the family retorted, "No; go and get your horse. James will go to church, as usual."

His face set in hard lines of resentment and "
Hume confronted his son. "Are you ill?" he aske

31

The younger man answered firmly, although his heart was racing, "No, but I feel as if I should stay home today."

The reply came back like a whiplash, "Oh, no! Hurry up, James, and dress. Sickness is the only excuse for not going to church."

"Well," answered Jim, "I am *not* going today, Father. Stevens will drive you to church, but I am not going." Boldly, although his knees were weak, he turned away from his stunned parent, went into the house, sat down, and began to read the New York *Observer*, the only paper his father allowed the family to read on the Sabbath.

Robert Hume, dressed in his best Sunday-go-to-meeting clothes and plug hat, stalked into the room, faced Jim squarely, and pounded the floor impatiently with his gold-headed cane. "Come, James. Hurry up!" he commanded. "We have little time, now."

Jim answered him patiently but resolutely. "But I'm not going, Father."

With growing astonishment, the older man demanded, "Do I understand that you are going openly to disobey my orders?"

Jim tried to be firm, yet conciliatory, explaining that he was generally willing to obey his father and certainly did not question his authority. In personal matters, however, he insisted that he be allowed to exercise his own preferences.

Robert Hume's answer was brief and sharp. "As long as a child of mine remains under my roof, I must be obeyed."

Jim said nothing but determined then and there to leave the family. His mind made up, Jim could allow himself to relax. Since the devout Stevens had abandoned the family to its quarrel and had ridden off to church, he said, "Very well, Father, I accept the terms. I will drive you to Lagrange today because Stevens has gone and I know that you and Mother and Kate wish to go. But I accept your terms." He then dressed hurriedly and drove his tight-lipped father and tearful mother and sister to the Presbyterian church. He refused to enter, and rejoined his family only when the service was over. Then he drove them to dinner with friends. The tension abated, but no reference to the morning's episode was made during the visit or on the drive back to the Pretty Prairie farm.

The next morning Jim rose and dressed in his Sunday clothes. He gave Stevens a second shock, announcing that he would have to take care of all the horses since he was leaving for good. Jim found that he could pack all his belongings in one small bandanna. Right after breakfast and family worship, he braced himself and turned to his father, "I suppose, Father, that the Dandy colt is mine?"

"Certainly the colt is yours."

"Well," continued Jim, "I am going away and if Dandy is mine I will take him with me."

When his father summoned voice enough to ask him where he was going, Jim had to confess that he had no particular destination in mind. In fact, he had no plans at all. He would simply saddle Dandy and let the three-year-old colt follow its nose. His father then asked how much money he had. When he learned that his boy's total cash reserve amounted to less than twenty-five cents, he tried to reason with him. "Well, I think this is a pretty bold step for a young man in your position. But if you have no plans, they will not suffer by any delay, so sit down and talk this matter over a little." For the sake of his sister and mother, who were crying, Jim said he would be glad to talk over his leaving, adding that, in fact, he was not really eager to go. But, he insisted, he had reached a point where he *had* to be allowed some liberty of thought and action, or else he would be forced to leave home for good.

Convinced at last that his son was in earnest, Jim's father became more paternal and less authoritarian than the boy had ever known him. He tried to make Jim understand his st⸀ ʰilosophy, explaining that he had found discipline essentiʲ so many children. But he admitted that he could ʳ relax the regimen somewhat, since only Jim anʲ mained at home. Choosing his words very carefully, he assured Jim that if he should decide to stay, he would never have cause to complain in the future.

The tense encounter was resolved. Glad to remain, Jim put on his work clothes and set about his chores. From then on, the father-son relationship was that of two equal adults. The older man consulted the younger about every aspect of their work, and Jim never disagreed with him. As each Sunday rolled around, Robert Hume would ask, "Well, James, do you feel like going to church today?"

Each time Jim felt a pang of remorse and simply said, "Yes." Years later, he explained, "I would have suffered anything rather than to have let them know that I felt I had gained a victory."

Having made his peace with his father, Jim Hume settled down contentedly to the life of a Hoosier farmer. The land was good and young, not worn out by years of cultivation. The grain yield was large, and there was plenty of work to be done. Although he was hardly an intellectual, Jim possessed a good mind and an excellent memory. He had spent the winter months, until he was fourteen, in a one-room country school and had capped his formal education with two winter quarters of twelve weeks each in the Lagrange Collegiate Institute at the neighboring township of Ontario. Although he had little taste for formal study, he devoured newspapers, and this reading kept his mind active. His brother John was a lawyer, but Jim did not seem cut out for a white-collar career of any kind. Farming was good enough for him.

Suddenly, during 1849, Jim Hume's placid existence was turned topsy-turvy. Northern Indiana, like every other cranny of the continent, received news of the California gold rush. Word was slow to reach Lagrange County, far from any railroad or steamboat landing, but when it eventually did, Jim Hume found that he was no more immune to gold fever than any other young Hoosier. There seemed to be no cure—short of going "to see the Elephant," that is, making the trip to the mines. Gold lust attacked Hume like the dumb chills and malarial ague of the prairies. While the older citizens of the county were applauding the new plank road built into Ontario from the south, he and his brother John had their heads together, excitedly discussing James Marshall's Coloma gold discovery. Soon they were licking pencil stubs and scribbling notes on scraps of paper. And their enthusiasm infected their acquaintances. Jim and John could have had dozens of recruits for the gold-mining company they had decided to form, but they settled for just six men and made plans to travel overland, through Indian country, to California. They did so in the face of opposition from their father, who saw Jim as his only hope of keeping the farm going.

CHAPTER II

———◄◆►———

EMIGRANT

IN THE spring of 1850, Jim Hume again risked—and accepted —his father's displeasure and dropped his plow handles for the last time. He was on his way to California by March 26. The eight-man Hume party outfitted itself in Chicago with guns, tents, canteens, and camping gear, then passed through the fertile savannas of Illinois to the Mississippi and Iowa, making for Maquoketa, 30 miles south of Dubuque. Jim and his trail mates halted in town for two weeks, ostensibly to wait for the grass to come up on the dry plains ahead so that they would have a good chance of getting all their horses to California alive. Probably they were equally motivated by good board, at only $12 a week per man, and the possibility of meeting some of the attractive young ladies in the Maquoketa Academy.

Two weeks later the Humes and their comrades tore themselves away from creature comforts and feminine beauty and pushed on for Council Bluffs, then called Kanesville. Here they laid over for three more weeks to make sure that the grass on the chancy portion of the journey would have attained sufficient growth. At last, Hume found himself on the fringes of the Wild West. Kanesville was a Mormon town, but its population was mixed. Tall, rough-looking backwoodsmen jostled pale, smooth-looking urban expatriates. For every man in a hurry Jim saw two loafing about, apparently with time to kill. Still others he observed in the ninety-nine stages of drunkenness. Watching three auctioneers selling the wagons and goods of "faint-hearted Californians"—those who feared to push any farther westward —he was amused to see some of his pals plant themselves in the crowd and run up the bidding when a member of their group was selling his gray.

Kanesville, though only half the size of Lima, was booming. Overland rations were in short supply and brought premium prices—flour, $7 a hundredweight, and hard bread, $10 a hundred pounds. Corn was scarce, and no oats or rice were to be had. Since spring was late, the Humes' party did not push on until May 7, although May Day was usually considered the optimum date, being neither too early for grass on the plains nor so late as to expose a party to snow in the Sierra Nevada toward the end of the journey. There was no cholera in Kanesville, smallpox was only a frightening rumor, and John found himself 10 pounds fatter and much healthier. It was a pleasant stopover, and Jim was glad to have exchanged Indiana for the Great Plains. He could bid a cheerful good-bye to what another Hoosier-Californian, Ambrose Bierce, would later describe as "the malarious farm, the wet, fungus-grown wildwood; the chills, then contracted, that since have remained."

Although perfect greenhorns, the Humes decided against crossing to California in the company of one of the large wagon trains they saw mustering. By forfeiting the security of a large party, they also lost the services of a guide, but they prized their independence and hoped to make a quicker passage of the plains and mountains. More important, they were free to forage as they pleased to find grass for their animals. They did not worry about the lack of a guide; Jim Hume knew that the sun, each day, headed for California. They would follow. In later years he characterized his party: "We were a hardy crowd. We could endure anything. No amount of hardship or fatigue counted with any of us. We cared nothing for hostile Indians and we could find roads. We did not know what fear meant and I would not have been the least daunted by having to start for anywhere in the world, on foot. We climbed mountains and swam rivers. When I think, now, of the chances we took, daily, I am almost surprised that we ever reached our destination."

From 50 miles out on the Nebraska plains, John rode all the way back to Kanesville to post a letter to his sister Kate that commented on his younger brother—"James is in fine spirits and keeps courage. He is a capital hand and gets along first-rate." Meanwhile, Jim was leading the party with its five wagons and eighteen to twenty horses. It was a well-equipped train since the Hoosiers had fought their way out of the 1837 depression into prosperity. The census taker who interviewed Jim in 1850, just before he left Indiana, listed his property as being worth $1,300, no small sum in those days.

On the plains Jim Hume really found himself, and he began to take over the command from his more than willing older brother. He decided to avoid the beaten path followed by both the Oregon and California trails on the south bank of the Platte River and to take the little-used old Mormon Trail of 1847 on the north bank. He found the grazing so plentiful here that he later commented, incorrectly but understandably, "We were the first emigrants who ever took the route north of the Platte River." But he spoke the absolute truth when he continued, "We found the country a perfect paradise. Grass was luxuriant and game of every character abounded." Progress along the Platte was easy and uneventful. Each day on the Great Plains shook down to a consistent routine. By seven in the morning the men, wagons, and stock were under way. After a drive of 12 to 15 miles, they halted for rest and food, whatever the hour. After having fed the horses with corn from the wagons, the men ate lunch and then took an hour's rest before driving on to find water, and if possible, timber, for the night's camp. While some of the men unharnessed the horses and secured them for the night, others were building fires, cooking supper, pitching tents, or laying out bedrolls. After chores and supper, the young men, now a dozen in number, sat around the campfire, talking and smoking as the shadows closed in around them. By eight or nine o'clock they had rolled themselves in their blankets and were ready to sleep.

Jim described a typical plains camp in a small strip of scrubby timber, separated by some 20 to 30 miles of open land from the next patch of cover. The wagons, ranged in a protecting circle, looked like white specters in the dusk. At the foot of a small rise, a slough of water provided tolerable refreshment for men and animals alike. "Above the fire sits, in a circle, a dozen rather rough-looking men, with boots drawn up over their pants, California wool hats drawn down over their eyes, striped shirts on and faces which, for weeks, have been innocent of a razor. Merry fellows, too, for Wicker has been telling a story and all are laughing in chorus."

Hume's route proved to be a good choice. Although virtually treeless, except for the willows and cottonwoods on the islets stranded in the Platte's broad and shallow bed, there were fewer streams to be crossed. There were a few sloughs, like medieval moats, athwart the Lima party's path, but only the Elkhorn and Loup rivers gave them any worry, and the Loup boasted a ferry by the time they arrived. As many as thirty-four horse-drawn wagons might be backed up at a slough, with men afoot and on horseback frantically searching for a good ford, and Jim Hume, more than once, saw horses floundering in these swampy spots. Breakdowns, too, were most frequent in the heavy going of the sloughs, but the Humes broke only a single kingbolt and a whiffletree. Just one of the party stuck fast and had to unload his wagon in order to pull it out of the mire.

The first major landmark of the trek was Fort Kearney, where the Mormon Trail joined the California-Oregon Trail. Here the Hoosiers had no lack of company. By May 11, 1850, 900 wagons had passed the fort, and the north bank was lined with emigrant trains from Kanesville. Jim thought the outpost—named (but misspelled) for Colonel Stephen Watts Kearny—to be a miserable collection of adobe and sod buildings, among them huts and stables, a smithy, a post office and a single store, where off-duty U.S. soldiers gathered. The garrison was assigned to protect travelers from the Indians and vice versa. That spring, for instance, a brutal Missourian had stupidly shot the first Indian he saw on the trail—a squaw nursing her baby. When the Indians demanded the murderer, he was handed over by his companions. In revenge, the redskins skinned him alive at a stream thereafter known as Rawhide Creek. The incident was all too typical of life on the lawless plains, and Jim Hume welcomed the sight of the troopers, drunk or sober, at Kearney.

When Hume and his companions moved on, they passed the 1773 Line—supposedly exactly 1,733 miles from San Francisco —in a barren and bleak area tenanted only by prairie dogs. Bones littered the trail now—and not all of them belonged to oxen, cows, mules, and horses. The skulls of buffalo gave the Hoosiers proof that they had reached the Far West. The party now relied on buffalo chips, or *bois de vache,* for their campfires, instead of on the driftwood gathered with difficulty from the river and the kindling extracted from abandoned wagons along the trail. Passing through the region of sandy ridges that J. T. Kearns, who followed two seasons later, would evaluate at 3 cents per hundred square miles, the boys reached the fork of the Platte.

Here Nebraska begins to heave itself up into dry-gullied, rolling, and sometimes rugged hills. And here the south-bankers were forced by the terrain to follow Hume's route with a number of crossings of the Platte. Beyond Ash Hollow, the tree-shaded ravine that caught every overlander's eye, the Lima company entered a high, treeless tableland where the dry air shrank the wagon wheels away from their rims. Looming above the bleak plain was the first of the great natural landmarks of the overland trail, Courthouse Rock. Next came even more awesome Chimney Rock, poking 200 feet into the air above the low-banked river and the grasslands bright with black-eyed Susans and dappled with pool water. About 20 miles farther on, the party reached Scotts Bluff, high country for Nebraska, and Robidoux Pass.

Thursday, June 13, 1850, found Jim Hume encamped with his men across the Platte from Fort Laramie. The river had been transformed by snowmelt into a raging torrent. Jim's self-confidence had grown with each mile. He had brought his party to Laramie without dissension or serious illness—and in a cholera year. Long afterward, John confided to Kate, "James and myself have got along admirably together. I cannot speak too highly of James's conduct ever since we left Lima. To me, he has ever been considerate and kind. From the first, he was, more than any, the leader of the company and in many cases when we were all in doubt what course to pursue, he did himself credit by his judgment and good counsel. I am writing not to praise but merely to do justice."

Jim examined the Platte crossing and found that the ford to the south bank lay under 20 feet of water. He watched as ugly whirlpools circled over the quicksand bottom and sucked at the tangles of floodwood rafted in the muddy water. The Humes were far too sensible to risk their lives in a hasty ferrying of the turbulent river. But more impatient and reckless emigrants made makeshift boats of their wagon boxes. Some failed to make it. Of those who attempted the brief cruise, five drowned between June 9 and June 13. John observed, "None but the most expert swimmers can live in it a moment."

During their enforced halt across from the fort, the boys wrote home. James and John collaborated on a letter to their father, joyfully reporting that they had passed the 500-mile mark of their journey from the Big Muddy. They had high praise for the Mormon Trail. "I do not believe there are 500 miles of as good road anywhere in the Union as between here and the Missouri River," reported John, and described the plentiful grass of the first 200 miles and the passable cover of the next 250 miles. With all the fodder gone, the horses were holding up well on grass alone, and both boys were confident that they would get their animals safely through to the gold country. John admitted that they had driven the horses hard, so far, in order to make time on the long but relatively flat stretches east of Laramie. But, well aware of the steep pulls of the Laramie Mountains and the Rockies ahead, they promised to move more easily.

Like so many other travelers both before him and after, John mistook the Laramie Peaks or Black Hills for the Rockies and wrote that the barrier range was already in sight. He described the Laramie Mountains, an eastern spur of the great massif, as rising "like a huge cloud" due west of their campsite. As for the notorious coffee-colored water of the Platte, a pailful left standing overnight, he told his father, would precipitate an inch of mud in the bottom of the container. And the water above the sediment would still be so murky that you could not see through a cupful to the bottom. Travelers told the Hume boys that it was healthful, however, and by the time they reached Fort Laramie, it tasted sweet enough to them.

John reported that the emigrants were becoming more vigilant now that they had reached Fort Laramie. Although they had not been bothered by Pawnees or Sioux, there were reports of marauding Blackfeet ahead. Neither he nor Jim had so far so much as glimpsed a wild Indian. Tamed Sioux, however, abounded at Fort Laramie. Their lodges lay in a great circle around the post, and the Indians flocked into town for handouts. On the whole, these Sioux were a drunken lot, debased by long contact with the corrosive environment of a trading post turned military fortress. They made a living of sorts by plundering the gear that overlanders, worried about the steep country ahead, which demanded lighter wagons, abandoned by the ton.

Wild game had been plentiful on the Humes' march to the Laramie River. They had, they reported, seen elk, antelope, wolves, and buffalo. Jim was the first of the company to kill a bison, a fine, fat, three-year-old heifer. His horse had overtaken the animal easily, once he had spurred it into a chase, but he was surprised when he had to put five rifle balls into the bison's shaggy side to bring it down. His efforts were richly appreciated, the boys swearing that buffalo steaks tasted better than beef. After recounting Jim's hunting exploit, John turned the letter over to his younger brother.

Jim, to avoid repeating John's observations, described his guarding of the grazing horses and the generally fine, cool weather they had enjoyed on the trail, with enough rain to lay the dust but not so much as to make the road slippery or miry. He told his father that he had counted 300 teams on the far side of the Missouri at Kanesville and 100 more on the western shore, as they had set out.

Before signing off with a promise to write again from Salt Lake City, Jim did his best to allay family fears for his and John's safety and health. He reported that both of them were in excellent physical shape. John, in fact, looked better than Jim had ever seen him. He ate three meals of pork and beans, hard bread, and water every day and was flourishing. "I never saw a greater change in a person in my life," said Jim. "He has stood guard one-half of every night since we left the States—and some very bad ones." Actually, the hard passages had been remarkably few, so far. Jim had seen only two fresh graves along the entire trail and a third at Laramie, where a young man had recently killed his brother in a quarrel. The dead man had been speedily buried and the murderer placed in irons in the fortress. With the exception of the treacherous river crossings, the overland journey had not seemed particularly hazardous.

The younger Hume, too, was thriving. John wrote: "I never saw James look so robust and stout. Even had there been no gold in California, I think that this, to me, would have been a profitable journey." John's worst day had occurred when he had ridden 25 miles and then had stood night watch. But this had been a simple matter of fatigue, not danger or illness. Neither he nor Jim had succumbed to even the slightest attack of the mountain fever that had afflicted their companions. They and their horses were in better shape than any others on the road West. Of course, the Hume brothers were no longer living high on the boiled rice, fat bacon, and flour pancakes they had enjoyed when they started from Kanesville. The flour had run out first, then the bacon and dried beef. While most emigrants were chronically short of supplies, the relatively affluent Hoosiers had been able to buy bacon at 50 cents a pound and rice at $1 the pound.

The river finally dropped, and the boys crossed to Fort Laramie. Before they left the old American Fur Company post after a brief rest, Jim got an Army officer to show him the fort's official register. He found that it had logged some 5,000 wagons already that season of 1850, about one-third of the estimated total. Not long afterward, on July 5, another West-bound traveler had looked the register over and noted a total of 37,171 men, 803 women, and 1,094 children who had been signed in since the record was begun. This was, however, a far from accurate accounting of the gold rush migration past Laramie, for many individuals went unrecorded.

Jim Hume knew that the 500-plus miles now behind them would not compare with those that lay ahead, but he felt prepared for anything. The long journey through the Platte Valley had made a seasoned traveler of him, and he had enjoyed following the mile-or-so-wide swath of riverbed threaded with shimmering sluices of turbid water and flanked by parallel sandhills.

No sooner had the Hume party left Fort Laramie behind than the terrain changed markedly. They began the uphill pull of the dry and alkaline Laramie Mountains, called the Black Hills because of their somber look. It was poor, barren country, like before, but steeper. The soil, sandy or stony, sustained only prickly-pear cactus, bunchy sagebrush, and a scatter of pines. On the south side of the river the road was more crowded than ever, the Mormon Trail having crossed the Platte at Fort Laramie to unite with the main Oregon Trail. The Humes, holding to the less-favored north bank, passed the meadow that served as a trail graveyard below the chalk bluff dubbed Register Cliff by the forty-niners, who used it as both giant autograph album and bulletin board. Just beyond lay Warm Springs, christened the Emigrant's Laundry Tub because of the 70-degree water it provided even in the dead of winter. The going was slow along the north bank of the Platte, but it was sure. And it proved more tiresome than dangerous to the Humes and their party.

Fifty miles beyond Fort Laramie, their progress was slowed even more by the season's single snowstorm. The squall blew over quickly, and most of the delay was caused not by the brief blizzard but by the snowball fights that sprang up among the men. Resuming their trek, they entered a windy wasteland of steep draws and gulches full of the rattlesnakes that hungry forty-niners called bush trout.

At (Jim) Bridger's Ferry, the Humes found the Platte Canyon rounding the obdurate mass of the north-thrusting Laramie Mountains in a wide curve. The terrain was now very different from the flat plains lying below Fort Laramie. From Laramie Peak and other snowcapped summits came breezes to cool their passage. Occasionally there were snowbanks alongside the trail. With La Bonté, Box Elder, and Deer Creek behind him, Jim Hume knew that he was approaching the Upper Platte Crossing. The Mormons ferried travelers across for $4 a wagon and two bits per head of cattle. The crossing was a great bottleneck for traffic, and traders of all kinds gathered there to sell to the impatient emigrants. The mass of men and animals churned and ground the sandy soil into a powdery dust, filling the air and everyone's already reddened eyes.

Here, without knowing it, Jim Hume probably saw Christopher "Kit" Carson. Kit was at the crossing by June, 1850, to sell a herd of horses and mules. There were so many potential customers for Kit—and the ferry—that the Mormons kept a register so that first come might be first served. Wealthy emigrants, of course, bribed their way to the head of the list. Hume was repelled by the bustle and crowding and shocked at the low value placed on human life by the gold-hungry emigrants. In a line of camps 25 miles long men maneuvered frantically to ford the Platte, at whatever cost. Many drowned daily, but the lesson of their deaths seemed completely wasted on the greedy mass hurrying up behind them to ferry the treacherous, flooding river.

To Jim, the right-bank road looked like a busy eastern turnpike. The trail was wide and worn down to the solid rock that underlay six inches of soil. Beyond the Upper Platte Crossing, the Hume party traveled over a fine road, paved by nature with solid sandstone as smooth as a ballroom floor.

As Hume advanced into the rain shadow of the Rockies, bypassing Red Bluffs and Fremont's Island, the countryside became higher and drier. Mountains loomed up into the sky in all directions. Grass was sparse, but there was no lack of litter, everything from boots to bookcases, discarded by emigrants amid the prickly pear. Those who had traveled the route had stripped the riverbanks of vegetation. For 25 miles at a stretch there was not a drop of drinking water, only an alkaline swill too toxic for man or beast, as dead carcasses of cattle by the hundreds testified. One bright aspect was the good-quality soda for baking that the Lagrangers secured from the saleratus lakes they skirted between Upper Platte Crossing and Independence Rock, the whale-like monolith guarding the Sweetwater River. Unlike many parties, the Hume caravan kept its collective temper during the passage of the blasted, waterless stretch that proved so abrasive to emigrant morale. There were no fights, no desertions, no mutinies among the Hoosiers.

Beyond the Fiery Narrows of the North Platte, the Humes crossed over to pick up the east-flowing Sweetwater. This stream, 20 yards wide, was a clear current cutting through country that continued barren except for a fringe of grass along the riverbanks. And the men welcomed the good, sweet drinking water after the near-poisonous liquid alkali of the upper North Platte. A mile beyond the point where they struck the Sweetwater, they reached Independence Rock, often called the Register of the Desert. By 1850, lazy but well-to-do travelers could hire Mormons living there to carve their names on the face of the 53-acre rock mass with stonecutting tools. The cost ran from $1 to $5, depending on the prominence—and difficulty—of the location of the engraving. What the emigrants did not know was that no sooner were they out of sight than the enterprising Saints erased the newly carved names in order to have a smooth surface ready for the next customer.

The Humes proceeded through an area cluttered with rubbish jettisoned by hundreds of wagons preparing for the mountains and canyons ahead. Six miles west of the monolith, Jim found the last of the great landmarks of the trail, Devil's Gate, a 330-foot-deep channel cut by the Sweetwater in the grey granite, with a dramatic streak of black granite extending from top to bottom.

West of Devil's Gate the Humes' careful precautions paid off nicely. They had raised the wagon boxes to keep their cargoes dry during river crossings and as a result, lost none of their gear and supplies to damp, although they had to cross the meandering Sweetwater nine times. Fords twice were within a few rods of each other but were separated by "mountains of rocks." The full-scale mountains on each side of the Sweetwater's 10-mile-wide valley began to retreat farther and farther from the river.

Across the sagebrush country west of Icy Slough and Split Rock, fragrant with Fremont's artemisia (sage) crushing under the wagon wheels, they followed the sandy track through a land inhabited only by antelope and sage hens to Rocky Ridge. From this point, later the St. Mary's stage and telegraph station, they skirted the Green Mountains' north edge to reach fabled South Pass. This passageway over the Continental Divide was so unimpressive that Fremont had compared it to Washington's Capitol Hill. Hume reckoned that it was 7,000 feet above sea level, and he underestimated by only 550 feet. He described it as a bald opening 19 miles wide between the Sweetwater Mountains and the Wind River Range. Below it, to the west lay a stretch of 100 miles of desert in which only sage and cactus grew.

From South Pass and its Atlantic and Pacific springs, the Humes dropped down into terrain as barren as a moonscape except for Pacific and Sandy creeks. Between them and Green River lay Greasewood Flat, Red Desert Basin, the Bad Lands Hills, and the sand dunes of Alkali Flat. Jim apparently followed the advice of Joseph Ware's *Emigrant Guide* and crossed the Little Sandy, or Dry Sandy, and then the Big Sandy, 12 miles beyond, bearing westward all the while, rather than heading south to pick up the Green at its nearest point. In the 35 miles between the Big Sandy and the Green there was not a drop of water for the Hoosiers, only heat and the insufferable dust that travelers called the smoke of Sodom blown by the ubiquitous evening wind.

The chaotic scene Jim Hume had viewed with such distaste at the Upper Platte Crossing was repeated at the Mormons' Green River Crossing. On the day he reached the Green (which he mistakenly called the Colorado of the West, of which it is a tributary), a boat capsized and threw twelve men, one woman and two children into the treacherous water. Luckily, an old French trapper pulled them out. The day before Jim arrived, another boatload of travelers had been less fortunate. All twelve occupants had drowned when their craft capsized in the Green. The banks of the river under the green cottonwoods were churned into a morass by wagon wheels and cattle hooves as men sought to cross at a dozen different fords.

The Humes' boat made the passage across the Green safely, although it required endless bailing by two men and constant calking by another just to keep it afloat. The great migration of 1850 had jacked up the $2-per-wagon price of ferriage. The Mormons and their Indian and half-breed sailors were now charging $5 per wagon. All cattle and horses had to be swum across, although sometimes the ferrymen would take a wagon with its four-horse team for $9. The price, Jim found, fluctuated with the amount of traffic.

From the Green, the Humes cut across shaley dry hills and greasewood flats under barren, lofty, snow-topped mountains. But the snow-born water was better. There was forage for the animals. And there were poplars, even a few spruce trees and strawberry vines, that promised better country ahead, although the temperature escalated from 30-40 degrees at dawn to 80 degrees by afternoon. At deep-cut Black's Fork of the Green River, where Jim Bridger and Louis Vásquez kept Fort Bridger, they found an eight-year-old trading post of mud-daubed poles hunched in the shade of cottonwoods. The stream alongside was full of trout, the wide bottoms covered with grass.

From the oasis of Fort Bridger, Jom Hume decided to take the Salt Lake Cutoff instead of the usual Fort Hall Road to California. It would prove, in the long run, to be the best route to California, but Hume always remembered it as the worst trail he and his comrades had to master—an arduous route through such steeply pitched, eroded, red sandstone gorges of the Wasatch Range as Echo and Weber canyons. The party slipped and slid its way down these canyons alongside rushing streams literally squeezed between snow-covered peaks.

Jim was awed by the Salt Lake Valley, a vast meadowland that yielded the Mormons from a ton to a ton and a half of hay per acre. It was a far cry from the hilly, barren west slopes of the Catskills, and Hume was amazed to find that hay was worth $20 a ton and that from 25 to 75 bushels of wheat per acre could be raised, depending on the irrigation.

Jim and his brother arrived in Salt Lake City on July 9, 1850. The cold, pure waters of the little Jordan River and other streams coursed through the streets of the Latter Day Saints' capital, and every day Jim saw men and women drinking or washing their hands and faces in the streets. A century ahead of their time the Mormon elders had strict regulations against pollution of their streams. It was not long before the brothers had made several Mormon friends. One, George A. Smith, gave John advice on where to settle in the semidesert of the great basin and range country: "No man has any business to think of living in this country in any place where he cannot see snow in summer."

Jim and John spent a week or two in Salt Lake City, boarding at 50 cents a meal, or $6 a week, in the home of Bishop Stephen H. Goddard and his two wives. They became close friends of the Mormon elder and relaxed completely during their stay. One enjoyable activity was bathing in the Great Salt Lake and in the more pleasant warm spring waters of the city's bathhouses.

While in the city, John met and impressed the great Mormon pioneer Brigham Young. Young urged him to settle in Deseret as a teacher and offered to build him a schoolhouse; John was tempted but declined. Another of the Hume party, however, decided to stay on and help build a dam. Meanwhile, Jim indulged in a bit of horse trading. He swapped a pair of matched chestnut horses, which he had kept in very good condition on the trail, for a pair of large, sturdy mules for the heavy going in the desert and mountains ahead. Everyone told Jim that the mules were easily worth $400 and that he had made $100 on the trade. Prices of stock, whether horses, mules, or oxen, were high in Salt Lake City because of the great demand by travelers who had already exhausted their animals in the high semidesert country of Wyoming. Jim learned that his little mare could have brought $100; good, fat, English horses commanded from $100 to $200, and even tiny Indian ponies sold for $60 to $100.

In the booming Mormon capital wages, too, were soaring. Men could afford to pay high sums for stock when laborers received $1.50 a day, plus board, and mechanics earned $2.80 in addition to their board. Teamsters also made good money hauling hay, and Jim, who had tired of the flavor of food cooked over pungent sagebrush campfires, was amazed to learn that even a wagonload of brush was worth $5 in Salt Lake City, where it was used as firewood.

Everyone had advised the brothers to sell their wagon and to proceed with pack animals over the very rugged desert and Sierra to California, and as their departure time drew near, Jim busied himself making pack-saddles. "At the end of about two weeks," he recalled years later, "we crossed the River Jordan on the south side of the Lake and struck for the Sunset Land without a guide, without a guidebook, with no knowledge of the country and with *Westward* for our compass and guiding star."

Hume quickly discovered that the penultimate leg of his long journey was to be the most taxing of all. He chose the Hastings Cutoff from Great Salt Lake to Skull Valley and Pilot Peak, 20 miles north of modern Wendover, Utah. This trail, pioneered by

Fremont and Kit Carson in 1845, had proved disastrous to the Donner Party in 1846, but it held little fear for Hume. Unlike the Donner group, he had no wagons to slow him down by breaking through the salt crust or bogging down in sand or sump. It was a gamble, to be sure, but not a reckless one. Jim Hume was betting that, because of the route's unpopularity, the sparse grass on either side of the Great Salt Desert would not be grazed-down. He was absolutely correct.

Hume led his men westward from the Jordan in a race against time, sun, and thirst. By traveling for twenty-three hours straight, resting for one hour, and pushing on again, they crossed more than 100 miles of barrenness, some 80 miles of it the dreaded Great Salt Desert, where they saw not a spear of grass or a drop of drinkable water. With a sigh of relief, Jim called a halt in safer country, probably at the springs under Pilot Peak. To his delight, none of his men, horses, or mules was used up. Others on the trail were not so fortunate. One man, just ahead of the Humes, died on the desert.

In a sense, the worst traveling of the entire route began when the party reached the reasonable safety of the Mary's, or Humboldt, River. The water in the turgid stream was both warm and bad. The road varied from sandy and dusty to miry along the river's bank. Poor footing everywhere made for very slow and uncomfortable progress through a bleak and drab country. The dust was worse than anything Jim had ever experienced. It rose over the entire caravan in billowing clouds obscuring the man directly ahead of Jim although they were close enough to converse. The 1850 season was wet, so there was grass, at least, and a few willows and cottonwoods gave shade on the banks of the miry Humboldt. As long as they followed the river, they could not get lost, nor would they die of thirst, bad as the water was. The major drawback of the Humboldt River trail was the frequent raids on stock by the Diggers (Utes or Paiutes), who also liked to fill oxen and horses with arrows and were not above picking off a human straggler. Four days before Jim and John reached Salt Lake City, Samuel Oliver of Waukesha, Wisconsin, had been ambushed and killed by an arrow as he stood guard on the upper Humboldt's sloughs.

But it was all downhill going, past Frémont's Canyon, Gravelly Ford—where James Reed killed John Snyder in the famous Donner Party quarrel—Battle Mountain, the tule marsh at present-day Winnemucca, Lassen's Meadows, and, finally, Humboldt Lake. Just above it lay its Great Meadow; just below, the bizarre Humboldt Sink, where the river moved sluggishly out into the desert toward the Carson Sink and disappeared into the sand.

At the Humboldt Sink, Jim's party laid over for two days to rest the animals. There they boiled and ate the last of their dried beef and beans, gathered grass to prepare as hay for the animals, and paid $3 a pound for a little flour, which they baked into biscuits, two each, for the crossing of the dreaded Forty Mile Desert stretching aridly between the Humboldt Sink and the Carson River to the south.

Setting out in the forenoon, the Humes traveled down to the last watering place on the edge of the desert. They arrived by three in the afternoon, rested and fed the animals a little of the dried grass, and ate the last of their own provisions except for unleavened bread and a canteen of coffee each. At seven o'clock that night, Jim again led the small train out of camp and into the forbidding Forty Mile Desert. He kept them moving steadily at a fast pace until midnight, when he called a one-hour halt. After feeding more grass to the animals and eating the bread along with a few precious swallows from their canteens, the men made ready for the last push to the eastern base of the Sierra Nevada. "I presume that each of us will long remember that Passover, eaten at midnight on the desert by the light of a burning wagon, and twenty to twenty-five miles from water," John Hume later wrote home.

By morning's light, Jim had put the Forty Mile Desert and its last 10 miles, Destruction Valley, behind them. He led his men into camp under the green cottonwoods of the Carson River. By the end of August that year, according to emigrant James Mason, there were 3,000 dead and from 600 to 800 wagons, besides tons of property, scattered over those 40-odd miles of sand. That same month, Dr. George Read, on the trail behind the Humes, counted 25 abandoned wagons in a single 100-yard stretch of the Forty Mile Desert.

At the Carson, Jim found Ragtown, a string of four or five trading stations, brush wickiups with canvas or cloth roofs. The isolated tradesmen were doing a brisk business selling beef at 50 cents a pound to famished emigrants. Flour brought from $1.50 to $3 a pound, and pork $1.50 to $2. Rice was $1 a pound, as was bacon, a scarce item even at that price. Some men were hauling Carson River water out into the desert to peddle to the thirsty at $1 to $1.50 a gallon.

Jim and John had somehow to raise money to buy food. Their horse, Old Jake, had failed in the Forty Mile Desert, but he was not worth even 3 pounds of flour. They declined an offer of $40 for their best mule. For their cream horse, they were offered, at first, a mere 15 to 25 pounds of flour. But just then a man appeared who needed a packhorse to haul a purchase of $552 worth of provisions out into the desert to sell to hungry travelers. He had seen the cream on the road and offered the brothers $50, which they quickly accepted. Bystanders told the Humes that it was an enormous sum to receive at that graveyard of broken-down stock.

The Humes put all their money into provisions. They packed their personal belongings on one mule and, with the mare and the other mule for riding, started off on the last lap of their journey to the mines. At the Carson they said good-bye to their friends, who were not yet ready to tackle the Sierra passes. Only Ahaez Young and Edmund Baker accompanied them as they started up into the Sierra via the canyon of the Carson.

The difficult, steep Carson Pass trail was child's play for the Humes. As they neared their goal, they were exultant. From the head of the Carson, they once again employed their successful strategy of avoiding the mainline trail, this time from Carson Pass to Tragedy Springs and across the shoulder of Iron Mountain to Hangtown. Instead, two old Californians they met guided them over a little-used shortcut, possibly Luther Pass or one nearby, which, they were told, had been blazed by packers for the U.S. Army. It took them three hours to climb just 3 miles at one point, but when they were atop the great ridge, they were rewarded with more than just the thrill of finally being in California. Below them lay the 50-mile-long azure expanse of Lake Tahoe. It was, in John's words, "the cleanest and purest I ever saw."

CHAPTER III

———◆◀◆▶◆———

PROSPECTOR

J IM HUME arrived in California on or about August 20, 1850, and, some five days later, ended a journey of three months and five days at a tiny settlement called Work's Ranch, in El Dorado County. There, he and John proved once again that luck was with them. Since their mules and the mare had just about given out, they sold them for $140. The price was high, and a little later, when the season's big wave of travelers dropped animals by the hundred on the market, it would have been impossible to get it.

Jim and his three companions left their possessions—a crammed sack of clothes—at Work's Ranch and set out, each with only a blanket slung over his back, across the high divides of the Sierra for the placers of the Middle Fork of the American River. When they reached the deeply etched gorge of Missouri Canyon, whose streams fed the American's Middle Fork, they halted. The word, locally, was that the tributary in the bottom of the steep canyon was rich in gold. So the impatient Hoosiers bought a secondhand shovel for $20 and a rocker, or cradle, for $10 and set up camp, cutting pine boughs to make beds.

For a day or two, their digging turned up no color worth noticing, although Jim had located almost next to a claim that had yielded $1,500 not long before. But just when they had broken their last eagle for grub, they came upon a tolerable lead and continued working in Missouri Canyon for some three weeks. Although neither of the Humes had so far suffered a single day's illness, Jim fell sick with dysentery or diarrhea. Since their prospect seemed to be about worked out anyway, the boys decided to pack up and head for Hangtown. This camp, originally Old Dry Diggings and later Ravine City, had been renamed Hangtown after the lynching of three men in 1849 for robbery. The Humes had been warned of the cold, wet season ahead, and they wanted a look-see at the camp to determine if it would serve them as winter quarters.

Neither Jim nor John knew the slightest thing about prospecting or mining. But few others among the newly arrived prospectors did, either. The forty-niners learned from experience. The only real miners were from Sonora, Mexico; from New Mexico; or from Georgia's mining towns, Auraria and Dahlonega. Jim and his brother merely imitated prospectors with a little more seniority and made up for their inexperience with hard work. When they broke camp at Missouri Canyon, they found that they had taken out more than $1,000 from the great arroyo's sandbars. This they split evenly with their two partners.

The Humes then broke up the partnership, intending to try their hands at storekeeping in Hangtown, which, growing in sophistication and propriety, was beginning to call itself Placerville. John explained the move and change of occupation in a letter home: "*Change* is written upon everything in California. You cannot rely upon any man's staying in one place or continuing in the same business for two weeks at a time. Thus, you will see that this letter is dated from a new place." He could have added that he and Jim were already tired of standing in icy water, sometimes over the tops of their boots, and of grubbing in sandbars for the dull glint of gold while shivering from cold, exposure, dysentery, and backbreaking fatigue.

In the opinion of Placerville's two newest residents, California was already full to overflowing in late 1850. John wrote his father, "The mining region is being turned upside down, like as a drove of pigs would turn up a clover field." Some of the miners were making money, but many more were taking out little or nothing and scores were abandoning the Sierra to return East with their pockets flapping. Still, prices were high everywhere, proof that the boom was still very much alive in the placer camps. Flour brought $30 a hundred pounds, as did pork. Potatoes were costly at 40 cents a pound and onions even dearer, at $1.13 a pound. Molasses was 8 cents a gallon; a luxury like pies, $1.50 each. But the real shock for John came in the shape of the homely shovel. When a new shiny shovel could be found at all, it set the purchaser back no less than $30.

After their long months on the trail, the Humes were delighted when letters from the family, dated in July, arrived. Reading them, they were assailed by homesickness and toyed with the idea of returning to Indiana after the rains. John wrote Kate that her "California boys" were both anxious to patch up any hard feelings at home over their departure. John, like Jim, had had to break with his father in order to migrate, and now feelings of guilt plagued him. He confessed to his sister, "We have not used him, or mother, always, as we should have done. I only hope that they and we shall live long enough to prove to them that we now appreciate their kindness and long-enduring affection."

Long before California's early spring, fresh and brilliant, swept winter away, the brothers had resolved that it would be foolish to return home having so little improved their fortunes. They decided to stay for at least one more season to see if patience and perseverance might not pay off. John, the better correspondent of the two, wrote home, "I would not advise anyone to come here; *but*, any energetic man can soon accumulate a concession." He added that he thought capital was needed in order to make money quickly on the Pacific Coast and volunteered the opinion that his prosperous brother-in-law Samuel P. Williams, Jane Hume's husband, could convert $10,000 into

$50,000 in a single year by operating a store or bank in Sacramento rather than in Lima.

One California phenomenon—the conspicuous lack of women—was difficult to get used to. The boys had to do all their own cooking and washing, and John once confessed their longings to Kate: "Sometimes, we think of home and the nice dishes that you used to get up for us and of the milk, corn bread, mush, pudding, good butter and a thousand other things which we had at home, but never here." However, he concluded, practically, "But money can be made here much faster than at home and, therefore, all make up our minds to care nothing for all these inconveniences."

To the still-provincial Jim Hume, California was fascinating but a bit frightening. With 3,000 or 4,000 men in and around Placerville, he saw more people on the streets on any given day than he had seen in his lifetime in Lima. Most were hard-bitten, and the only ones who dressed like gentlemen—the 300 professional gamblers who preyed on the miners in the area—were anything but. Jim guessed that almost everyone except himself frequented the ubiquitous gambling dens, as much for amusement as for gain, because—aside from getting drunk—there was no other recreation in the mines.

In the elegant first-class saloons and gambling houses like the El Dorado, thousands of dollars changed hands every night. In a permissive atmosphere, the professionals went about the business of separating men from their money without interference from sheriff or court.

In matters of religion and morals Placerville and Lima were worlds apart. Jim found few, if any, prospectors honoring the Sabbath. On one Sunday in October, 1850, he saw a man mount a stump in the street to harangue passersby on the subject of Hangtown's proper observance of the Lord's Day. But Jim could barely hear him over the secular din of the day. Pins in a nearby bowling alley continued to clatter and crash, music rickey-ticked from saloon pianos, and a blacksmith was setting the rim of a wagon wheel so near the evangelist's perch that the little crowd of curious spectators could not stand on one side of him because of the intense heat of the smithy fire. The final irony, for Jim, was the harsh litany of a nearby auctioneer hawking a horse at the top of his lungs—"Forty-one dollars! Do I hear any more?"—which became entangled with the evangelist's words.

After only three weeks as Placerville businessmen, the Humes were confident of success. They had an excellent location and a good-looking building—at least in comparison with Placerville's characteristic shacks and shanties. Business was so brisk that they expected to clear $1,000 by spring, while in contrast with the miners, living dry and comfortably all through the wet season. They needed to make money, for they had left Kanesville with a total of $50, and had arrived in California with only the cash made by selling their animals. Jim could not decide whether to continue as a trader, return to mining, or have a go at the lucrative business of truck farming. He was even ready to go home if his father was to request his assistance in running the farm. His indecision was not prompted by difficulties in the store. Even taking into account the excessive freight charges on their Sacramento purchases, they still sold everything (except, possibly, flour and heavy articles) at a profit of at least 100 percent, and they turned over their entire stock every ten days.

On the other hand, neither brother felt himself cut out for a merchant's life, even should the market continue to be so scandalously profitable. And both wondered whether in a year or so the days of a clear profit of $8 on a single barrel of apples might be over. Prices in the fall of 1850 were dreamlike: apples worth two bits for two, oranges a quarter apiece, pies going for $1. Practically everything Jim sold across the counter went by the pound, whether tobacco, flour, nails, or candy. Even lowly turnips, beets, and cabbages were netting 37½ cents a pound, and hay in times of scarcity brought them 15 to 20 cents a pound! Both boys decided to postpone a decision on their future until the following year.

The combination of good climate—only three or four rainy days between August 25 and October 18—and the less strenuous work of storekeeping agreed with the Humes. They were dismayed, at first, by the strangely parched appearance of the California countryside, but they enjoyed winter weather as warm as early September in Indiana. Questioning the old-timers, they learned that the rainy season might hold off until December. John probably spoke for both of them when he wrote Kate, "I think the climate will agree with me, first-rate."

Both Jim and John continued, however, to be lonesome, homesick, and a little apprehensive about their aging parents as another sickly season approached back in Indiana. Jim complained to Kate that she did not write enough, urged her to send him a note every two weeks, and reassured her that he did not mind paying 40 cents postage, per letter, since nothing less than $1 in the boomtown of Placerville was considered to be worth even "a man's notion."

As 1850 waned, Jim's old Indiana friends were beginning to scatter. Ahaez Young, closest to the Humes and easily the best miner of the group, was living 10 miles out of Placerville, throwing up dirt for winter washing and happy and fat as a gopher. Jim and John acted as bankers for Young, who had been grubstaked by their brother-in-law, Sam Williams. From time to time, they reported on Young, telling Williams how well he was doing. Gold was still to be found in abundance. John observed, "It is the most unusual thing in the world to find a man without some of the dust." On the other hand, he had to add, "No one can live comfortably; that is, few do live very comfortably." An irritant to both brothers was the mobility of the population. "There is no such thing as society, at present," complained John; "men can no more know who their neighbors are, and take no more pains to get acquainted with each other, than passengers in a steamboat or omnibus." Shortly, however, he wrote that men with high standards of morality were not as scarce as he had thought. He and Jim were heartened by California's admission to the Union in September, 1850. On October

7, 1850, they participated in their first California election, confident that it was a harbinger of more peaceful and settled days.

The brothers were a little worried, that fall, about the possibility of an Indian attack. Indians had raided a nearby mining camp on October 20 and then had swept through Diamond Springs township as far as Mud Springs, shooting a miner in a cabin near Martínez Creek and driving off his stock. In their retreat up Weber Creek toward the High Sierra and a crossing of the American River near Brockliss's Bridge, the braves had murdered one or two other miners. The raid was, in fact, the second Indian scrape of the year. Earlier they had killed some miners in revenge for the shooting of redmen near Johnson's Ranch.

A company of volunteers was mustered at Placerville under Sheriff William H. Rogers, but the Hume brothers remained at home. Neither was thirsty for blood, and Jim was still not feeling in top form. Besides, John had hung out his shingle and was making far more money as an attorney than he ever had at home. Jim was pleased but rather surprised at his brother's success, for there were already two lawyers in Placerville, and two more soon came in. But John wrote the folks, "We never show our faces in court for less than an ounce, and a regular charge for a common case before a justice is $25, sometimes more. I have, two or three times, made $50 per day, cash down. I wish you had the gold watch which I got lately for attending to one case." He told the family that he was husky and healthy. But Jim was ill again, and John tried to alert his parents without alarming them—"James's health is tolerably good. I think he will go home next fall. I shall endeavor to persuade him to do so."

In the same letter, John reported on the farcical El Dorado Indian War: "We have for several weeks been in the midst of an Indian war and troops are marched almost daily through our streets, to and from the seat of war. Several skirmishes have already been had and several have fallen on each side. The Indians are living on every side of us and we frequently hear of their attacking mining parties within three or four miles of town. We enlisted in this place some 200 men for the army and since they have been gone, I have seen, on a sudden alarm, at least 400 men turn out at an hour's notice, armed to the teeth. No place in the States could equal this, for here the population is composed of men fit to bear arms and all have arms at hand."

The militiamen did march out, in fact, with Bob Carson, reputed to be Kit's brother, as a scout. But they went no farther than an encampment at Johnson's Ranch, where Jack C. (Cockeyed) Johnson kept a trading post and an ample supply of rotgut. Reports of a bloody battle soon drifted back to Placerville, as John indicated in his letter, but sometime later Carson declared the story a hoax. Commander Rogers got Thomas L. (Pegleg) Smith to negotiate with the Indians, and the almost bloodless war came to an end—except, of course, for the ubiquitous claims, real or fancied, that follow on the heels of all such wars. Expenses for the campaign—really a reconnaissance in force—came to $19,060, the cost of horses and mules supplied the troopers.

Not all the violence in El Dorado County occurred during Indian clashes with militia units. In October, 1850, a newcomer from the "States" was stabbed to death in the El Dorado gambling house on the corner of Main Street and Quartz Alley. A mob of some 2,000 to 3,000, intent on lynching the murderer, a gambler and desperado named Richard (Irish Dick) Crone, got him away from Sheriff Bill Rogers and two town constables by force. The mob was about to hang Crone from a tree in the main plaza when someone complained to the ringleaders that the noise was disturbing a sick man in a nearby house. They obliged the invalid by taking Irish Dick down Main Street and up Coloma Street to a suitable oak tree, where they strung him up without further disturbance of the peace and quiet of Placerville. John, as an attorney, was even more appalled than Jim by his first glimpse of vigilantism. He wrote his sister, "Such a fearful storm of popular fury I never witnessed."

By the time the spring of 1851 was brightening the manzanita-clogged ravines of the northern mines, Jim Hume had abandoned storekeeping, but he did not turn to truck farming. Instead, he went back to prospecting. There was a lot more wanderlust and gold hunger in Jim than in his brother. Still lonesome, he urged Kate to send his letters directly to Placerville. He advised her that letters addressed to him via Sacramento cost him $1.25 extra, above the 40 cents postage, and were not received a day sooner. Finally, in his April 10, 1851, letter, Jim confessed to his sister what she may have guessed from reading between the lines of his and John's earlier letters. His health had not been at all good during his first six months in California. "In fact," he wrote, "about the first of January, I had almost made up my mind to return home on account of my health." But he hastened to assure her that he now felt first-rate —"Today I was weighed and I find I am twenty pounds above my weight, at home, of 150, making 170."

With his health back and the warm sun drying out the slopes of the Sierra, Jim Hume turned energetically to prospecting again. The winter had been relatively dry, denying many miners the water needed for washing their gravel. But many had gone ahead and thrown up huge piles of dirt for future washing. Jim joined three other miners operating long toms some 50 feet in length. Since it took seven to ten men to manage one of the cumbersome contraptions, he and his partners hired helpers, paying each $4 to $5 a day. Still, Hume and his associates each cleared from $6 to $8, day in and day out, and they could expect to do so as long as the water supply lasted. On a single April day the foursome made $12 each, but on other days they made no more than their wage hands. Jim hired an old Indiana acquaintance, who eventually earned enough to buy out one of the original owners of the long toms and, thus, become his partner.

Like his brother, Jim sent nuggets home to Kate. One was large enough, he thought, to be made into a pin. The other was a curiosity, a nugget shaped like a fowl. He also mailed her a photographic view of Coloma, noting, "The gulches you see in the mountains are what we call dry diggings; the flats on the river, wet [diggings]."

During the summer of 1851 Jim boarded comfortably in Placerville with a Boston-born merchant, a true Yankee. Probably for his father's benefit, he wrote home that his landlord was the only man in town who refused to do any business on the Sabbath. Jim, himself, had become a churchgoer once again. When Ahaez Young made the seven-mile hike into town to visit him, Jim missed seeing his friend because he was at Sunday meeting. Business had slackened in Placerville over the winter of 1850-51, forcing Jim's landlord to take in a dozen boarders. The New Englander recommissioned his Yankee clerk as cook, and Hume rated his cooking as good as any he had tasted in California. In fact, every Sunday he enjoyed the luxury—virtually unheard of in California—of milk and mush. Milk was so rare it brought $1 a quart. However, the remarkable Yankee kept his own cow and provided Jim with fresh milk in his tea and coffee three times a day. His bed was made up of a straw mattress, three blue blankets, a quilt brought from Indiana, which he used as a sheet, and his rolled-up coat, which substituted for a pillow. He liked to brag to the folks at home—"I have not seen a bedstead in the country [but] I rest as well as I ever did on the nicest feather bed."

There was now only one other Lima man in Placerville, besides Jim and John. That was Wicker, a member of Hume's original party who, after having devoted himself to gambling and liquor, was trying to turn over a new leaf. And Ahaez Young was only 7 miles out of town. With few ties binding him to Placerville, Jim tried some of the more northerly mines during the summer, without much success. In September, 1851, he decided to make a major move. He formed a company, which marched 150 miles overland to try its collective luck in the southern mines, or the Mother Lode, itself. Perhaps, thought Jim, fortune would be kinder to him in Sonora, Tuolumne County, than in fabled El Dorado.

By November, 1851, Jim Hume was enjoying fair-to-middling luck as a prospector. He was in Sonora but thought of returning to Placerville, of which John was now writing home: "Our village begins to assume the appearance of life and bustle which it puts on at the approach of every rainy season. A large share of miners from the North, where they have snow during the winter, come here to a mild climate to spend the rainy season, as they mine here throughout the year. I have seen no snow, except on the mountains, since I left home." He told the family that he, but not Jim, expected to be going home for a visit in June or July, 1852.

John apologized for the lack of news of Jim and himself, explaining: "Everything is full of life but you would scarcely take any interest in the account of how such and such a tunnel is paying, or such a one struck a new lead or made a good raise, or another made a fortune in a good operation. Nor in our various public meetings, of which we have an almost infinite number. Or that such and such ones had a fight or were drunk, which is a daily occurrence with a certain class. Or that another made or lost such an amount at the gambling table. Yet such is the status of our news."

Jim was so pleased to receive three letters from Kate and a surprise letter from his sister Mary, forwarded to him by John, that he was prompted to write to the family on November 24. He hoped that their visit to Delaware County, New York, had benefited their uncertain health. He confessed to a lack of success at prospecting, but revealed his usual optimism: "I have now got a claim which I think will pay very good wages for two months or so." He sent his sister a locket, a present for his mother. It contained photographic miniatures of John and himself, made by their friend John Salmon, now a daguerreotypist. Salmon had taken John's picture at Coloma, Jim's at Sonora. Jim assured Kate that the locket, made of pure California gold, was an example of the best jewelry to be had in the state. Along with the locket he mailed two nuggets, and he also sent the family an artist's view of Sonora and a large photograph of himself.

He apologized for his unkempt appearance in the picture, explaining that it had been taken before he had shaved his beard off and when he was not in clean clothes but in his everyday rig, rough pants and two shirts—a cotton under a flannel one—the uniform of all Tuolumne miners. "The flannel shirt outside answers the purpose of a coat and also to keep off the dirt and mud which a miner is daily in contact with." In return, Jim asked Kate for miniatures of herself and his father and mother. He suggested that all could perhaps be on one plate.

Jim reassured his sister about living conditions in the Farthest West. "People in the Atlantic states are very much mistaken in regard to the hard fare in California. It was, indeed, *hard* a few years ago but, at present, a person can live as comfortably here as at the East. Vegetables of all kinds are now plenty at all seasons of the year and prices are moderate." He then reeled off the prices of potatoes, turnips, cabbages, onions, tomatoes, and parsnips. He enjoyed nearly all these vegetables daily at his boardinghouse, for only $10 a week. Although almost everything, including hay, was still being sold by the pound, he told Kate that, with the variety and moderate prices of beef, pork, venison, beans, peas, sugar, and molasses, there was no need for anyone to suffer from hard fare in the California mines as of November, 1851.

On the other hand, admitted Jim, religious fare was scarce indeed. The Sabbath in Sonora was characterized by business as usual and gambling, with more of each carried on that day than on any other because the miners customarily came into town on Sundays for supplies, rest, and recreation.

By this time Jim had a new partner. They were working two 16-foot claims on the bank of Wood's Creek, about 40 rods from the extreme west end of Sonora. In a claim only a few rods from Hume's, a piece of gold weighing 28 pounds had been taken during the summer, and more recently he had seen a miner, only 60 feet away, getting out nuggets ranging in weight from 1 ounce to 20 ounces, each. "It may be my good fortune to light on some like lumps, but I have given up expecting any very heavy showers [of gold], for I have been disappointed so often," he told his sister. Yet on the very day on which he wrote, Jim found a lump of gold worth $15. This sort of find kept his hopes alive, but it was an exception. Mining was becoming increasingly difficult. He explained, "The claims are so deep that we are obliged to work underground all the time except when washing, which occupies about one-fourth of our time. This kind of mining is called coyote diggings and is very hard on the eyes, as we are obliged to work, altogether, by the light of a candle. It is, however, considered perfectly safe, the ground being very hard and the drift made in the form of an arch."

Meanwhile, John was prospering in Placerville as a partner in the law firm of Robertson, Sanderson and Hume. Like Jim, he turned a deaf ear to Kate's pleas that he return to Indiana to live, although the violent character of California life was still distasteful to him. "The constant excitement of a life here is wearing and tiresome. The county is full of crime and bloody tragedies. Within the past week, two men were hung by the mob for stealing at Coloma, the county seat of this county, 13 miles from here. Today, I have obtained warrants for two men on a charge of larceny and when I close this letter I shall go straight to the Justice's office to prosecute them."

With the gold fever still raging uncontrolled in him, Jim Hume moved through the placer camps in search of a strike. He must have stayed in or near Diamond Springs that year because El Dorado County historian Paolo Sioli recalled that Jim had turned out in 1852 for the grand immolation of the Indian chief called Digger Jim, whose body was brought by his tribesmen to the holy ground behind the stables of Ham Hawley and Bob Shirley in Diamond Springs for the kindling of the funeral pyre. The ceremony took ten hours, and the stench of the burning body was almost intolerable by nightfall. Some prankster notified Coroner Tommy Daugherty that he was wanted, and he galloped to the scene from Placerville on his mustang, unaware that his customer was a "dead Injun." But he joined Hume and the crowd of at least sixty-five miners who stuck around to witness the funeral ceremony.

On May 1 Jim was rounding out two months of mining in Pine Grove, near Sonora. He wrote Kate: "You speak of looking for us at home in June but I believe I have not written anything to warrant you in expecting *me* so soon, nor has my mind changed on that point since I last wrote you. It would afford me the greatest of pleasure to see you all once more, although I am quite certain that I never can live contented again in the States. . . . My principal objections to living in Indiana are, in the first place, the unhealthiness of the climate; secondly, the uncertainty of crops and the very low price of produce; thirdly, the extreme length and severity of the winters."

Pine Grove, known also as Camp Martínez, was not the well-known town between Jackson and Volcano, but one four miles north of Sonora. Jim described it as lying "in a most beautiful little valley about a half-mile in length and forty rods wide." He and his partner were living in a log cabin about the size of one that stood on his father's Indiana farm. It had a door on the west side and a large fireplace on the north end. He wrote in detail about this home of his, describing the three-foot by two-foot bale standing some six feet from the hearth, directly in front of it. Its oilcloth-covered top was graced with three tin cups, three or four tin plates, a small box of sugar, another of salt, a jar of pickles, a bottle of molasses, and a small bottle of pepper. Also laid out were knives and forks, a wooden candlestick, a clay pipe, and a good-sized chunk of tobacco. Under the table squatted a camp kettle, a fry pan, and a coffeepot. The dirt floor and the small gold scales on the table were the only features that distinguished the interior of the Pine Grove cabin from that of a similar cabin in Indiana or New York. The utensils Jim listed made up his and his partner's entire cooking gear. But with a baker supplying bread every other morning, the cooking duties were fortunately light.

Jim and his partner had suspended a shelf in the middle of

the room, hanging it on ropes from the rafters. This shelf held all items they wished to keep secure from the rats and mice that also called the cabin home. In the corners of the hut adjoining the fireplace there were two bunks, really cots, made by stretching canvas between two poles set two feet apart. Jim had Kate's quilt on his straw-and-feather mattress and a pair of Mackinaw blankets. His coat still served as pillow. "You will undoubtedly think my bed a pretty hard one but I assure you, I never rested better in my life than I do in this." At the head of his bunk was Jim's tiny library—the Bible, Ollendorf's *Spanish Lessons*, a few newspapers, and some novels from the "States." Also there were the comb and the needle book Kate had sent him. And finally, the small package containing all the letters he had received from Indiana; most important to the homesick Hoosier, these he reread evening after evening.

Jim then explained why his possessions were so few. He reminded Kate that a miner changed locations often and had to carry all his goods on his back when he moved. Therefore, it was best to travel light. Then he mused, "I often think of a remark which Father used, frequently, to make. 'Boys, you should not be so difficult about your food. Learn to like such as is set before you. You may see the day when you can't get such as you like best.' Well, I have learned that it would have been better for me if I had paid more regard to this, as well as to all other advice given me by my parents. When I left home, I thought that while crossing the plains would be a good time to leave off the use of tobacco. But, as there was plenty to be had, I continued to use a little—*to kind of neutralize the effects of the poisonous water.*"

After bragging a little bit about his prowess at walking—"I have become so used to traveling on foot since I left home that I now think it no hardship to take my blankets on my back and walk twenty or thirty miles in a day"—Jim signed off by saying, "I leave it entirely to Father to do with the farm as he thinks best. Perhaps, if [sharecropper] Kelly does well, better let him keep it, another year at least."

71

During the summer of 1852 Jim's brother Charles came to California and located at Placerville. In July Jim made the trip to El Dorado County and stayed with his brothers until the end of October. All three were shocked by the news of the death of their sister Mary, but none was willing to return to Lima. John felt that he could not succeed at law in Indiana. As for Jim, John observed: "I do not know what James's ideas are about going home but I do know that he has a strong disinclination to spending the remainder of his life out of California."

Jim Hume's mother wrote him on September 14, 1853, to complain that she had not had a word from him since she had written a year before. Her letter of the same date to John had been answered promptly, likewise her note to Charles. She had important news for Jim. His father had attempted to sell the farm for $4,500 to Samuel Selby, who wanted it because he had just bought the adjoining 40-acre Croy place. But Selby's lawyer had persuaded his client not to buy because of Jim's part ownership of the property. Robert Hume had suggested that Selby pay only one-half the price until he could secure Jim's title, but Selby had finally dropped the whole idea. Jim's disappointed mother told him, "We were sorry, as we thought the farm well sold." She informed him that men were working the farm on shares but were not doing well. They did not even keep the barn and fences in repair. "The fact is, men working on shares never do things right and to keep a farm to let is the worst of folly."

With understandable urgency and annoyance, Mrs. Hume asked Jim to attend to the matter of title immediately, while Selby was still interested. His parents planned to give Jim one-third of the price of the farm, upon their deaths, and one-third to Kate. She asked him to show the title to John, who could make certain it was in proper legal form.

Mrs. Hume had bad news for Jim. His father's health had failed. Although his appetite, hearing, mind, and memory were good, he was hardly able to walk and no longer able to write. "Your father will not be able to write another letter," she stated and closed her letter by asking, "James, when may we expect to see John and yourself in Lima? When you answer this, do not fail to say what your intentions are in regard to returning."

The distressing news from home persuaded a dutiful son—reluctant as he was to leave California—to return to Indiana, via ship to the East Coast. His visit was hardly a holiday. Although in letters home he later tried to refer to it as a pleasurable experience, it must have been a trial. He was a stranger in the old household and was not sorry when it was time to leave again for California. By July 5, 1854, Jim had left Lovejoy's Hotel in New York and was in a first-class cabin on the steamer *North Star*.

On Monday, July 31, 1854, James Hume and fellow passengers, including actor Edwin Booth, arrived in San Francisco after a fine run from Panama. He wrote Kate, boasting about the speed of his steamer, which had arrived ten hours ahead of the Pacific Mail Line ship and far ahead of the Nicaragua Line steamer; in fact, the latter had not yet arrived. Jim reviewed the voyage. The Pacific had been mirror-smooth, and there had been relatively little sickness aboard—only four men died and had to be thrown overboard, three of them in one day. He himself had come down with the Isthmus fever, but thanks to the intensive care of new friends on board, particularly Dr. Winslow S. Pierce, former controller of California, Jim had recovered nicely. He was especially grateful for Pierce's services, since the doctor was returning to the coast not as a physician but as an office seeker.

On disembarking, Jim ran into a friend who gave him the first news of John's nomination for state senator and predicted his election. But John must have withdrawn from the race. (A few years later, he ran for the Assembly and won.) Jim immediately took the steamboat up to Sacramento and joined John and Charles in Placerville the following day.

Despite the high hopes of everyone concerned, Jim felt more estranged from his family after this visit than before. He tried to explain: "Thirteen or fourteen thousand miles is a great distance to travel merely to make a visit. Yet I do not, at all, regret going, for I am safe back and enjoyed my visit very much." But he felt it necessary to add, "More, perhaps, than my friends there. But, everything there is so very different from California that a man who cannot sit down quietly for days without excitement or amusement of any kind is lost to everything that is good. He has no affection for his friends and relations and is no more worthy of confidence." Probably, his mother and father had wanted to turn over the farm to him. Just as likely, he had flatly refused. He told Kate, "I am quite certain that Father has lost confidence in me but equally certain that if I ever had any principles of honesty and integrity, I still retain them, although I have been, and am again, in this 'awful country.' "

Jim was delighted to be back in California. He resumed his mining operations and was in good spirits even at the loneliest time, the Christmas holidays. Charles had left for home on Christmas Eve, John was 30 miles away in Placerville, but Grizzly Flat, Jim's new home, was blessed with May-in-Indiana weather. Almost a month later, on January 23, 1855, he wrote to Kate, now Mrs. Sanford Halsey, to congratulate her on her marriage and to express the hope that her new role would not alter their close relationship as correspondents and friends. He admitted that he had neglected to write her since leaving Placerville but hoped that John had kept his promise to write often. Reviewing the year just past, Jim found it the most eventful of his life: "My departure from San Francisco and first voyage on the perilous ocean; crossing the Isthmus, that terror to California voyagers; being on foreign soil for the first time; my first view of New York; Crystal Palace; Barnum's Museum, etc.; traveling by railroad for the first time; our meeting the morning I reached home and my very pleasant visit while there; my departure from home again; my return voyage and, finally, my safe arrival in Placerville and the mines."

What Jim neglected to tell Kate about 1854 was the fact that it marked his final decision to become a Californian. He would

visit Lima in later years but would never consider living anywhere outside the state that his friends and family in Indiana
called that "awful country." More important, he was, at last,
almost ready for a fresh start.

CHAPTER IV

————◄◆►————

CONFEDERATE ROAD AGENTS

THE New Year's Day rain of 1855 that had heartened Jim Hume with the promise, in *poco tiempo, mucho oro,* turned to snow, then faded away before clear and sunny skies. It was pleasant to walk about outdoors without coat or tie in January and to sit writing to Kate with cabin door and window thrown wide. But had he foreseen the rainless winter, Jim would never have moved his operations to the dry diggings two miles out of Grizzly Flat. With no water for washing the gravel, time hung frustratingly on his hands. So, on January 23, he wrote his sister a newsy letter. Christmas had been bleak and lonely, although the weather had been fine. His partners had gone away for the day, leaving Jim to consume on his own an entire mince pie, which he had baked. He described his current situation: "Myself, with five other *hombres,* are living here in the mines 30 miles east of Placerville, and one mile or more from anybody, keeping 'bachelor's delight.' Our business is mining or, rather, *banking—* but the bank as yet refuses specie payment and will not discount without a supply of *agua* and the application of elbow grease. There have been no runs as yet but the stock holders and owners expect a desperate one as soon as water can be had, which has been looked for, in vain, for a long time."

Jim was, of course, doing his own housework again, and he bragged to Kate that he had that morning washed four shirts and two pairs of socks. Commenting on his role as a housewife led Jim to discuss his sister's marriage and his own unlikely prospects. He called the idea of his ever getting married "a crazy notion." He swore, "The course I have marked out for myself is to press through life without ever forming any such connection."

By the time he next wrote his sister, on April 22, he and his five partners had pulled up stakes and were mining at Mount Pleasant, near Diamond Springs. He had walked to Placerville to visit John, a six-hour hike. From him he learned of the death of their brother Wilson. Much younger than Wilson, Jim could hardly remember him except as the parson in the pulpit of Pretty Prairie Church, and he was not much moved by his passing. However, he was conscientious enough to worry over the support and education of his deceased brother's family. After his visit with John, Jim transacted some business in Placerville and then walked home, the 25 miles proving rough on his socks, although he had patched them with parts of old pants in order to get optimum mileage from them.

On August 12, Jim began a brief vacation from mining. As a delegate to the El Dorado County nominating convention of the American (Know-Nothing) Party, he had to go "below," to Coloma, the county seat. After winding up his political business, he returned to Mount Pleasant, but only for the night. The next day he started out on another prospecting tour with some friends, still seeking a major strike. He was back at Mount Pleasant by August 30, after a very rugged expedition. He told Kate, "This was the hardest jaunt I have ever taken in the mines. After the first day, the route being impassible for mules, we sent them home and took the packs, which consisted of two weeks' provisions, cooking utensils, blankets, picks, pans, shovels, guns, pistols, etc., etc., on our backs. We traveled in this way, more or less, every day, prospecting favorable-looking places while we rested from our loads until our stock of provisions was nearly exhausted. Then we left everything but our firearms, some baked dough and a few pounds of bacon, and made our way home. None of us had a coat or vest with us. We slept on the ground every night, caught no cold (which is not at all remarkable in this climate), for eight days did not see a white man or any trace of one, found gold as far as we went, and got one piece of $12. But such mountains it has never been my lot to travel before and 'if I knew myself intimately,' will never be again, especially with a load on my back."

When Jim visited John in Placerville, he noticed that his brother was not only tidying up his dwelling, curiously enough, but was also refurnishing it and building on an addition. John volunteered no information, and Jim was too polite to ask. But his curiosity was soon satisfied, for on Thursday, September 6, 1855, John married Martha Tackaberry of Placerville. Jim was unable to attend the wedding, although he received a pressing "invite" from the groom. Unfortunately, duty called, for Jim, now an inspector of elections, was kept busy at the polls until it was too late to reach town in time for the ceremony. But John Salmon, who had attended, gave him the details later. It had been a very select gathering, and the Reverend James Pierpoint, the Presbyterian minister in Placerville, had performed the ceremony. Martha was about eighteen years old, handsome, and highly spoken of by everyone. Jim knew her only slightly but was sure that she would make John a capital wife. "Hope so," he wrote Kate, "for John is one of the best of men."

John's marriage made Jim Hume more a loner than ever. But he immersed himself in mining and in his new interest, politics. The elections of 1855 delighted him. The American Party had inherited the role of loyal opposition from the collapsing Whigs, and its success was overwhelming. As Hume noted, it swept the state and put an end to Democratic gubernatorial rule dating from 1849. The American Party candidate for governor, J. Neely Johnson, received 49,078 votes to the incumbent John Bigler's 44,708.

After the election, Jim returned to Grizzly Flat to try his luck there once more. On September 16 he wrote to Kate, instructing her to send all mail directly to the flat, since it was to receive a post office shortly, and reassuring her that he had not been delinquent in his letter writing. "You complain of not receiving letters, regular. It cannot be my fault for I believe, with one exception, I have written home every month and, many times, oftener." During the last hour of the last day of 1855 Jim wrote home to his brother-in-law Samuel Williams, lamenting that he could not greet him, face to face. He added, "Christmas came and passed as other days with us. We worked as usual, ate and drank as usual, nothing more. Tomorrow we expect to do the same, except *chicken pot pie* for dinner. We are working real hard now. We have not realized anything from these claims, yet, but will soon if we do not freeze up entirely." (Frosty nights left up to an inch and a half of ice in buckets and mud puddles by morning.) Jim sold a half-share in his claim to Fred White, a first-rate fellow and steady worker who also worked half time for him for $30 a month.

Hume's hopes were sustained at Grizzly Flat by the success of his neighbors. A quartz mill near his "Lagrange" claim had taken out $39,000 in a month, and its expenses had been only $30 a day. All three mills in the area were paying well, and there seemed to be plenty of room for others to come in. Still burning with gold fever, Jim kept digging away. He also tried to reinterest Sam Williams in California gold. "Would you not do well to visit these parts before the good chances are all taken?" he asked. However, he astutely commented, "I think the quartz business is *the* business," and enclosed a newspaper clipping that listed the gold discoveries in El Dorado County.

Even in his isolated Sierra cabin, Jim must have been aware that the boom days of California gold were fast drawing to an end. Bad times were on the way, but the panic and depression of 1857 would hurt the city dwellers more than the miners. More lonely than ever after John's marriage, Jim was ravenously hungry for news from home. On March 1, 1856, he wrote Sam Williams that he read his letters from Lima first at the post office, then at his cabin, and then over and over again until "I verily believe I could transcribe from memory every letter from home." He renewed his subscription to the Lima paper, hoping that its recent change of editors might improve it. Although it contained little of value, it was a link with home that Jim badly needed.

In a letter home, John wrote, "In the mountains of California we feel no effects, good or bad, from the financial embarrassments otherwheres . . . [for] we have no paper currency, a bank bill is seldom seen and is of no possible use (I have not seen one for years). . . ." But Jim was beginning to lose his optimism. He predicted hard times ahead for miners like himself and wrote Kate, "There are quite a number of persons in Grizzly Flat who are to start for the Atlantic states in the morning and, to use a common saying, I have half-a-mind to join them. Was it one month later, nothing but the enormous rates of passage would prevent me again visiting you. But fare now is *exorbitantly* high, being $350.00 in the cabin."

Perhaps Jim's gloomy prospects also soured his view of the present. He was now in partnership at Grizzly Flat with two other men, a bachelor and a young married man. They all shared a cabin, and the wife of Jim's younger partner took care of all the household chores. Each of the single men paid her $1.25 a day, plus two-thirds of the general expenses. But the married couple's two-year-old daughter and five-year-old son soon got on the nerves of perennial-bachelor Hume. "I am heartily tired of it," he wrote his sister, "and shall, in a few days, commence building a small home that shall be wholly and *entirely* my own, in which I take up my abode and be, myself, the housekeeper. I don't feel at home with them. The woman does the housework very well and is very kind to me but unruly young ones I cannot endure. No peace or quiet about the house, for them." At the ripe old age of thirty, Jim Hume seemed to be turning into a misanthrope.

Jim did not see much of John now, and both pleaded lack of

news for their faltering correspondence. However, Jim did visit his older brother in February, 1857, and John reported him to Kate as being not only robust, but heavier, filled out. Politics, particularly the Kansas question, was of vital interest now to both Humes. It seemed to them, as they exchanged notes, that Stephen Douglas and Senator David Broderick had solid backing among the mining population and that the federal administration had few supporters in California beyond officeholders, because of its views on Bleeding Kansas. John explained it to his sister: "We are all squatters here. The law of our mines is squatter law and each ravine and cañon makes its own laws and regulations, which are recognized and enforced by the courts. Therefore, from our habits and position, we are, perhaps, a little ultra in favor of Squatter Sovereignty in its broader sense."

Jim was now somewhat ambivalent about California. He still liked to tempt his brother-in-law to come, writing Williams that he wished that they were together. "But that is impossible while I entertain such favorable notions of the Pacific Coast and dislike of Indiana, unless you conclude to take up your abode here, which I am certain you would do, should you but once visit and spend a season here." Yet at the same time he was thinking of abandoning California for Mexico. He thought that there he might find the golden success that had so far eluded him in the mines of Sonora. He would wait until the political disturbances in Mexico were settled, basing his plans on the hope that Uncle Sam would take possession of the area, either by purchase or otherwise. He admitted to Williams that mining had been very dull all winter, but he still insisted that things would improve—perhaps in 1858.

During the severe winter of 1858-59, Hume finally got the rain he wanted so badly. At last he had sufficient water to work his claim. He kept at it diligently although when he visited John and Martha in October, he got the disturbing news that his father had died in August.

When news of Nevada silver discoveries broke, Jim was not

ready to join the rush, but he was sure that the riches were not illusory. He predicted that the rock would yield from $4,000 to $7,000 a ton, mostly in silver but partly in gold, too. He foresaw vast migration to the Comstock, and he was right. But his own confidence in mining as a way of life was flagging. He had mined longer than most forty-niners—for almost ten years—and had little to show for it. When a close friend gave up and started for Wisconsin on October 20, 1859, Jim nearly joined him. "I thought strongly of going with him," Jim wrote Williams, "and I should have gone [home] had I not feared your cold winter weather. I have now given up all thought of going at any time." This was an old sentiment to Williams, but Jim's discouragement was a jarring new note. He ended the letter, "The Prince of Ill Luck seems to have followed me unceasingly ever since I returned from there [Indiana] in 1854. In my operations, this summer, I have not made a dollar."

To keep himself in beans and coffee, Hume took on other jobs, and one of them turned out well—a brief stint as a deputy sheriff under E. B. Carson, although his duties were collecting taxes in eastern and southern El Dorado County, rather than tracking down dangerous outlaws.

The gold fever died hard in Jim Hume. He seemed to cling to the dream of instant wealth as the only way of justifying his traumatic break with his father. Guilt hounded him all the way to El Dorado, and even the knowledge of his father's death did not shake it off. If anything, it tightened its grip. But after a decade of fruitless searching, Jim finally recognized his dream for what it was—a chimera. On March 4, 1860, he chucked aside his miner's pick and shovel forever and began a new career in public service. Never again would he be nagged by self-doubt. Although his start in office was modest he had found his niche at last and was on the road to much better times and to fame itself.

Jim Hume was appointed deputy tax collector in Placerville, charged with securing, particularly, the Foreign Miners' License Tax, a levy originally so unfair and punitive—even confiscatory—that all aliens with the exception of the meek and long-suffering Chinese, had protested violently against it. In 1850, some 4,000 French, Mexican, and *Chileno* miners had gathered in protest in Sonora in such mob force that it took the sheriff, backed by 180 armed men, to disperse them. The tax had been too much for even the most bigoted Know-Nothing to swallow—$20 a month, with nonpayment punishable by up to three months in jail, a $1,000 fine, and the sale at auction of the offender's property after only an hour's notice by proclamation.

The tax had been virtually uncollectible and had poisoned relations between American and alien miners. It was repealed in 1851, and a new one was substituted the following year with the monthly fee dropped to a fraction of the original figure. By the time Jim Hume took on the job of collecting the tax in El Dorado County, it was still bitterly resented, although only $4 a month, payable in "good, clean gold dust" valued at $17 the ounce—and it was being paid.

The law's apologists masked their xenophobia by arguing that the tax was a way of equalizing the burden of the cost of government and pointed out that foreigners did not normally own taxable land. (They failed to say that many Yankees owned no land, either.) In reviewing the license, the State Supreme Court upheld the state's right to require it, leaning on the legal fiction that it was not a tax, but merely a license fee. Therefore, it could not be discriminatory taxation. So in 1860 Hume joined the throng of peace officers who collected the monthly fees and pocketed the 15 percent commission. He was able to keep his tax collector's job in 1862, when he accepted appointment as city marshal and chief of police of Placerville. It was at this time that he adopted the middle name Bunyan, after a Scots ancestor on his mother's side of the family, as a device for keeping him from being confused with his well-known brother, the attorney. (Both boys had, at birth, been given the middle initial "B." but no middle names.)

Some of Hume's time was taken up with the pettiest of policing chores—dogcatching. The *Daily News* liked to rib him about his canine funeral processions up Center Street and warned its readers: "You had better 'tag' your dogs!" But the paper was serious when it applauded the City Council for having selected Hume for the multiple offices. "Order begins to 'reign in Warsaw.' The streets are being thoroughly cleansed, nuisances are slinking out of sight, and crime is lowering its flag." The editor meant cleansing in a literal as well as a figurative sense. For, in addition to his duties as lawman and tax collector, Hume was also street commissioner. In July, 1862, for example, he had all the gutters in town cleaned out, and he graveled Main Street from the plaza to Stony Point. He also repaired or replaced all broken sections of the board sidewalks on Main and Sacramento streets, leading the *Daily News* to cheer: "The streets and sidewalks are now beginning to look 'niff.'" The editor crowed in August, "OUR CITY, under the administration of our able, efficient and energetic Marshal, James B. Hume, presents a fine appearance. Order and cleanliness is manifest everywhere. Main Street, with its new coat of gravel, laid down with care and precision will soon be the finest street in the County." That winter, Hume had a posse out, clearing snow, slush and mud from the boardwalks in order to keep the town looking "nifty." The following spring, although he had announced his candidacy for reelection as marshal, tax collector, and street commissioner, he did not fear to threaten to have the law on Coloma Street property owners who failed to remove rubbish from in front of their establishments by the deadline he had set. The citizens were pleased with the shipshape way Jim Hume was running the county seat and in the April 21, 1863, election, gave him 466 votes, to his opponent's 185.

Hume continued to play his threefold role in civic affairs for several years, announcing regularly in the press that he could be found in Esquire Bush's old office, upstairs in Douglas' building. Tax collecting, street cleaning, dog pinching, and prying fees from Chinese miners constituted his basic training in public service and law enforcement. While the routine work palled, he did his duty and bolstered his income by means of the tax commissions. He usually turned over $100 to $500 monthly to the city treasurer, but in July, 1862, for example, he deposited $1,464, of which $250 was from the sale of dog tags.

The sheriff's office normally handled the big cases—murders and robberies; Hume and his deputy marshals dealt with the leavings—incidents of drunkenness, indecent exposure, and the obstruction of Hangtown Creek. One of his cases proved rather embarrassing, too. In February, 1863, the Chinese celebrated their New Year with shouts of *"Gung hay fat choy!"* the firing of crackers, and general bedlam. They started on the fifteenth and were still at it on the seventeenth, when several of Placerville's residents appealed to Hume to put a stop to the din, which was causing teams to bolt in the daytime and making the nights "hideous and sleepless." Jim called on the leaders of the Chinese community and asked them to refrain from using firecrackers. In every "celestial" store he was answered, "Very good, John, we stop-ee," but no sooner had he turned his back than crackers started exploding, some popping at his very boots. Finally, Hume had to arrest one of the celebrators, lodging him in the station house. But when he returned to the Chinese section, the noise was worse than ever. He arrested a second man and attempted to haul in a third, who resisted, forcing Jim to display his revolver. The celebration was turning into a riot when Hume got help from Officer Higgins, but the two were met by fifty chattering and angry Chinese, who gave them a rough handling until they began hitting out with their billies and clubbed pistols. A stagecoach driver, Coon Hollow Charlie, rushed to Hume's rescue with some of his cronies. The Chinese were subdued and their leaders taken into custody. A Mexican then threw his support to the Chinese side and hurled several chunks of wood at the beleaguered city marshal. The *Daily News* took advantage of the Chinese imbroglio to needle its rival, the *Mountain Democrat*, reporting: "During the battle, a Greaser (one of those peace-loving citizens so ably defended by the Secesh sheet uptown) was observed to throw sundry billets of wood at Marshal Hume, thus showing a determination on the part of the native to defend the adopted citizen." Things calmed down, and Hume quietly released his prisoners.

In time, Hume's cases became more interesting. In March, 1863, he investigated the bold rustling of a horse right in Quartz Alley. A gentleman was riding up the alleyway when two Mexicans grabbed him, pulled him to the ground, and made off with his mount. That same night someone dug a hole through the brick wall of Hunt and Chance's Store and absconded with $20 in coin, a flask of quicksilver, and other valuables. Hume was sure that the culprits were Chinese because of the quantity of tea stolen. He found a package of it that had been dropped and began a search of Chinatown, turning up six Oriental thieves and much of the stolen goods. He was sure that he had found the gang of petty larcenists that had plagued both Coloma and Placerville for a long time. His editor friend wrote, "We hope he will succeed in cleaning the last one of the pilfering horde out and that after he gets through with the job he will make a reconnaissance of the Greaser lines." Although, in May, he arrested a daring Mexican robber armed with a formidable knife, Hume was not playing any favorites; he was after all wrongdoers, whether Mexicans, Chinese, or *fan kwei* (whites).

Jim Hume's effectiveness as municipal peace officer, backed by his work as secretary *pro tem* of the Confidence Engine Company Number One of the Volunteer Fire Department and as delegate to the Union Party's county convention, soon brought him to the attention of county officials. On March 4, 1864, Sheriff William H. Rogers appointed him under sheriff. The *Mountain Democrat* cheered him as a clever gentleman who would make a good officer. But Hume was not adept at politics. He made a major blunder as city marshal when he chose Seneca Davis as a policeman to replace Constable J. G. Bailey, whom he raised to deputy city marshal. Davis had served earlier as a reliable officer, but he was now under general suspicion, accused of being a Copperhead, or Confederate sympathizer. Since Hume leaned toward the Democratic Party, though not its so-called Chivalry (Southern) faction, he had not worried about Davis' politics. The maverick *Mountain Democrat,* a lonely opposition sheet in a world that seemed peopled entirely by superpatriotic Republicans and Unionists, gleefully poked fun at the town's fears: "Our citizens were never dreaming of danger but sleeping through the pleasant nights in fancied security. Last week, however, it was reported that Semmes, the buccaneer, had threatened to sail the *Alabama* up Hangtown Creek and throw Greek fire into Chinatown to punish one of our aldermen for his loyalty and enmity to the Southern Confederacy."

Hume was wise enough to rectify his mistake and dropped Davis from the force. The *Mountain Democrat,* fond of Hume, spared him its usual barbs when it reported the City Council's impassioned debate on the incident, merely remarking, "Mr. Hume said he had employed Davis because he knew him to be well qualified for the place, honest, capable, and faithful, without thinking about his politics, but that he had just learned that he was a Copperhead and he was, therefore, snakebit." Civil War politics were deadly serious in the Sierra. When Hume's Greek friend John Cartheche ran for city marshal, to succeed him, he lost to the administration (Republican) candidate, Samuel J. Ensminger. The loyal opposition had to content itself with the *Mountain Democrat's* predictably sarcastic story. The editors showered tongue-in-cheek praise all over Ensminger, "the unobtrusive, patriotic, faithful, irrepressible, loyal Samuel. We breathe freer and easier. . . . Copperheads, hunt your holes! His loyalty is of the genuine stamp and manifests itself in the genuine manner, by constantly seeking office."

Hume was not superstitious, but Friday, May 13, 1864, seemed to be jinxed for him as he led a pursuit of the McCollum gang of robbers—Ike McCollum, Scotch Tom, and another, nameless, desperado. They had escaped from the Marysville jail in April and fled to El Dorado County. Constable John D. Van Eaton, first to hear of the escapees, notified Under Sheriff Hume, Sheriff Rogers, and Deputy Joseph Staples. Hume took Staples and Van Eaton out of town and then split the party.

Each man took a different route toward Mud Springs, where Hume thought he might surprise the gang. Van Eaton saw them first and joined Hume. Staples was left to guard the road, while Jim and Van Eaton pushed on. They found Scotch Tom at the head of Irish Creek, near Kelsey, sick and abandoned by his pals. Hume arrested him but found no trace of the others. On Sunday he heard that the outlaws were robbing the Chinese in Big Canyon, near Frenchtown. It was Monday evening when he and his men overtook the two bandits near Fiddletown in Amador County. The robbers hid in the brush, shooting at the officers, who returned the fire. Although the bandits were no more than 60 feet away, they were so well concealed in the thick manzanita that Hume soon realized that they had a distinct advantage. After some forty rounds had been fired, Jim was pretty sure that he had hit McCollum, but Van Eaton was wounded in the right side, near the hip, and Staples' horse had been struck in the right leg. When darkness fell, the robbers escaped. Hume found no sign of them the next morning. He left Van Eaton to rest in a settler's cabin and reported to Sheriff Rogers, who sent a doctor to treat him. Although both the *Mountain Democrat* and the influential Sacramento *Union* praised Hume, the former saying, "For the faithful and fearless discharge of their duty, all three officers deserve the thanks of the community," Jim was thoroughly disgusted with himself for letting McCollum slip right through his grasp. He realized that he still had much to learn but vowed that he would not be outmaneuvered again.

Early in June, Jim Hume cleared up the robbery of Nachman's Store within a few hours. It was a satisfying case, but a minor one. On the last day of the month, however, the most farfetched of all stagecoach holdups in the West occurred, and right on Hume's beat, the Placerville to Nevada stage road over the Sierra. But Hume's streak of bad luck held, and he was in Stockton on sheriff's office business when the Bullion Bend case broke. He read about it the next day in Sacramento as he was returning to Placerville. The capital was buzzing with rumors that the take, in bullion and specie, totaled anywhere from $5,000 to $40,000. Wells, Fargo had made no statement, but finally an agent told newspapermen that the coin stolen did not exceed $3,000. No estimate of the worth of the stolen Nevada silver bullion was made public.

Stagecoach robberies were becoming numerous in California, but this one, Hume agreed, was unique. Not only had two stages been held up at once, but also the robbers had been identified as Confederate irregular soldiers! Hume read in the *Union* that several posses had set out from Placerville, and he hurried home to join the chase. On arrival, he learned of the curious holdup's tragic sequel, the gun battle of July 1 in which his friend Deputy Joseph Staples had been killed.

Under Sheriff Hume carefully reconstructed the robbery: At about ten o'clock on the night of June 30 two of Louis McLane's Pioneer Stage Company coaches were winding their way over the Sierra from Lake Bigler (Tahoe) toward Placerville. Only a few minutes apart, both were crowded, as usual, with Nevada passengers, fourteen to a coach—seven inside and seven on top. Ned Blair, driving the lead Concord, has slowed down to ease around the narrow blind curve high above the canyon of the South Fork of the American River, screened by a mountainside covered with ponderosa pines and towering incense cedars. Blair had considerable respect for the curve because of the steep drop-off to his right and the mere foot of running room on his left, between the wheel tracks and the 10-foot inside bank of the stage road.

Suddenly Blair saw seven men in the road and on the upper bank. All were armed and wearing masks. Jamming on the brakes, he brought the Concord to a shuddering halt, throwing the passengers inside into a startled knot and almost tossing those topside into the dust. The road agents immediately surrounded the coach, ordering Blair to throw down the Wells, Fargo box.

"I don't have one," he lied.

"Then throw down the bullion!"

90

"Come and get it!" was the driver's hot retort.

While two men kept him covered, two others secured the bags of silver bars. When Blair asked them not to rob his passengers, they said that they had no such intention; all they wanted was Wells, Fargo's treasure. Their leader, addressed as Captain by the others, reassured the passengers quietly and politely that he was no robber but the commander of a company of Confederate soldiers.

When he heard the drumming of hooves, followed by the creaking of a thoroughbrace and the rattle of undercarriage and wheels that signaled the approach of the second stage, the captain ordered Blair to pull up to the side of the road. Charley Watson, founder of the Sierra settlement of Strawberry, was the second driver. He stopped when he saw Blair's coach, motionless, ahead of him. Thinking that his friend had had an accident, Watson handed the lines to a passenger seated on the box next to him, got down, and walked up to the other Concord, only four or five rods away. He was brought up short by a terse command: "Hold on, or I will put a ball through you." Watson did as he was told and resumed his seat while the bandits finished robbing the first stagecoach. Blair was then allowed to start off. As he did so, one of the passengers—an ex-policeman from Virginia City—pulled out a pistol and blazed away at the masked men. One shot went wild, but a second knocked the revolver from a bandit's hand. The furious robbers did not even have time to snap off a shot in return before the coach swung around the next curve and disappeared into the black Sierra night. They began to threaten Watson and his passengers, but the driver managed to calm the bandits by reminding them that neither he nor his passengers had made the slightest resistance and should not be blamed for the foolhardy actions of one man on the other stage. Later Watson recalled the tense moment—"They seemed excited and said they would kill the last son of a bitch of them. I talked good to them and got them into a good humor." Charley ordered his customers to make no resistance. He wanted to keep them from being shot and also to prevent his team, jittery from the shots already fired, from tumbling coach and passengers down the canyonside. But he need not have worried, for the only arms among them were a single revolver and a couple of derringers. An anonymous passenger later told the *Daily Alta California* why prudence had prevailed so completely: "I can assure you, pistols never before seemed so formidable to me, as well as others, for in the dark, the bores seemed at least as large as a six-pounder's."

The captain was a stabilizing influence, too. He again spoke politely to the passengers, assuring them that no harm would come to them as long as they remained quiet. "We won't detain you but a moment. All we want is Wells, Fargo's treasure," he declared, then added, "Gentlemen, I will tell you who we are. We are not robbers but a company of Confederate soldiers. Don't act foolish. We don't want *anything* of the passengers. All we want is Wells, Fargo and Company's treasure, to assist us to recruit for the Confederate Army."

Watson handed down two sacks of bullion, gambling that the highwaymen would think that was the entire consignment. But one, cursing him through his black beard, demanded, "We want it all!" He climbed aboard, elbowed the driver aside, and threw down another sack of bullion, the wooden Wells, Fargo treasure chest, and a small box of expressed freight. During the looting one of Watson's passengers, a young girl of about sixteen, seated on top near him, kept up a barrage of questions and banter with the outlaws. She asked the captain if he had a Confederate flag and how he planned to get away with so much heavy silver. Apparently fearless, she was annoyed, not frightened, when the muzzle of the captain's pistol accidentally grazed her face. She chided him, lightly, for his carelessness and asked him to be more careful, as the gun just might go off. The flustered captain was suddenly all chivalry; he apologized profusely and said that she had no cause for worry since he and all his men were Southerners, who would rather protect young ladies than injure them. Finally, the Rebels passed the hat, asking the passengers if they would not care to "contribute" a few dollars to advance the cause of the Confederate States of America. The travelers had little choice but to add their silver to Jeff Davis' coffers. During this levy, the girl continued her repartee. She asked if the Rebels would take greenbacks and joked that she had five cents of postal currency (postage stamps) in her pocket but that she would not give it up without a fight.

Before ordering Watson on to Placerville, the captain warned him that any shooting from the coach would be returned, with interest, by his men. Then one of his aides handed Charley a slip of paper. When he had time to steal a glance at it, the driver found that it was a receipt for the loot just seized: "This is to certify that I have received from Wells, Fargo & Co. the sum of _____ cash, for the purpose of outfitting recruits enlisted in California for the Confederate States Army." It was signed "R. Henry Ingrim, Captain, Com'g company, C.S.A., June 1864." Hume noted that the captain, in his hurry or nervousness, had neglected to fill in the blank space where the amount of treasure requisitioned for the South should have been indicated.

Once they were safe, the passengers asked their Jeanne d'Arc why she had chattered so much with the robbers, and her reply proved her to be as quickwitted as she was plucky. Since all the holdup men were masked, she engaged them in conversation in the hope that some of the passengers would later be able to identify them by their voices. One of her fellow passengers gave the story to the *Alta*, saying, "She was smarter than we men were . . . and I might add, considerably more self-possessed. If I knew her name I would give it to Chief Burke [San Francisco police] with a recommendation that she be employed on detective duty."

At Thirteen Mile House, Blair gave the alarm. He was soon joined by Watson, and word of the double holdup was flashed to Placerville by the original telegraph line over the Sierra, Colonel Bee's "grapevine." In the absence of Under Sheriff Jim Hume, Sheriff Rogers took personal command of the pursuit of the bandits. He awakened Deputy Joseph Staples, constables George

Ranney and John Van Eaton, policemen J. G. Bailey and J. Y. Williamson, some Pioneer Stage Company employees, and other civilians, and they galloped off in search of the Secessionist raiders. But all the posse found was one of the bandits' horses in the pine woods near the holdup curve. The animal was saddled and bridled, a pair of Mexican rawhide hobbles hung on the saddle horn, and behind the pommel was a blanket roll, inside of which were two cans of powder, some bullets—and a bologna sausage.

Sheriff Rogers had then divided his posse, sending Van Eaton, Ranney, and Staples on horseback to check out the junction of the Placerville-Diamond Springs road with the shortcut that ran from the holdup site—ever after called Bullion Bend—while he hurried in a fast freight wagon to the bend itself. Rogers was sharply and unfairly criticized for heading for the one spot where the robbers would not be found. But Hume would have done the same thing, in order to pick up their tracks. The three officers detached by Rogers cut the trail of the fleeing guerrillas, heading across the North Fork of the Cosumnes River. Van Eaton, still suffering from the bullet wound he had received in May, was sent back to the sheriff for reinforcements while Ranney and Staples trailed the horsemen through the buckthorn to a dusty, hillside clearing, spiked with weedy, candelabralike mullein, and dominated by the two-story frame inn called Somerset House, run by Mrs. Maria Reynolds. It lay just beyond the North Fork on the road to Grizzly Flat. Since it was a major stopping place and only a dozen miles from Bullion Bend, the two lawmen halted, dismounted, and asked Mrs. Reynolds if there were any men in the house. "Yes," she replied, "six, upstairs."

Staples led the way to the porch and examined a shotgun propped against a wall near a door. As he turned back, Ranney passed him and boldly entered another door, which led to a bedroom. Inside, he found a half-dozen startled men, several of whom put their hands to their sides as if to draw weapons. But Ranney put them at ease with sheer bravado. "Good morning!" he began cheerily, and when a dark-complexioned man with

94

bloodshot eyes mumbled a reply, the constable, playing dumb, asked if he had seen anyone passing the inn, toward Grizzly Flat, during the morning. The man said no, so Ranney left the room, his heart twisted into a tight knot as he turned his back on the gang of Johnny Rebs.

Outside he met Staples, carrying the shotgun at full-cock. Ranney put a hand on his shoulder and whispered "Hold on! We are right on them!" But the deputy made no reply and continued along the platform. Stepping into the doorway of the bandits' room, he leveled the gun at one of them and said, "You are my prisoners. Surrender!" Why had Staples, alone and silhouetted in a doorway, acted so recklessly, bearding six outlaws in their hideout? Hume knew exactly why. Staples was smarting from loose talk about his courage—or rather, his rumored lack of it. In the battle with Ike McCollum near the Amador line, Staples' horse had run away with him when it was shot in the leg, leaving Hume and Van Eaton pinned down by the fire from the thicket of chaparral. Hume knew that later some saloon hero in a Placerville barroom had said, contemptuously, while the deputy was present, "Staples took damned good care to keep out of danger." Stung, Staples had sworn publicly, "The next time I go, I'll be brought back dead or I'll bring back my man."

Staples' command was answered by pistol shots from the crowded room. The deputy swung around in the doorway but was able to fire once before he fell, the charge of buckshot catching one of the band, Tom Poole, full in the face. The outlaws quickly turned their attention from the dying Staples to Ranney, filling the room with the cordite stink of gunsmoke and the air with flying lead. The captain—Ingrim—fired eight shots, bandit John C. Bouldware fired six more, and Alban Glasby shot at Ranney twice from the porch. Their comrades joined in, too. Ranney retreated, seeking cover in the canyon oaks, the Ceanothus, black locust, and prickly toyon that formed a thicket behind Somerset House. There was no time to reach the ponderosas, or yellow pines, on the hill. Ranney later recalled the panicky moment: "I had lost the range of the man in range of

95

my pistol at the moment of firing. He had crawled into the corner. I could not get in the door as Staples took up the room. . . . I commenced backing down the steps and fired two shots at them. They were firing at me. I got behind a tree. I got behind a small building. They fired at me as I went. I started to go up a raise of ground. I had been hit and the blood was coming out of my mouth. I threw up my hands. They then ceased firing."

Hemorrhaging, Ranney almost choked on his own blood as the outlaws angrily demanded to know who he was. When he was able to tell them that he was a constable, they refused to believe him. They could not conceive of lawmen being so close on their heels so soon. One demanded that he show them proof of his authority. Another blurted, "How in hell did you find us so soon?" A third placed his pistol against Ranney's head and shouted, "God damn you! I will blow your brains out. You have killed poor Poole!" A robber who stood on Ranney's right interceded, saying, "Hold on! Stop!" and Mrs. Reynolds also interfered, crying out, "Ain't you ashamed! Shooting a dead man!" At that, the would-be murderer lowered his weapon, but continued to bluster, "Do you suppose that a Confederate officer is going to surrender to a damned Yankee? We are Missouri bushwackers, all of us!"

Another of the gang rolled Staples' body over and went through his pockets, taking $40, a watch, and his pistol. Then he cursed the corpse and bragged to no one in particular, "There's one Union officer less!" Another tore up one of Mrs. Reynold's tablecloths in order to bandage a man wounded by Ranney. The five men then exchanged two of their poorer horses for those of Ranney and Staples, mounted, and prepared to ride off. Tom Poole, covered with blood from his blasted left cheek, staggered out of the house and begged them to take him along. His comrades had to refuse but promised to send a buggy for him as soon as they got to Fiddletown, to take him to a doctor. They ordered him to stay out of sight and to crawl off into the brush if any peace officers should arrive at the inn. Before the five rode off, Alban Glasby took Poole's two pistols and gave them to Captain Ingrim.

This was the situation when Hume arrived back in Placerville on July 1. That afternoon, alerted by Van Eaton, Jim and Sheriff Rogers hurried to Somerset House and found Mrs. Reynolds tending to Ranney's serious wounds. One ball had lodged in the muscles of his lower back, and opposite his heart another was causing considerable internal bleeding. The same evening he was moved to Placerville and in just ten days, he was back on his feet, having made a fantastic recovery. Although Ranney carried one pistol ball in his lower back for the rest of his life, the incident left him with no permanent handicaps.

Hume examined the Rebel bandits' gory room. Bullet holes pocked the wall two feet above the beds bloodied by Ranney and Poole. Rogers handcuffed Poole and sent him to the county seat in the custody of one of his possemen, and Staples' body was also taken to town, where it was laid out in the engine house and washed for interment. The Irish-born deputy was buried on the afternoon of July 2 by his fellow members of the Neptune Engine Company Number Two, with the Reverend Charles Caleb Pierce preaching the funeral sermon to a large crowd.

Hume was, according to reports, "frantic with grief and rage," because Staples had been a friend, as well as a subordinate officer. He took out a posse, which included driver Charley Watson, and vowed not to come back without having avenged his friend. But although he fanned his men out over the brush-clogged hills and ravines of the lower Sierra, he lost the Confederates' trail. After seven days of exhausting pursuit Hume had to give up. His posse was relieved in the field by one from Jackson, Amador County, attracted by Wells, Fargo's reward of $500 for each robber convicted—or killed while resisting arrest —plus 20 percent of any treasure recovered. Even though he had failed, Hume and his men were praised by the state's press. On October 7, 1865, the *California Police Gazette* commented: "So continued as untiring a pursuit, we venture to say, as has ever been made in this state. Over mountains and through gulches, these officers pursued their way, night and day, across the roughest portions of the State of California, including Amador, Calaveras, and San Joaquin counties, often without food or rest, until the robbers, being forced to travel on foot, of course could not be followed. The chase reflects the greatest credit on Sheriff Rogers and all concerned."

Much later Hume learned that the Ingrim band had given him the slip by holing up atop a thickly wooded mountain, from which they were eventually frightened away by their lookout's report that the under sheriff's horsemen were ascending the slope. They fled, leaving horses, blankets, and even some of the stolen silver, unaware that the posse closing in on them was really the remnants of the McCollum gang, still hiding from Hume and heading for the same hideout selected by Ingrim.

By July 6, the Sacramento *Union* claimed, five sacks of bullion had been recovered, including the most valuable bag, leaving only three still missing, plus $700 in coin from Wells, Fargo's strongbox. The *Union* predicted that "the chances of the 'good Jeff Davis men' for escape are rather small." Hume tried to make the editor a good prophet. He interrogated Poole, who was more painfully than dangerously wounded. At first Poole insisted that he knew nothing of any stage holdups. He claimed to be the ex-under sheriff of Monterey County and said that he had met the other men, strangers all, at Somerset House. However, stage driver Watson was pretty sure that he recognized Poole's voice and named him as the one who had handed over Ingrim's receipt. At this point someone tipped Hume that Poole was one of the so-called *Chapman* pirates, a band of plotters led by Asbury Harpending who had secretly outfitted the *J. M. Chapman* as a Confederate commerce raider on the San Francisco Embarcadero in 1863, and Hume later found this to be correct. But San Francisco dispatches to the *Union* persuaded that paper, if not Hume, that the captive was a bogus under sheriff, since a Confederate sympathizer and ex-Monterey lawman named *John* Poole had just been brought to San Francisco from Fort Crook for violation of parole.

Hume grilled the prisoner and got the truth. He was, indeed, Thomas Bell Poole, a Kentuckian who had settled in the Pajaro River Valley near Watsonville. He had been appointed under sheriff of Monterey County by Sheriff De Grau, who had turned over so many of his duties to him that he had been, for all practical purposes, sheriff for the two years ending in 1860. Under Hume's relentless questioning, Poole finally admitted his role in the Bullion Bend and Somerset House affairs. But he insisted that he had been acting under the authority of a sovereign govermnent, the Confederate States of America, and demanded to be held as a prisoner of war, not as a common criminal.

Under Sheriff Hume already had a pretty good description of the gang, having interviewed Mrs. Reynolds at Somerset House right after the gunfight. Thus he knew that Glasby had effeminate mannerisms and that Ingrim's hair and beard were dyed. But when Poole broke, he really spilled the beans on his comrades, giving Hume a line on each of them. Captain R. Henry Ingrim was really Ralph Henry. John C. Bouldware, or Bulwer, used the alias John Creel. Alban Glasby was sometimes called Al Gillespie. Others in the gang were George H. Baker, Thomas J. Watkins, Henry Jarboe, George Cross, John A. Robinson, James Wilson, James Grant, Joseph Gamble, John Gately, Preston Hodges, John Ingraham or Ingren), and three men whose first names Poole did not know—Jordan, Ward, and Marshall. There were also two brothers, John and Wallace Clendenning.

Jim Hume traced the fleeing partisans to the San Joaquin River as they tried to rendezvous at one of the stations of California's little-known Confederate underground railroad, perhaps Cherry's Ranch on the Kings River in Fresno County or in the Visalia stable kept by J. P. Murray and J. E. Dewey, two Copperheads who, in the words of the *California Police Gazette*, "talked Union louder than anyone." But they changed their plans and headed directly for the hotbed of Secessionist sentiment, Santa Clara County. Hume was on their trail, but it was still cold, and he could not prevent the next Rebel raid. Bouldware, Glasby, and John Clendenning decided to hold up the payroll shipment scheduled for delivery to the New Almaden quicksilver mine, just south of San Jose.

On July 14, 1864, the three Southern sympathizers approached the Hill Ranch on the Guadalupe River near the outskirts of San Jose. They planned to lie in wait there on the New Almaden Road. Telling Hill that they had been looking for some friends, without success, they asked for dinner. The rancher prepared them a meal and when they asked if he could put them up for the night, he told them they could use the shack next to his house.

Overconfident, the three boasted to Hill of their scheme to hold up the Almaden payroll stage and threatened to kill him if he did not help them. The rancher agreed, then told them that it was time to feed and water his cattle. Once outside, he slipped through his wheat field and took the trail to San Jose. There he informed Sheriff John Hicks Adams, who hastily organized a posse and surrounded the shack.

Sheriff Adams strode boldly up to the door and knocked. As it swung open, a bandit fired point-blank. The slug struck Adams' watch and glanced into his side. Reeling, he still managed to empty his shotgun into the room. His men followed suit with their handguns. When the shooting was over, one Deputy was suffering from flesh wounds, but Bouldware, alias Creel, lay dying, and Glasby had surrendered, unhurt, although his clothing was shredded by bullets. Under Sheriff R. B. Hall, investigating some groaning from a thicket, found the last of the trio, John Clendenning, who died on the way to the San Jose jail.

Hume read in the *Mountain Democrat* that Bouldware had been a Kansas Jayhawker and a worthy pupil of Senator Joe Lane, who had commissioned him a lieutenant in Bleeding Kansas. The editors added, "We doubt not that many of the thieves now at large in this state are graduates of the same school." Van Eaton brought Glasby to Placerville, where he, like Poole, insisted on being treated as a captured soldier, not as a bandit. Hume questioned Glasby as closely as he had interrogated Poole and got the young man to turn state's evidence, although he was not promised immunity from punishment.

Putting together the information he had received from Poole

and Glasby, plus tips and rumors, Jim Hume traced the remainder of the gang to San Jose. He laid his plans carefully, and on August 1, the day before the grand jury formally praised him and Rogers and their deputies for their exertions in the Bullion Bend case, he sprung his trap. Backed by Van Eaton and a fistful of bench warrants, Hume crashed a mass meeting of Copperheads and arrested Jarboe, Cross, Robertson, Gamble, Ingraham, Gately Hodges, James Frear, Thomas Frear, Joseph Jordan, and Wallace Clendenning. Although the California irregulars had patterned their unit after Quantrell's Blood Raiders in Kansas and, according to Glasby, had sworn a solemn oath never to surrender but to fight to the death, they gave up meekly when Hume covered them. In San Francisco he released Jordan when he became convinced that he was innocent.

The Sacramento *Union* reported that 200 Placerville citizens were mustering to help Hume get his captives safely to jail from the Folsom terminus of the Sacramento Valley Railroad. The word was out that Secesh (Secessionist) partisans were going to take them away from the under sheriff. When the captives arrived, Hume by himself guarding six in one coach and Van Eaton watching the other four in a second, the *Mountain Democrat* blasted the *Union* for peddling such rumors. The *Democrat*'s editor interviewed Jim Hume, who said that he and Van Easton had had no trouble during the transfer. "No attempt was made to rescue the prisoners, nor did I hear any rumors of the kind, nor did I anticipate a rescue," said Hume.

All the bullion, except two bars, was found cached near a spring close to Bullion Bend. One other was discovered on the mountain near Railroad Flat from which the Rebels had been flushed by McCollum's noisy appearance; the last was hidden under a sill of the barn at Somerset House. Glasby directed Van Eaton to it.

Hume had brought in all but two of the surviving Bullion Bend men. Ralph Henry—Captain Ingrim—escaped his net entirely. John Grant, having quarreled with Ingrim, took off by himself. He successfully robbed two stages in a single week near

San Juan Bautista. However, he was betrayed by his girlfriend, who lived at Forbes's Mill near Los Gatos, and captured in bed by Under Sheriff Hall. He made a break from the building, seizing Hall's pistol even though he was handcuffed. The irons prevented his firing it, and he was grabbed again just as he caught the charges from both barrels of a shotgun held by one of Hall's men. Grant confessed and implicated still another pro-Rebel, R. F. Hall, who had sheltered him on his ranch near Gilroy between the two holdups. Hume had to admire the courage of Hall's wife. On the verge of tears, she testified effectively in her husband's behalf. She asked the judge, "Just suppose you knew of a band of two hundred and fifty desperate men, bound together by the most solmen oaths, sworn to take the life of any person who should disclose their purposes or betray any of their number into the hands of officers of the law, and suppose one of their number should seek the shelter of your roof, as did this man who robbed the stages. What would *you* do in these premises?" The judge freed Hall.

The courtroom conclusion to the Bullion Bend case broadened Hume's understanding, if not his respect, for the legal process. He was witness to what really amounted to a miscarriage of justice but could do nothing about it. In later years, however, as a Wells, Fargo agent, he resolutely took the side of outlaws whenever he felt they were not being treated fairly by the law. Since he had not been at Somerset House during the fight, he played only a minor role in the trial of Thomas Poole, his diagram of the inn being introduced as evidence. (All the suspects had pleaded not guilty, demanding separate jury trials.) The most damning testimony came from Constable Ranney and the turncoat, Glasby, whom Hume had softened up originally with his relentless questioning.

Glasby stated: "I think each of us had two pistols, in the party fourteen in all, and a shotgun that belonged to Clendenning. . . . Ingrim assigned us to our places and instructed us to keep cool and, if there was any firing, to empty every shot we had. When the stage came up he took the shotgun. . . . Poole held one of the lead horses of the first stage. We got some bullion, gold dust, coin and papers. We hid the bullion. Two bars of bullion we carried off with us, and the coin and chest. . . . An hour or so after we arrived at Somerset House, the Deputy Sheriff and Ranney came. . . . There was an alarm raised just before the officers came. Bulwer [Bouldware] was in a different room and came in, waked us, and told us to get up, someone was after us. . . . The Deputy Sheriff then came to the door with the shotgun. He pointed the gun toward Poole and I and said we were his prisoners. Ingraham made a move to get his pistol. Staples pointed his gun toward him, and Poole and I drew our pistols. Poole held his pistol down at his side on the bed, in position for firing. I then heard a shot after Staples changed the gun to Ingraham the second time."

The defense tried to get Glasby to say that Hume had promised him immunity in return for testifying against his pals. But he would admit only to having been questioned by Hume—"I have not been promised I would be discharged. No inducement has been offered me."

The Frear brothers had been released before trial. Judge Samuel W. Brockway granted the others, except Poole and Preston Hodges, a change of venue to Sacramento County, where, to Hume's amazement, they all were released on legal technicalities. Hodges got twenty years in San Quentin at hard labor. Slowly it dawned on Hume that Poole had been chosen scapegoat for all the Bullion Bend raiders. Glasby had not testified that the ex-Kentuckian had shot Staples. "I don't know who fired the first shot," he told the court. "*I* did not fire the first shot; don't know whether the first shot was fired by Poole or not; think not. I don't know where the shot came from." If Glasby thought that Poole had probably not fired the killing shot, the *California Police Gazette* was *sure* that he had not fired it and blamed Bouldware.

Hume was puzzled. Why was young Poole being singled out for vengeance? He was the most likable and least vicious of the whole gang. Yet on July 26 he was convicted of first-degree

103

murder and on September 10 sentenced to be hanged. His case was appealed, but the Supreme Court sustained the lower court's decision. Poole was hanged on September 29, 1865, after he had thanked Hume and others for their kindness during his imprisonment. The *California Police Gazette* editorialized after the execution; "Thus ends a tragedy which at one time threatened to drench the State in blood, for it is positively ascertained that had not the party been so vigorously followed and broken up, others in large number were preparing to take the field and make a second Missouri of California. To Sheriff Rogers and Deputies Hume and Van Eaton belongs the credit of its abrupt and final failure. Better officers were never entrusted with the execution of the laws."

Such publicity was flattering to Under Sheriff Hume, but he was nagged by the knowledge that Poole had paid the ultimate penalty almost accidentally, through the application of the old principle of an eye for an eye, not in respect to Staples' death but to an earlier tragedy. Governor Frederick F. Low had refused to reprieve Poole not only because in those Civil War days "the times were too hot," as Poole's son claimed later, but because the prisoner, when under sheriff of Monterey County, six years earlier, had hanged a Mexican bandit, José Anastasio, even though he had received a reprieve from Governor John B. Weller. Why? Weller had made out the man's name incorrectly on the document, calling him Gregory Jesús Anastasio. The callous Poole had checked with the district attorney and county judge, to protect himself, then had ruthlessly executed the Mexican. His despicable action was not forgotten, and it brought him to the gallows in 1865, demonstrating to Jim Hume that in Civil War California two wrongs *did,* apparently, make a right.

CHAPTER V

SHERIFF OF EL DORADO

THE Bullion Bend case held the attention of many Californians in 1864 and into 1865, but Jim Hume soon had to direct his thoughts to other matters. Life went on during the prolonged judicial process, and he watched over his beat, the main highway to Carson City, Nevada, and the "States." Louis McLane, President of the Pioneer Stage Company, had graded the stretch from Placerville to Tahoe's Lake Valley into a veritable turnpike. The travel writer J. Ross Browne could hardly recognize it as the rough track he had followed in 1860. Still twisting and turning, it was now wide and leveled, and its margins were bounded by the great clutter of civilization. Browne wrote, "There is probably not an acre of ground, possessing a water privilege, on the entire route between Placerville and Virginia City which has not been taken up and settled upon by some enterprising squatter or speculator."

Under Sheriff Hume shared with Ranney and other officers a host of routine cases after the Bullion Bend affair—telegraph tappers and Copperheads who shouted, "Hurrah for Jeff Davis!" on Main Street were typical. And Hume's sharp watch on trans-Sierra travel seemed to be paying off. There were no stage holdups, although Wells, Fargo, in just a half-dozen shipments of Nevada bullion that season, moved 7,271 pounds of it, valued at a whopping $209,003.07. Hume's duties were increasingly varied as 1865 progressed. He became a notary public and was on the board of delegates charged with choosing a chief and several assistants to run a professional fire department in Placerville. He shared with Rogers the conducting of sheriff's sales, auctioning lots and houses on the courthouse steps in settlement of court judgments. In one sale he had to "give away" a tract on Lake Tahoe's magnificent Emerald Bay in order to clear a judgment of only $1,054.30.

That spring Hume became involved in an unusual case of cattle stealing, which, to date, had not much troubled the Sierra hill country. Acting on a tip, he and Van Eaton rode to a house near Clarksville, a town with an evil reputation. A decade earlier, highwaymen Mickey Free and Tom Bell had made the Railroad House in Clarksville their hangout, until they were lynched, and it was no more high-toned in 1865. Concealing their horses, Hume and Van Eaton lay in wait until two strangers rode up and entered the cabin. Hume signaled to Van Eaton and headed for the horses, but he made his play too soon; the men inside had not yet relaxed, and one of them saw him at the hitching rack. Both rushed outside, firing as they ran. Hume's hand dove for his Colt, and he wounded one of the rustlers. Under hot fire, the other soon surrendered. By the next evening, cattle thieves Jones and Hawkins were locked in the Placerville jail.

Hard on the bootheels of this case, which again made his name news, Hume succumbed to friendly advice and ran for sheriff. A popular figure, he was chosen to make the formal reading of the Declaration of Independence at the Fourth of July ball and celebration at Strawberry Valley, to which many of Placerville's citizens migrated for the day, thanks to the free transportation offered by the Pioneer Stage Line. The line also provided free sight-seeing trips by coach to the Sierra summit for an eye-popping view of Lake Tahoe. Two weeks later, at its

California convention, the new Peoples Union Party placed Hume on its ticket as candidate for sheriff in El Dorado County. The *Mountain Democrat,* always friendly toward independent Hume, did not want to come out against him, but neither could it support him, since it was committed to Democratic candidates. Editor Gelwicks joked about Hume's slim chances, comparing his nomination to an indictment: "The late Grand Jury [convention] found a true bill against James B. Hume, Esq., as a candidate for Sheriff. We believe Jim is guilty but in these degenerate days, conviction is not always consequent upon guilt. We fear the trial jury [electorate] may not see it and will acquit him. Indeed, we have heard it hinted that there is a strong possibility that Ensminger, or Barber, or Stroud will quash the indictment." But the winner was not Barber or Stroud or the ex-meat-packer, Ensminger. But neither was it Jim Hume. It was the Democrat, Maurice G. Griffith, riding the victory wave of his party. Hume received a meager 371 votes to Griffith's 2,114, and runner-up Barber outpolled Hume badly with 1,821 votes.

Hume was learning that, clearly, law enforcement was one thing, politics another, but his bruised pride was soothed by a minor victory—in a hotly contested race he was elected chief engineer of the Fire Department. The *Mountain Democrat,* delighted, predicted that Jim would soon rouse the department from its apathy.

Sheriff Griffith hired a new deputy, James D. McMurray, and a new jailer, Hume's friend John Cartheche. Cartheche was Greek, a rarity in the mines. He spoke English and Italian as well as his native tongue, and was a forty-three-year-old ex-sea captain who had lost a schooner on the coast of Greece when he was only twenty-one. Griffith, however, knew that his election rival was indispensable in the key position of under sheriff, and he swiftly reappointed Hume. Jim was soon in the field, trailing a Chilean *bandido* and double-murderer, Pedro Pablo, but another officer brought him in.

At the end of July, when Hume received word that three men

107

were on a rampage of robbery on the Carson City road, he wired Constable Charley Watson, the stage driver, to be on the lookout. Watson answered at 3 A.M. on August 1 that the robbers had passed Strawberry, heading for Nevada. Since Griffith was away, Hume took full charge. At 10 A.M. he left town and, riding like hell, got ahead of the fleeing men and cut off their retreat into Nevada. Between sundown and dark he reached the little Echo Creek bridge in front of Osgood's Toll House at the base of the Kingsbury and McDonald Grade. There, just south of Lake Tahoe, at the best bottleneck on the entire road, Hume posted Watson and the tired men who had galloped after him. All night the peace officers waited in the pines and underbrush flanking the stream, but in vain. The next morning Hume learned that the trio had pulled off another holdup between Strawberry and his ambuscade. Although his men were grumblingly impatient, Hume settled them down to wait.

At twilight on August 2, 1867, Hume ordered his men to increase their vigilance, and at 11:30 P.M. he saw the robbers, armed with rifles, riding right into his trap. They were Hugh DeTell, Walter Sinclair, and their partner, known only as Faust. They were in high spirits after their unhampered spree of robbery during which they had even taken a small sum from the poor driver of a water cart. As they approached, Hume called out an order to stop, telling them that he was an officer and ordering them to surrender. They halted, all right, but only to take aim. DeTell's first bullet hit Hume in the fleshy part of the arm. He and his men returned the fire, and when the gunsmoke had drifted away from the Echo Creek bridge, the under sheriff found Faust dead and Sinclair on the ground, unhurt. He had a brief glimpse of the third fellow falling or jumping off the bridge into the creek below. In the dark Hume could find neither DeTell nor his body, so he retired to Osgood's, where he bound up his wounded arm and rested until daylight. He then led a search which turned up two coats but no owner. Soon they picked up DeTell's tracks, which led back toward Placerville, and galloped after him. The Sacramento *Union* picked up the story from the wire, predicting that the bandit would not elude Hume for very long. "As we have so good a description of him, and Hume is on his track, no doubt he, too, will throw up the sponge."

Hume led the pursuit until he reached the fork of the Placerville road, 25 miles west of Osgood's. There he split his party, sending two men on the old county road while he continued alone along the American River road. (Apparently he had left two men to guard Sinclair and to hold the bridge in case DeTell gave him the slip and doubled back to Lake Valley.) Hume ordered his men to meet him at Pacific House, east of Sportsman's Hall. When he arrived at the rendezvous, he learned that they had cornered and captured DeTell just above Brockliss's Bridge over the American River. Hume jailed Sinclair and DeTell and received flattering attention from the papers, especially the *Mountain Democrat,* which sang his praises to the pinetops: "The masterly manner in which the affair was conducted, throughout, reflects the greatest credit upon our Under Sheriff and we mean it as no empty praise when we say that in this, as in his official acts in general, he has exhibited in high degree those qualities that are requisite in a first-rate executive officer of the department to which he belongs. We congratulate him and his fellow citizens of El Dorado County at the good fortune that spared his life. The wound in his right arm, though a painful one, was not a dangerous one and had he not been forced to return to Placerville on horse back before getting it dressed, it would by this time have been almost healed."

At the inquest Hume learned little about his mysterious adversaries. Sinclair, a twenty-one-year-old from Arizona, testified willingly but did not know the age or even the first name of the German, Faust. He had met him in Sacramento for the first time about July 1 and had joined him in the business of highway robbery. Nor did he have much of anything to say of DeTell. Charley Watson's testimony followed. After Hume had been hit, Watson had fired both loads of his shotgun, and the rest of the party had followed suit. He and Hume had then found Faust dead from two bullet wounds in the right chest. The coroner's jury wasted little time in finding that "while armed and resisting the attempt of said Under Sheriff to arrest him and two other highway robbers . . . the killing of said Faust was justifiable and necessary."

On November 5, 1867, a rainstorm ushered in winter with a vengeance. At higher elevations snow began to fall. Normally, the winter would have brought a respite, but in January Hume had to investigate the mysterious murder of a forty-five-year-old French miner. His skull caved in by a sharp instrument, Joseph F. Roland was found lying in the bed of Weber Creek, a half-mile from Webertown and 200 yards below his cabin. Sheriff Griffith was sure that the homicide was the work of Indians, so he sent Hume to arrest a lame, English-speaking brave who was rumored to have some knowledge of the crime. On January 25, 1868, Hume took Cartheche and rode up into the Sierra. On the trail between the American River and the main road near Nine Mile House, Hume found his Indians—much to his regret. There were three of them, armed with rifles—cocked and aimed at the two lawmen. Hume and his Greek friend had only pistols, which were, at that moment, pinned down under their heavy overcoats and raincoats. It was a tense moment, as Hume noted that the several inches of snow on the ground would hamper his maneuvering on horseback. There was nothing to do but sit his horse calmly and try to parley with the redmen. The Indians refused to powwow, but were in enough awe of his office not to shoot the white men. Instead, the three backed off and disappeared into the cedars and pines.

The under sheriff and his aides were not foolish enough to test their luck again that day and did not give chase. They made for Sportsman's Hall, where they calmed their nerves with drinks and prudently telegraphed Placerville for reinforcements, whom Hume ordered to come properly armed with rifles. The next day, Hume led his strengthened party out and, without difficulty, arrested the gimpy Indian, Bob, who confessed that he was one of the four who had killed Roland on January 12. He implicated White Rock Jack; Lazarus, alias O-Lan-O; and Dick, or Indian

Dick. In contrast with most lawmen of his era, Hume spent considerable time interrogating his captives. While others would have leaped on horses and charged off, to follow up the first clue that dropped, Hume patiently garnered descriptions of the wanted men. He learned that White Rock Jack was five feet, six inches, had very big feet for an Indian, and always wore an imitation Peruvian hat with a stiff brim. He carried a long-barreled rifle. Lazarus was short and slightly built, about twenty years of age, and was never without his Yager rifle. Dick, about five feet, eight inches, was tall for an Indian and light-complexioned. He was about eighteen, and he carried a heavy rifle with a bright, nonblued, barrel. Bob also told Hume that Indian Dick was the leader of the gang and the man primarily responsible for Roland's murder. Before the month was out, Hume had Dick and Lazarus in jail but had not been able to trace wily White Rock Jack.

About a month after their arrest, the Indians were tried. Although it stayed out for twenty-four hours, the jury disagreed. Eight of the veniremen were for a guilty verdict of murder in the first degree, but four thought that it was second-degree murder because all the Indians had been drunk at the time of the killing. The *Mountain Democrat* sided with the minority and demanded, in an editorial, that those who had sold wine or whiskey to the Indians be held a party to the crime. Indian Dick was eventually found guilty of second-degree murder and drew twelve years at hard labor in San Quentin Penitentiary. Lazarus, found guilty of manslaughter, got ten years on the rock pile. Bob withdrew his not-guilty plea and, because of his cooperation with Hume, was given only one year in prison, for manslaughter. On February 28 Sheriff Griffith started for San Quentin with his prisoners, leaving Under Sheriff Hume to keep an eye peeled for White Rock Jack. (The elusive Indian was finally captured, in 1870, but not by Hume.)

When Griffith was reelected and began a new term in March, 1868, he reappointed his right-hand man, Hume, to the post of under sheriff. The two had been busy since 1866; 196 prisoners were in the county jail during their term. Two of them were hanged, 20 were sent to the penitentiary, and surprisingly, 16 were assigned to the insane asylum. Thirteen remained in the cells as Griffith and Hume began their second term. Crime had gone down during their tenure—Sheriff Rogers had had to accommodate 371 prisoners during his 1864–66 term—but there were numerous routine cases to occupy the lawmen. None was very important, but one did provide Hume with a little exercise. He arrested a burglar named Wilson, alias Blair, alias Durham, alias Price, in Lake Valley and was bundling him into a stage, where he would be handcuffed for security, when the fellow decided to make a break for freedom. That was his first mistake. His second was to try to overpower Hume. Let the *Mountain Democrat* sketch the scene: "The prisoner made it lively and sensational in a brief but spry little struggle in which the tableau of Officer Hume quickly and strongly clutching the prisoner's throat was speedily followed by a closing scene in which the prisoner, well manacled, was conducted towards the Placerville jail." Most of Jim Hume's cases were like this, as, of course, were those of every other peace officer in California. A Bullion Bend case—even an Indian Dick case—was an exception. Much of Hume's time was spent escorting prisoners to San Quentin, and he had to investigate a whole gamut of crimes, from sluice robbing to arson and burglary. During his free time Hume was becoming more prominent in the Democratic Party, to which he had shifted his allegiance. The ex-Unionist was firmly in the loyal opposition now, and named chief marshal of the Democratic Club in October, 1868, he appointed aides for a political parade and mass meeting.

Perhaps after dunning them for taxes for so long, Hume was growing fond of the hardworking and much-put-upon Chinese of El Dorado County. In the summer of 1869 he set out to crush a gang of cowardly outlaws who for years had been pillaging the Chinese with impunity. There had been arrests but not one conviction because Chinese testimony was not allowed in California courts. The outlaws were canny enough to make use of county lines, too; they raided the Chinatowns of Coloma, Georgetown, and Greenwood in El Dorado County but holed up in Sacramento County. First, Hume identified the members of the gang —S. D. Emmons, alias Vern Emmons; Bill Howard; David Jacobs, alias Little Jakey; and George Martin. He then swore out warrants for all of them but kept this quiet. With supreme cunning, Hume got the gang to convict itself. Since Chinese witnesses were useless, he had to find a weak link in the outlaw band itself, apply a little pressure to make the man talk, and then round up the others. Hume decided that George Martin was his man. Because he himself was too well known in the area, Hume sent Deputy Cartheche to scout around Folsom. But the gang spotted the Greek as a lawman and laid low. Cartheche had to give up and return emptyhanded. However, this was only a temporary setback to Hume's well-laid plans. When the gang surfaced again, Folsom officers whom Jim had primed tipped off Constable J. G. Bailey at Shingle Springs. He made the arrest. With Martin safely in jail, Hume put the rest of his plan into motion. He wired the Sacramento County officers who were cooperating with him, and they picked up Howard. Hume suspected that Jacobs had fled to Grass Valley, so he telegraphed Steve Venard, the deputy sheriff, who arrested Jakey pronto.

To trap Emmons, Hume planted a phony news story in the Sacramento papers—a device new to California—to the effect that Martin and Howard had been discharged after examination because of the incompetency of the only testimony against them, that of Chinese. Hume then notified Sacramento County officers of his ruse and dangled a reward of $50 in front of them for Emmons' arrest. No sooner did Emmons come out of hiding than officers grabbed him. Martin, who had been in solitary confinement all this time, finally broke down and talked. When Hume told Emmons, Howard, and Jacobs that their pal had peached on them, they philosophically gave up. The grand jury indicted them, they were convicted, and Hume had the pleasure of escorting them on a one-way trip to Marin County's San Quentin peninsula. There, starting on June 23, 1869, Emmons began a nine-year residence, Howard eight, and Jakey four.

As usual, the *Mountain Democrat* had something nice to say about Jim Hume and his breaking up of the systematized looting of Chinese in the mining camps: "All thanks are due to the officers of Sacramento and Nevada Counties who had a hand in making the arrests and for their promptness in carrying out instructions. Especially are the thanks of El Dorado County tax-payers due to our own officers who planned and carried out, with so little cost to the County, this whole affair. We should have made mention of this matter in the *Democrat* ere this but were requested by the officer [Hume] not to do so until the trials have been held."

Between criminal cases, life was good and easy in the Sierra foothills. On July 4 Hume was assistant marshal of the day, handling the grand parade from the plaza to the Methodist Episcopal Church, where Independence Day speeches were delivered. On August 6 he began a brief vacation, a fishing and hunting trip into the High Sierra, with Judge Charles F. Irwin and a half-dozen of the town's prominent citizens. When he returned, two weeks later, the editor of the *Mountain Democrat,* George O. Kies, observed in his column that Hume and his companions had never looked better. In fact, he said, they were much improved by their expedition. Hume and his pals repaid Kies for his kind words with a fine mess of trout, fresh from the Sierra.

When John Cable, a storekeeper at Indian Diggins, was killed by burglars, Hume performed a dual role. He helped organize a committee to raise funds for the distraught widow and her children—and for a long time kept the appeal going, by means of notices in the papers. Meanwhile, he quickly arrested four prime suspects, Mexicans living in the area. A run-of-the-mine peace officer in California's Sierra would have been content. But not Hume. Intuition told him that these were not the right men. He kept poking about Indian Diggins and came up with three fresh suspects, all Chinese. He kept the Mexicans locked up in order to lull the Orientals into relaxing their vigilance. After several days of intensive searching, he found their trail, followed them right across the Amador County line, but finally lost them. However, regular search parties took up his work and arrested two of the suspects on the Cosumnes River, near Latrobe. One escaped temporarily but was reapprehended and handed over to Hume. Try as he might, though, Hume could not run down the third member of the gang. Not until November, when he was studying the robbery of the Coloma Wells, Fargo express office, did he learn that the Coloma robber was also the man he wanted in the Cable murder case. And he got him. Once more, the local press was generous in its praise of Jim Hume, saying, "Few officers would have been able to trace out these murderers as Hume has done. At the first, everyone thought he must be crazy when he said the murder was committed by Chinamen. But, heedless of what others thought or said, he kept steadily on until he had succeeded in lodging the parties in jail and getting such a chain of evidence as can hardly fail of convicting them of the crime." Hume kept a bargain with one of the men eventually convicted, Chung Ah Cum. In return for his cooperation—he had confessed and implicated the others—Hume saw to it that he received a reduced sentence.

In 1868 Hume was elected sheriff of El Dorado County. He took office on March 4, 1869, and immediately rewarded his loyal friend John Cartheche by naming him deputy sheriff and jailer, while he appointed Adam Simonton under sheriff. When Simonton resigned, Hume replaced him, in April, with the experienced Deputy James D. McMurray. That June, the brand-new sheriff of El Dorado was, for the first time, completely stumped on a case. Jesse Hendricks, an employee of the South Fork Canal Company, disappeared mysteriously. His coat and tools were found on the section of the ditch which he patrolled about eight miles above Placerville. But a search of the county, stimulated by Hume's posting of a $100 reward for information, turned up absolutely nothing. Even when the Canal Company added another $100, there were no results. Although Hume could not supply a corpse, he was almost certain that Hendricks had been murdered, and he strongly suspected White Rock Jack, the Indian who had given him the slip in the Roland murder case. Hendricks had helped Hume pursue White Rock Jack in that case and there were rumors that his life had been threatened. Editor Kies agreed with the sheriff: "This White Rock Jack is a thoroughly savage and desperate Indian, who is feared even by men of his own tribe. The Indians look upon him as a 'big brave' from the fact of his escaping punishment for his crime and they undoubtedly assist him in keeping out of the way and warn him when danger approaches."

The El Dorado County Board of Supervisors showed their faith in Hume's judgment by offering a $500 reward for the body of White Rock Jack. This bounty prompted Kies to fire a blast at the capital: "This reward should have been offered by the State, and that long ago, but the State authorities did not seem to think the lives of our people were of sufficient importance to warrant the offering of a reward for this savage outlaw. . . . If this reward rids the County of this notorious murderer, it will be one of the most economical things the Board has ever done, not taking into account the lives of our people." The sting of Kies' words was apparently felt in Sacramento, for the governor soon added $300—but for conviction, not for a corpse—to the price on White Rock Jack's head. Jim Hume chose the wrong time to take a rest from the case when he went on a July fishing trip just prior to Jack's coming out of hiding. When he returned, Hume found that two Indians, with the help of a white settler, had captured Jack after he had drunk himself into a stupor at a local Indian fiesta. Hume quickly went into action and arrested three Indian witnesses, including lame Bob. It was his only way of protecting them, for all had been threatened with death by White Rock Jack's friends.

White Rock Jack's case dragged on, and Hume's interest was temporarily distracted by a case that started out as a simple matter of arson. Late in 1868 or early in 1869, Hume had learned that a young man of Placerville, identified only as Johnny, had received a badly misspelled note, all in small letters to disguise

116

the writer's hand, along with $150 in greenbacks. His unknown correspondent asked Johnny to set fire to the harness shop next door to the Phipps House, which was then standing empty. Johnny was promised an additional $50 if he would drop a line to one John Alpine in San Francisco, telling him when he could come to the city to see him. Hume suspected that John Alpine was James Phipps himself, who had moved from his Placerville home to San Francisco in 1867. Unfortunately, Hume had been absent from Placerville when the young man received the note and was unable to stop him from returning the money to "Alpine." But at least Johnny had held onto the evidence for the sheriff's return. Hume hurriedly telegraphed the San Francisco chief of police to ask him to observe who picked up the letter from Johnny, but it was too late; it had already been collected by "Mr. Alpine." Hume hunted up samples of Phipps' handwriting that convinced him of the man's guilt, despite Phipps' attempts to camouflage his hand in the bribery note. Next, Hume sent the fire marshal a memorandum on the arson plot and asked the Hamburg and Bremen Insurance Company to cancel its policy on the Phipps home. The company complied, but when Phipps wrote it a little while later to ask for a renewal of his $1,200 policy, Hamburg and Bremen somehow overlooked the cancellation and issued a new policy, reducing the valuation to $700. (Hume estimated that the building was really worth about $500.)

On September 10, 1869, Phipps left San Francisco for a visit to Sacramento, telling friends that he was going to the State Fair. By sheer coincidence, Hume was a passenger on the same train, between Stockton and Sacramento, and recognized Phipps. He did not have enough evidence to arrest him, of course, so he just stayed out of his way and laid over in Sacramento that night before continuing on to Placerville. The next day he learned that a fire had destroyed the Phipps place. Hume hurried home and immediately began to circle the town in hopes of picking up Phipps' trail. Twelve miles out on the Folsom road he learned that a stranger had hired a horse at 7 P.M. the

117

night before, to go to Wall's Diggings, 7 miles away. Incredibly, the man had told the stable hand that he was a Chinese detective—whatever that was supposed to mean. And he had left him a gold watch as security for the horse. The man had returned the horse at 5 A.M., after having ridden it, hard, most of the night. (Curious, if he had gone only the 14 miles to Wall's Diggings and back.)

This was enough for Hume. He went to San Francisco and arrested Phipps, who swore that he had not ventured a foot beyond the city limits of Sacramento on the night in question. Hume discovered that Phipps had arrived in the capital at 2 P.M. but had left at 3 P.M. for Folsom, arriving there at 5 P.M. He had hired a horse in Folsom and witnesses had seen him on the road to Placerville. Shortly after the blaze broke out, at 1 A.M., he had been seen galloping toward Folsom. There was no doubt, from the hostler's description, that the man who had returned a sweat-lathered mount at 5 A.M., was Phipps. He admitted to Hume that he had returned that morning to San Francisco but insisted that he had gone no closer to Placerville than the Sacramento fairgrounds. Piece by piece, Hume demolished Phipps' alibi and replaced it with convincing evidence of guilt. The *Mountain Democrat* cheered him in its accustomed fashion: "There is a great credit due Officer Hume for tracing out and getting evidence in the matter." Hume was more pleased when Phipps was given seven years in San Quentin but absolutely disgusted when the State Supreme Court reversed the decision and allowed the arsonist a new trial. When he withdrew his not-guilty plea on October 22, 1870, he was resentenced, to six years, and Hume took him back to prison. But not for long. To Hume's astonishment, Governor Henry Haight ignored the loud complaints and signed protest of Placerville's best citizens and gave the firebug a full pardon.

The big case of 1870 and 1871, however, was not the miscarried arson conviction but White Rock Jack's murder indictment. Hume agreed with Editor Kies when he declared, "The arrest of Jack was attended with more difficulty than that of any other offender that has figured on the criminal calendar of this County in years." The twenty-three-year-old Indian was hardly forbidding in appearance; in fact, he was a good-looking fellow, and Hume understood why the press labeled him "a superior specimen of the Digger race." He was 5 feet, 10 inches in height, weighed about 180 pounds, and gazed on the world with sparkling black eyes. But on March 7, 1871, Judge Amos Crandall Adams gave Jack life at hard labor for the murder of Joseph E. Roland in January, 1868. He was not charged with the murder of Jesse Hendricks, since Hume had never been able to find the body of the missing canal inspector, much less any evidence to link Jack to his murder—if, indeed, he had been murdered. At first Jack accepted the sentence with the customary stolidity of his race, but Hume later found him weeping in his cell at the prospect of spending the rest of his days behind bars. On March 8 Hume took him to the penitentiary to start his life residency in Marin County, but he was not able to write finis to the Hendricks' case until 1876, long after he had left El Dorado County for employment with Wells, Fargo. On December 19 of that year a deer hunter found two pieces of a human skull about 7 miles above Placerville. Coroner Collins inspected the site on December 21 and found a shovel, boots and foot bones, a leg, and the rest of the man's skull. A pocketknife, clothing, and $2.25 in half dollars and two-bit pieces suggested that robbery had not been the motive for the killing. A knife and some strips of a woolen shirt supplied proof that the remains were those of the long-missing Hendricks.

As sheriff, Jim Hume presided over the Placerville jail, which he referred to as his Gridiron Hotel. During the summer of 1871 his "guests" included three murderers, four burglars, and two witnesses. One man was in for assault and battery, two for assault with intent to commit murder, and one each for petit larceny, grand larceny, and "threats against life." The most

119

distressing lodger of all was a madman, turned away from the hospital, to whom Hume gave shelter until he died, raving and violent.

Rarely did Hume lose a prisoner, but in the summer of 1871 he nearly lost three at one swoop. He had investigated the robbery of a safe belonging to Dr. R. H. Duncan of Nashville (south of Placerville). The thieves had been able to push the safe across a 40-foot-wide street before bashing it open with a crowbar and axes. The din of the local stamp mill had drowned out the noise, and they had made off with about $1,800 in buckskin pouches. Within a month of the May 14 robbery Hume had his men, three Chinese. At approximately 2:30 A.M. on June 21, they decided to part company with Jim, although he had clapped them into a strong cell with a heavily grated window facing the jail's courtyard. The sheriff's suspicions were first aroused when he noticed that his dogs showed signs of having been scalded. He guessed that the Chinese had doused the dogs in their tea water in order to intimidate them so that they would not interfere with the planned jailbreak. His suspicions were reinforced when the prisoners suddenly took up singing. Hume figured that the faltering harmony was meant to cover up the noise of tunneling, sawing, or filing. He decided to give the schemers a little rope—and very nearly gave them their freedom, by waiting too long. Somehow they had succeeded in slicing off the heads of the rivets in their cell door. Unknown to Hume, each door hung by a thin, uncut bit of metal. On the night of the twenty-first the Chinese knocked the rivets off, slipped through the door into the adjoining room, and tore from the floor a 5-foot iron bar attached to a chain, which Hume used as a sort of ball-and-chain. Muffling the chain with strips of cloth, the prisoners used the bar to dig away the stone and mortar beneath the wooden sill of the iron-grated window. Next, they set the plank of the sill on fire, using pieces of wood and paper for kindling, in order to speed up the breakout. They even pushed a blanket through the grating and adjusted it outside to silence falling fragments of masonry and timber. They had succeeded in breaking the charred sill in two with their prybar and had only to knock away a few stones to be free as birds. However, embers from the burning sill had set the blanket afire and the smell of smoke roused Jim, who appeared and restrained the prisoners. He had been caught napping, but the local paper declared, "Thus has a most ingenious attempt to break jail been thwarted by one of the most vigilant officers and intelligent detectives in the State."

As a new election rolled around on September 6, 1871, Jim Hume was reasonably confident of being returned to office. He was the incumbent; he had a good record of arrests and convictions; the grand jury had found his jail first-rate, his books balanced, and his prisoners contented. He was an officer of the Association of Territorial Pioneers and had been reappointed to the arrangements committee for the annual Fourth of July celebration. Moreover, the *Mountain Democrat,* politicking in his behalf since April, was reminding its readership that horse thieves and cattle rustlers were out of business and added, "It is to be hoped that the people will be ever as successful in selecting good officers as the County has at the present time, from Sheriff down." Probably Hume was lulled into a sense of false security by the *Democrat,* which, seeing all Republicans as "Rads" (Radicals) fronting for what it called the Railroad Subsidy Party, gave them little chance for victory. Candidate W. H. Brown would never be sheriff, said the paper, but would be returned to private business. The El Dorado (town) correspondent ventured, "Having been successful in business, we will see that Hume protects him in the enjoyment of property acquired by his honest transactions, through life. No thief, burglar or felon shall molest his home while Jim is Sheriff, and roam at large, unwhipped of justice." Similar sentiments came from the editor's stringer in Lake Valley. But even though Brown found nothing in Hume's record to attack and had to praise him as a good and faithful officer, he insisted at the same time that Jim had held the office long enough, and the Republican won! Hume was stunned when he was swept into oblivion with the rest of Governor Henry H. Haight's Democratic slate. When the chips were down, the popular Hume could muster only 1,414 votes to Brown's 1,635.

It was Editor Kies' sad duty to write Jim's political obituary: "Personal spite and sore-headed disaffection in our own ranks have defeated one of the best and most deserving officers this, or any other, county has ever had in its service." He praised the 100 or more Republicans who had crossed party lines to vote for Hume and then alluded to the prejudice in the Democratic ranks that had doomed Jim's chances. Kies lamented that the switch-voting Rads were not numerous enough to offset "those claiming to be Democrats who, from the standpoint of narrow-minded prejudice, cast their votes and influence against him."

So it was that Jim, due to be ousted on March 4, found himself in the uncomfortable position of lame-duck lawman during the winter of 1871-72. The *Mountain Democrat* tried to ease the pangs of defeat by making light of it: "Jim Hume, Sheriff of El Dorado County, went to Newtown on Thursday. Came home safe and was greeted by an immense number of friends in a very enthusiastic manner. . . . It is not true that the Trustees of the Presbyterian Church are painting that building such a dark color on account of Jim Hume's defeat."

But Jim resolved not to slacken his efforts. On November 28, only three days after the paper ran the item above, the Georgetown and Auburn stage, carrying the U.S. mail and Wells, Fargo express, was stopped by a bandit between Georgetown and Greenwood. At first the driver thought it was a joke, that someone was just trying to "sell" him. So, when ordered to throw down the box, he countered, good-naturedly, "Go to the devil!" His mood changed abruptly when he looked into the muzzle of a gun which suddenly seemed as big as the end of a pickle barrel. He threw the box down and at the road agent's command, drove on, through a barricade of brush.

When Jim Hume learned of the robbery, of about $1,000 in gold dust and $50 to $60 in coin from Wells, Fargo's green strongbox, he hurried to the site, three and a half miles from Georgetown and two and a half from Greenwood, examined the barricade and the emptied box, and picked up the robber's trail. He followed it into the brush and timber country but lost it when a storm washed it away ahead of him. Even Jim's friends were dumbfounded when he told reporters that there were no clues and dropped all attempts to continue the search. Critics muttered that Hume had gone into an awfully early retirement. Actually, Jim was bluffing. He secretly sent a description of the stolen treasure to thirty Wells, Fargo agents, asking them, in turn, to notify all gold buyers to keep a sharp eye out for the loot and to keep mum. His patience paid off. Three months later a telegram informed him that the gold dust had been sold at Michigan Bluff. Hume sent men there who identified the gold and arrested the bandit, E. G. (Kentucky) Watkins.

It was a bittersweet victory. Jim Hume would be a longtime civilian before Judge Charles F. Irwin gave Kentucky four years in San Quentin. But the *Mountain Democrat* gave him several fine parting salutes: "From the Sheriff's office we lose one of the best officers that the Coast has produced. . . . If any further proof was needed of Hume's detective ability, which is state-wide, the working up of this case would furnish it. Had he listened to the urgent appeal of others and arrested parties on suspicion, the chances are that neither the gold dust nor the man who committed the robbery would ever be discovered. The whole credit of ferreting out this affair belongs to Hume and is freely accorded to him by all those conversant with the matter with whom we have conversed."

Placerville did not intend to let Jim Hume off easily on March 4, 1872. The townspeople bought a fine gold watch and chain, reserved the courtroom secretly for an 8 P.M. get-together, and got R. J. Van Voorhies to steer Hume in the right direction at the right time. Chairman H. F. Page greeted Jim and called him forward, then launched into a sentimental farewell. "Mr. Hume," began Page, "I have been deputed by some of your many friends in this city to make a few remarks upon this, the

123

close of your official term as Sheriff of this county, and it is a pleasure to be permitted to address words of friendship to one who, during a long residence in this city and county, has endeared himself by his many acts of kindness to the people as you have done. Years ago, you left your native state and, with pioneers like yourself, settled in this county. . . . Here you have spent the latter years of your youth and a portion of your manhood. Here, with others, you have assisted in building up a great and glorious state."

Warming to his audience, Page continued, "During your residence here, you have often been honored by our citizens with important public trusts. For the past eight years, you have been connected with the Sheriff's office of this county and in all the public positions you have discharged the duty with fidelity to the people and honor to yourself. And as you are about to retire from office, your friends, without distinction of party, deeming this a proper occasion that some fitting testimonial be made you for the distinguished manner in which you have discharged your duties as an officer and a citizen, have selected me to present to you this beautiful gold watch and chain as a slight testimonial of their esteem and regard. Which we ask you to accept as an offering of friendship to one who is entitled to the enduring application of 'Well done, good and faithful servant!' We do not present it for its intrinsic value but as a memento of an enduring friendship and when you place it beneath your pillow, and in the silence of the night you listen to its incessant ticking, may it ever remind you that true hearts will ever beat in unison with it for your future success, and whether in this or other lands your lot may be cast, true friends will ever rejoice in your prosperity and sympathize with you in adversity. . . . May your successors imitate your example. . . . Permit us, one and all, to extend the hand you have so often pressed in friendship, and wish you a hearty Godspeed."

Later Page recalled that, all the while he was speaking, Hume fixed him with the penetrating gaze of "the practiced detective" and all but shouted aloud to him, "What are you driving at,

124

sir?" When the wild applause died down, Hume responded. Either he was a master of the ad lib or had anticipated the ceremony, for although he was obviously moved, he spoke well and effectively. First, he bowed to Page and said, "You have taken me wholly by surprise. You have got me." He was here interrupted by laughter and applause. "And I can only say, in the language of Watts, 'A word fitly spoken is like apples of gold in pictures of silver.' " (Probably no one knew or cared that Hume had mixed Watts and the Old Testament.) "But more precious to me than 'apples of gold' are the generous sentiments with which you have surprised me out of any fitting response. And more highly prized than 'pictures of silver' are the generous donors of this valuable and tasteful present. You, sir"—turning to Page—"and the inscription upon it unite in testifying that it is the gift of friends. From *them* I accept it with emotions so heartfelt and gratitude so profound that they baffle my power to express them. And the further assurance that this massive and magnificent testimonial of respect and friendship is tendered to me irrespective of party—by friends above all personal meanness for partisan purposes—greatly enhances its value. For, if it were otherwise, I could neither cherish it as a keepsake or value it as a time piece. You have got me, sir!"

After another storm of clapping and laughter, Hume went on: "But considering the occasion of this presentation, sir, it may not be improper for me to respond briefly to the very flattering allusions to my residence and official life in El Dorado County. Many of you have known me here during a residence of about twenty-two years. During ten years of that time I have been connected with the office of Sheriff. The first eight years as Deputy or Under Sheriff, I tried to do my duty at a cost to myself far exceeding my income. The last two years, I have been Sheriff and with the help of J. D. McMurray and John Cartheche, each of them the very soul of truth, honor and manliness, I have labored to discharge the duties of the office faithfully and efficiently. And I leave it now with no honor or emolument I will not share with them and with true-hearted

125

F. M. Fletcher, too. Again, thank you for this unexpected testimonial of friendship. I can say no more."

Editor Kies warmly endorsed the meeting: "The whole affair was an honor to all concerned, and gave a touch of religion to political and official good faith. Men without distinction of party vied with each other to render an act of personal friendship, significant of public justice."

Hume was not unemployed for long. He had several good offers of jobs and accepted Wells, Fargo's invitation to head a detective bureau. But although he was hired in March, 1872, the express company gave him a year's leave so that he might accept the appointment of deputy warden of the Nevada State Prison. Since the lieutenant governor was titular warden, Hume was virtually acting warden and faced the task of cleaning up a disastrously run penitentiary. The incompetent prison administration had reached its nadir on September 17, 1871, when almost thirty cons escaped after attacking the lieutenant governor and killing guards and citizens.

Jim Hume located a house in Carson City, then returned to Placerville for a visit with his nephew, Wilson Hume. Although he came unannounced and arrived at a late hour, a large crowd of well-wishers was on hand to welcome him to the Cary House. Drawn up in front of his hotel, too, was the Placerville Brass Band, ready to celebrate his homecoming and five-day stay. The *Mountain Democrat,* of course, bubbled with enthusiasm: "Although brief, it was a season of rare social and spiritual enjoyment. No man was ever more universally and deservedly beloved by our citizens than the subject of this notice. A pioneer resident of our city, his long residence, fine social qualities, lavish generosity and high sense of honor have made him a household word among us. In all his public and private relations, he has acquitted himself with unspotted honor and eminent ability and has endeared himself to all who know him."

Hume's job was to reform the administration of the Nevada State Prison and to restore its morale. Working in the shadow of Carson City's notorious politics, he more than earned his year's salary of $3,600, and he did enjoy at least a modest degree of success. Hume was not able to get the prison out of politics, but at least he kept the lid on and the penitentiary out of the press, most of the time. Just before he took effective control, the Virginia City *Territorial Enterprise* reported, on April 17, 1872, that Deputy Warden James A. St. Clair had suddenly resigned. This was the signal for new chaos in the penitentiary. The next morning, while the prisoners were at breakfast, six of the guards refused to go on duty and, in fact, immediately decamped. The remaining officers hurried the cons into their cells before the lack of personnel was noticed. The *Carson Register* blamed the guards' desertion on the continuing mismanagement of the institution. Warden Denver, on the other hand, insisted that he had proof that St. Clair had induced the guards to desert and had promised—even guaranteed—that they would be rehired under the "new management"—that is, for Hume's term as deputy warden.

The angry *Territorial Enterprise* accused the recalcitrant guards of being guilty of a crime in walking off their jobs. The paper insisted that they had no right to leave until their positions were filled by new men. The editor asked for a law prohibiting prison guards from quitting without due notice. In the meantime, the paper urged the State Prison Board to demand an oath of all guards that they would not quit their jobs until successors were appointed. "Almost as well might they have thrown down their rifles and deserted their posts while the prisoners were at work in the quarries."

Jim Hume survived the St. Clair contretemps, which coincided with his appointment, and strove to push the prison off the front pages. To a great extent he succeeded. Regrettably, however, Governor L. R. Bradley claimed all of Jim Hume's ideas as his own and gave him no credit for his year of determined effort. But at least the governor called for reforms in the laws that had created a conflict of authority between the unsalaried lieutenant governor, who was ex-officio warden, and the State Prison Board. The press supported the governor's bill

127

(very likely, Hume's, too) that would take control of the prison from the lieutenant governor and give the board full power to choose a qualified warden. The *Territorial Enterprise,* feeling sorry for Denver, added, "The Wardenship of the State Prison was given him in charity, that he might not starve," and suggested that if he could not be salaried that he be given, at least, the extra post of state librarian.

The governor's bill passed, but to Hume's anguish, Denver flatly refused to relinquish his post when Bradley asked him to resign and make way for a warden under the new law. When the board visited the prison, Denver all but set the dogs on the commissioners. Under his orders, Captain of the Guard McSweeney refused to admit them. Denver reminded them that the election of a warden could not take place, by law, until the first Monday in April; therefore, he was still in charge. When Governor Bradley ordered Major General Van Bokkelen and sixty-three militiamen from Virginia City to Carson City, Hume decided that things had gone far enough. Blood just might be spilled. He had already resigned as deputy warden, but he tried to rescue Nevada from another spectacle of comic-opera politics. He hurried to the governor's office on March 13, 1873, with word from Lieutenant Governor Denver that he would hand over the prison if His Excellency would be there personally to receive it. Unfortunately, Hume carried only a verbal message, and Bradley angrily told him that he had gone to the prison once already (as a member of the State Prison Board) and had been denied admission. He would not go again until he took over the institution, whether Denver liked it or not. Hume gave up at 4 P.M. and left the governor, discouraged.

Van Bokkelen did not want civil war in Nevada any more than Hume did. Leaving his three-inch cannon at the railroad station, he marched his men only as far as Capitol Square, where he ordered them to stack arms rather than prepare a frontal assault on the state pen. He sent his adjutant general into the prison with a summons to Denver to surrender. When the besieged Denver capitulated, Hume drew a sigh of relief.

128

He was aware that Van Bokkelen's commander in chief, the governor, had given him orders to place the prison in the hands of the new warden, P. C. Hyman, even at the cost of lives, if necessary. Denver, in the tradition of defeated military men, composed an eloquent surrender message: "Under military necessity and from the fact that you have a superior force in numbers, and that if I should stand by my rights, by meeting force with force, innocent blood might be shed and the convicts escape, I hereby surrender to you as Commander of the military force." To Hume's amusement, Denver then ruined his swan song by tacking on a request that an inventory of state prison property be made, and a receipt given to him.

After a political defeat in El Dorado County, Hume had blundered into the bitterest political crossfire in the West. He made enemies as easily as friends in Nevada, and probably because as a peacemaker in the farcical war he was identified with Denver, he was not given so much as a nod of recognition by either Governor Bradley or Warden Hyman in any of their reports or public messages. This ingratitude so angered El Dorado County historian Charles E. Upton that he scolded his fellow Nevadans publicly in 1906: "Captain Hume took charge of the Nevada State Prison at a time that few would have cared to have anything to do with it. The imbecility of the Warden had caused the people of the state a large amount of trouble and dread. But the management of Mr. Hume was able for the occasion and had he but received the reward of his doings, he would have been tendered the office of Lieutenant Governor of the State of Nevada and doubtless so have been, but for overwhelming political influence antagonistic to him." Although in many respects Hume was really apolitical, he never seemed able to avoid ending up in the middle of partisan squabbles, whether in Bradley's Carson City or, later, in Willie Hearst's San Francisco.

CHAPTER VI

WELLS, FARGO DETECTIVE

I N SOME quarters of the Old West, Wells, Fargo's express charges were regarded as exorbitant taxes exacted by a ruthless business monopoly. Consequently, the activities of highwaymen were tolerated by too many citizens of, at least, fair-to-middlin' honesty. They saw these affairs simply as instances of one thief robbing another. This view of Wells, Fargo & Company as a corporate robber—a league of high-handed extortionists—was a convenient conscience balm, too, for the company's own agents and tellers who were dipping their hands into the till. This line of spurious reasoning did not, of course, affect the attitude of Jim Hume. He saw his duty as plain and simple. It was to pursue, to apprehend, and to bring to conviction any and all persons,—in or outside the company—who preyed upon his employers. He was, of necessity, a plainclothes officer, and to provide him with an inconspicuous cover, the company seldom addressed him as Detective, but simply as, Special Officer, or Chief Special Officer, Hume, as if he were an efficiency expert rather than a sleuth.

Jim Hume was an ideal choice for the new position. He was not only a devoted and diligent worker, who had proved himself completely in law enforcement, he was virtually indefati-

131

gable in his pursuit of wrongdoers—as obsessed with getting his man as the most legendary Mountie of the Royal Canadian Mounted Police. He knew most of the peace officers in northern California and could enlist their cooperation in a case; he knew many of the state's criminals and their *modus operandi*; he was familiar with a large part of the California countryside, particularly the Sierra mining country in the north and its important stage routes. Best of all, he was blessed with great natural ability as a detective. As early as March, 1866, he had demonstrated some talent in this direction when his examination of greenbacks passed in El Dorado County by one David Lindsay showed them to be bogus currency. Hume was aware, too, of the great advances being made in crime detection, advances that had already created Vidocqs and Pinkertons. In December, 1867, Professor Thomas Price of San Francisco, an assayer-chemist, had made a major breakthrough in scientific detection when he proved, by microscopic analysis, that the dried blood on the shirt of an Indian murder suspect was of human origin and not that of a turkey the suspect claimed to have killed. (The *California Police Gazette,* which picked up the story from the *Pacific Medical Journal,* immediately predicted another breakthrough, which not even a Sherlock Holmes would ever be able to bring about—the capture of the picture of a murderer believed to be "photographed" on the retinas of every victim's eyes.)

Hume knew that almost as much of his time would be spent tracing internal corruption as in running down wily stage robbers. The first robbers of express shipments in California had not been highwaymen. Alexander Todd, whose Reynolds, Todd & Company Express was absorbed by Wells, Fargo in 1853, reported that one of his Stockton clerks in 1852 had relieved the firm of $70,000 while his Mariposa counterpart was making off with $50,000 and the Mokelumne Hill clerk was contenting himself with a mere $40,000. Almost a half page of the San Francisco *News-Letter* on September 22, 1866, was devoted to wayward Wells, Fargo men. The story, hot enough to be reprinted in the September 26 San Francisco *Weekly Recorder,* mentioned four enterprising employees. One of them had withdrawn from public life; another had been a suicide. The remaining pair were charged with embezzlement. The *News-Letter* jokingly accused the growing company of hardheartedness: "When another agent, and yet another, proved to have spent a few thousand dollars of the Company's money, this same firm, conceiving that it had a right to its own property, forgot that patience which every man habitually displays under such circumstances, and declared that these things must have an end. . . . It is urged, in justification of this step on the part of Wells, Fargo and Company, that employees have really no right to take the money of their employers without their consent . . . !" The sarcasm was rather heavy-handed, but the newspaper made its point about the number of agents who would rather speculate with company funds than suffer them to lie idle in Wells, Fargo strongboxes. The *California Police Gazette* was led to observe, on January 5, 1867, that "Wells, Fargo must do a profitable business to stand the losses by defaulting agents."

Eventually, Hume would have his hands full with incidents of Wells, Fargo embezzlers, but his first cases involved that breed of men with whom the ex-sheriff was already so familiar —highwaymen. His first major investigation after he had settled into the Sacramento office that would be his headquarters for ten years (until his transfer to the company's main office in San Francisco) was called, by the press, the Grass Valley Holdup. It was an absorbing case with a bizarre twist.

Because there was as yet no Nevada County Narrow Gauge Railroad to tie the mining towns of Nevada City and Grass Valley to the main line of the Central Pacific Railroad, two six-horse, sixteen-passenger stages were run daily, except Sunday (when only one coach made the connection), between Colfax on the CPRR and the two towns. On the sunny afternoon of July 23, 1873, eleven men and one woman boarded the coach at Colfax after Wells, Fargo agent William B. Story had placed $7,788 in coin in the iron strongbox, which, built into the back of the

133

coach and cushioned on top, formed the rear inside seat. At 4 P.M. the driver, Bob Scott, shook his team into a trot down the curving road to Bear River, glimpsed now and again by the congenial group of passengers through a screen of pines and incense cedars. Beyond the Bear, the pace slowed for the long ascent up manzanita-clad slopes, and when the lively conversation lagged on the uphill pull, attorney E. Black Ryan took up the slack by singing in a passable Irish tenor.

As the Concord reached the lower acres of Sheet's Ranch, only 5 miles from the Grass Valley terminus, four men—all masked —stepped into the road in front of the lead animals and beckoned to Scott to stop. The driver, deeply respectful of four double-barreled shotguns, halted the team, which had been at a walk. Ryan broke off his rendition of "The Low Backed Car." Abruptly, there was a brief and total silence, except for the sighing of the wind in the cedars and pines.

"What do you want?" asked Scott.

"The treasure box," came the answer.

"It's on the other stage," stalled Scott.

"Well," said the bandit, "we'll keep you until the other stage comes up." Then, all business, he added, "Climb on down and unhitch your team. Two coaches don't run on Sunday." Two of the bandit's men, leveling their shotguns, herded Scott, his assistant driver, and the passengers some 30 yards down the road and ordered them to sit down, cross-legged, in a row. Meanwhile, the leader and one of his men attacked the double-locked Wells, Fargo box with a miner's pick. They broke the outer lock but were balked by the second padlock.

When the leader got a canister of powder and some fuse, young Eleanor Webber, the lone woman among the passengers, spoke up nervously. "Gentlemen, it is evident that you are going to use powder to blow open the safe, and my trunk, which is on the deck of the stage, will, in all probability, be blown to pieces. It contains all that I own in the world, and while its destruction will not benefit you in the least, it will be an irreparable loss to me. I beg of you, take it down."

134

The black-masked bandit leader gallantly reassured her. "Certainly, miss—with the greatest of pleasure." He set the can of powder down, climbed up onto the deck of the stagecoach, and carefully slid the lady's trunk down over the boot to his waiting companion, who carried it to safety. As the chief of the outlaws hefted the trunk, the wind tugged at his mask and the girl had a momentary glimpse of his face.

The two men resumed tamping powder about the lock, attaching and lighting the fuse. They then retreated to where the others stood, flinching in anticipation of the explosion. When, after a full minute of waiting, no blast came, the impatient bandit leader walked up to the coach to see what the trouble was. After a quick glance inside, he jumped back and took off at a dead run. The warning hiss of the burning fuse was swallowed up by a red flash and a great echoing report, which bounded and rebounded off the enclosing hills. When the smoke cleared, the bandits rushed up to collect the contents of the ruptured strongbox, scattered over the roadway. "All right, boys," shouted the leader, once that chore was completed and he had replaced Miss Webber's trunk in the shattered coach. "Let 'em hitch up and go on."

Although the top of the treasure box, after having been bent double, had been blown right through the roof of the coach, and portions of the lock had whistled like grapeshot through the box and floor of the Concord, shredding the lining of the coach and making kindling of much of its fine woodwork, Scott found the running gear undamaged. He hitched up the team and resumed the drive to Grass Valley, while the bandits disappeared into the chaparral that edged the road.

At Grass Valley, Scott made an unscheduled stop to let Miss Webber alight, with her trunk, at the address she had given him in Colfax. It was a neat cottage on the outskirts of town, surrounded by a white picket fence, which gleamed in the lamplight streaming from the windows and the door, left open as if in expectation of a guest. As the coach halted, a woman came out of the house, made her way to the street, and welcomed Miss

Webber, leading her back into the cottage. The curious passengers noticed that the attractive young lady was more upset now than she had been during the holdup.

James Hume, who began his investigation the next day, learned why the girl had been so distraught. The one person who should have been there to greet Eleanor Webber—her fiancé, Louis Dreibelbis—had been absent. The reason for the girl's concern over her trunk was that it contained her trousseau. She had come to Grass Valley to marry Dreibelbis as the result of a courtship by mail. The lady of the house told Eleanor that her fiancé had been called away by an emergency but was expected momentarily. After Eleanor had eaten some supper, bathed, and changed into fresh clothes, her hostess reappeared, all smiles, to announce that Louis had returned. She led the girl to the dimly lit living room, where a clergyman and a witness were sitting with her future husband. They rose as she entered, and no sooner had Eleanor set eyes on her husband-to-be than the clergyman was arranging the couple in the proper positions for the wedding ceremony. Louis' voice sounded strangely familiar as he greeted her. And for some reason—perhaps shyness, she thought—he averted his face and did not embrace her. Eleanor demurely bowed her head during the ceremony and made the appropriate responses. When the preacher said his final words and bride and groom drew together, at last, to seal the compact with the traditional kiss, the girl's outraged cry astounded the others in the room. As Dreibelbis bent over to kiss her, the light of the kerosene lamp shone directly on his face, and Eleanor recognized him as the leader of the highwaymen who had robbed the coach. She tore herself from his arms and ran sobbing to her room. Dreibelbis, in an equal panic, rushed out of the house. To the bewilderment of the witnesses, Eleanor Webber—now Mrs. Louis Dreibelbis—locked herself in her room and refused to come out. She persuaded her hostess to book her passage on the downward-bound stage. Red-eyed with humiliation, she left Grass Valley forever, sadder but considerably wiser.

Meanwhile, Hume was already on the trail. The day after the holdup, he had a suspect, Charles Thompson, alias Bill Early, whom he arrested for complicity in the robbery, although he had far more hunch than evidence to go on. Hume's skillful questioning soon elicited a confession—not only to a part in the Grass Valley affair, but also in the holdup of the Downieville stage on June 23, 1873, near Oregon House, in Yuba County. Almost as important to Hume as the confession was the description Thompson gave of the loot taken in the earlier robbery. The Wells, Fargo box had yielded $100 in gold dust, $381 in coin, and a gold bar worth $2,200.

The next break came on August 9. On a tip from a Coloma friend, Hume investigated the activities of a man named Robert Walker, who was living in a Coloma hotel. Walker, who claimed to be the ex-superintendent of a Grass Valley mine and the St. Patrick Mine at Ophir in Placer County, was well fixed. He had given his landlady a small bar of solid gold and some hundreds of dollars in gold coin for safekeeping. Though he seemed to be habitually sad and preoccupied, he had won the sympathy of the townspeople by his kindness. Not only did he hand out candy to the children in generous quantities, but more than once, he also bought shoes for barefoot youngsters. It was with sincere regret that the people of Coloma watched Walker begin to drown his unexplained sorrows in the local saloons.

By telegraph, Jim Hume made a routine check on Walker, and when he learned that no man of that name had ever worked in the Grass Valley mine or the St. Patrick, his interest in the good samaritan of Coloma doubled. He drove there with a team and persuaded the landlady to show him Walker's valuables. He recognized the gold bar as having been cold-chiseled from a larger one fitting the description of the bullion taken at Oregon House. When he examined the gold coins, he found that many were bent and smoke-blackened, obviously the survivors of a recent explosion. Hume had no difficulty in apprehending Walker. In fact, he found the robber so badly disturbed that Hume placed him in a doctor's care at Placerville before jailing him there temporarily while en route to the Nevada City jail. When Walker recovered sufficiently, Hume questioned him and learned that he was really Louis Dreibelbis, the wandering bridegroom and a well-educated Midwesterner who had come to California to make his pile. Failing this, he had drifted into crime. Dreibelbis tried to get Hume to promise him immunity from punishment, in exchange for a confession. Hume, of course, could make no such deal. However, the outlaw soon became convinced of Hume's fairness and told him everything, implicating not only Thompson but also James Meyers, a Grass Valley saloonkeeper; Nat Stover, a miner; and George Lane, alias George Lester.

Hume telegraphed Sheriff Joseph Perrine of Nevada County to meet him at Grass Valley, which he reached shortly after dark. They took Perrine's team to the Coe Mine, where Stover worked, and roused Superintendent Hill at midnight. He cooperated fully with Wells, Fargo's special officer but flatly refused to believe that Stover was a criminal. Why, he told Hume, Stover was the most industrious and reliable man on the payroll—even if he was living with a woman not his wife. Hill showed Hume the cabin to which Stover had just returned from a "hunting expedition" of several days and said that he would get Stover to come out by telling him that he needed help to repair a pump at the mine. Perrine decided to lie in wait for their man at the mine, but Hume, uneasy, decided to shadow Hill up to the house. Finally, he resolved to take his man. Stover made no resistance, even restraining his savage dog at Hume's orders. But Hume took the precaution of checking the pillows on the bed and came up with the miner's loaded six-shooter. Stover's distracted girlfriend leaped out of bed and threw her arms around her lover's neck. Perrine took him to Nevada City handcuffed to the seat of the wagon. Like Thompson, Stover talked, telling Hume that Meyers' share of the loot was buried under a log in Boston Ravine. When Stover led them to the spot, the officers discovered that the money had already been dug up. A trail led to a cabin nearby, but its owner insisted that she knew nothing, and no one could get her to alter her story. Hume and Perrine quickly convinced Meyers that the game was up, and three of the four culprits were soon safe behind bars.

Although he had confessed, Meyers was persuaded by his attorney to stand trial. He drew ten years in San Quentin. Stover pleaded guilty and received a similar sentence. The jury failed to agree in the case of Thompson, but in a second trial he was sentenced to fifteen years in the penitentiary. He served out his term but later burglarized the safe in the Drytown Wells, Fargo office and was returned to San Quentin from Amador County. Hume finally traced the last of the gang, George Lane, alias George Lester, to Virginia City in 1874. He secured his arrest and removal to California, where he stood trial and drew a sentence of fifteen years in prison.

Meanwhile, Dreibelbis had sung like a bird. According to the press, he was the "prettiest" (most obliging) witness ever put on the stand. Besides his confession to Hume and to the grand jury, he testified six times in various examinations and trials. His turning state's evidence, along with his handsome appearance and apparent candor, won him his freedom. Hume furnished him transportation to his old home, Galena, Illinois, where, Dreibelbis claimed, he had been county sheriff before leaving for California.

Hume's first case for Wells, Fargo had gone well—but not perfectly. Politicking and personal recrimination ruined what might, otherwise, have been an exemplary case. Normally, Hume did not care much about publicity, but when Deputy Sheriff J. G. Bailey of El Dorado County skimmed off some of the credit for breaking the case, Hume decided that this time he just had to speak up. He wrote to the El Dorado *County Republican* to remind its editor that *he,* and not Bailey, had suspected Dreibelbis, had arrested him at Coloma on his own responsibility, and had arranged with Sheriff W. H. Brown for the use of a cell in Placerville to hold his prisoner en route to Nevada City. He specifically asked Brown not to permit either of his aides, George Burnham or Bailey, to speak to the prisoner. Hume explained that he had no real objection to Burnham, only that "too many cooks. . . ." But of the man who was jealous of his success, he wrote, "To Bailey I objected because I have no confidence in him." Perhaps still smarting from his defeat at the polls in El Dorado County or his lack of recognition in Nevada, Hume complained, "I care but little that the [newspaper] item denies me credit to which I am justly entitled, thus doing me an injustice but this, and another, similar item in the same paper concerning another recent arrest, deal in falsehood for the evident purpose of making political capital for a person who is not entitled to it and I, who am familiar with all the facts, should feel as though I were a party to the fraud if I should suffer it to go uncontradicted."

Hume then had to air some rather soiled linen, some of which belonged to Sheriff Brown, as well as to Deputy Bailey. He reported that when he had checked on his prisoner, he had found that the deputy, mistaking Dreibelbis for a bandit nicknamed Grizzly, had been pumping him. Furious, Hume was on the point of bundling his prisoner off to Nevada City in a wagon until Brown reassured him that it would not happen again. But then the real blow fell. Sheriff Brown took Hume aside and asked him, pointedly, if he was likely to "make anything" out of the case. It was obvious to Hume that his onetime election opponent was referring to the rewards posted by Wells, Fargo. Hume answered yes. To his astonishment, Brown then suggested that he could help him identify the prisoner and work up the case—*if* Hume would give him a cut of the reward. Later Hume wrote, "The proposition was so unprecedented, so unprofessional, so unlike anything that I had ever been asked or had ever solicited that, for a moment, I was so shocked as to hardly know what to say." Finally, he had explained that if anything were due anyone, it would go to his friend Cal Montgomery, who had passed along the original tip on Dreibelbis. Brown had then backed down, saying that he did not want to share the pay of anyone for what had been done but hoped that Hume would "let him in" on any future cases on which he might collaborate. Since Brown was holding Hume's prisoner in his jail, the detective had to consent, but grudgingly. "He would have been blind not to have seen that I consented with reluctance and almost on compulsion," recalled Hume. As for Deputy Bailey's statement that he, and not Hume, had got the information out of Dreibelbis, Hume branded it false and got Sheriff Brown to back him up. Thus, Hume's well-handled case ended on a bitter note of greed.

But many other investigations demanded Hume's attention, and he had no time to spend pondering man's easy corruptibility. It would be tiresome, even if possible, to list every case Hume investigated after his debut. However, 1875 is worth looking at in some detail as a typical year in the life of Wells, Fargo's head detective. According to a list of thirty-one robberies compiled by the *Expressman's Monthly,* Wells, Fargo lost $87,000 that year and posted rewards totaling $23,500. The driver of the Shasta to Redding coach was shot in the eye; other drivers were fired on but escaped injury. Of the robberies, two were burglaries of Wells, Fargo safes in Quincy and Newcastle, but all the rest were stage holdups in the classic pattern. Virtually every route in the state had proved vulnerable. Coaches were stopped on all of the following runs: Bakersfield-Kernville (January 15); Shasta-Redding (February 16); San Diego-Julian (February 22); Lodi-Mokelumne Hill (March 1); Sonora-Milton (March 23 and July 26); Visalia-Goshen (April 1); Marysville-Downieville (April 14); Grass Valley-Colfax (April 16); Ione-Galt (May 3); Soledad-Paso Robles (May 28, August 11, August 12, and October 22); San Luis Obispo-Santa Barbara (June 27); Fiddletown-Latrobe (July 5); Oroville-Laporte (August 3); Quincy-Oroville (August 17); Bakersfield-Sumner (October 4); Downieville-Marysville (October 5); Calistoga-Lower Lake (October 9); Milton-Sonora (October 12); Redding-Yreka (October 18); Caliente-Kernville (November 29 and December 7); Caliente-San Fernando (November 30 and December 4); Chinese Camp-Milton (December 1); and Marysville-North San Juan (December 16).

Since these holdups occurred so frequently, in every month of the year except, inexplicably, September, and from San Diego in the south to Redding, hundreds of miles to the north, no man —not even Jim Hume—could expect to bring them under control. In fact, the *Expressman's Monthly* was able to cite captures in only six of 1875's thirty-one Wells, Fargo robberies. California had no monopoly on holdups, either; there were many more that year, and every year, in Arizona, Nevada, and elsewhere.

Typical of these cases was the heist of December 16, 1875, when the North San Juan to Marysville stage, with five passengers, was halted at 10:30 A.M., some four miles from Smartsville. Driver Mike Hogan was half an hour ahead of time, so he had slowed his team to a walk—which was just what the waiting highwayman wanted. A masked man jumped out on the road from behind a bush, with rifle aimed, and cried out, "Stop! And hold up your hands!" Hogan was a trifle slow. The bandit roared, "Hold up your hands or I'll blow your brains out!" Quickly Hogan dropped the reins and whip and grabbed at the sky. "Hand over the box and be quick about it!" came the next command, and when Hogan fumbled with a valise in the way, the highwayman snapped, "Hurry up!"

After Hogan threw down the box, he asked, "Shall I drive on?"

"Yes," said the bandit, his voice quavering a little. Hogan began to suspect that the fellow's courage was evaporating. "Drive on or I'll blow your brains out!" was the highwayman's adieu.

A passenger, Robert Williams, agreed with Hogan that the outlaw was in a sweat. After a short distance he had Hogan stop. Drawing his pistol, he went back to stalk the robber. However, he was observed and ordered away by the highwayman, who had now been joined by a companion who had been waiting in ambush in case Hogan had shown fight.

Normally, bandits did not molest passengers. They at least pretended that their only quarrel was with the moneybags of

Wells, Fargo & Company. Once in a while, however, they robbed passengers. This was usually when they found not so much as a token in the treasure box. Thus, the occupants of the Grass Valley-Colfax stage were relieved of their valuables on April 16, 1875, and in the December 22 holdup of the Downieville-Marysville stage, the masked bandits lined up the passengers and took $165 from a Chinese and $200 from a white man.

Rarely did Hume actually ride shotgun on a stage. But he thought it wise to do so when the Temple & Workman Bank was foundering late in 1875. To rescue the Los Angeles bank, the sum of $240,000 in gold pieces was rushed south from San Francisco, under Wells, Fargo guard. The Southern Pacific Railroad was not yet completed to Los Angeles and the end of the track was Caliente, in the Tehachapi Mountains southeast of Bakersfield. There, at 7 A.M., Hume joined S. D. Brastow, Division Superintendent for Wells, Fargo, as the trainload of gold rolled into the station. Aiding Hume and Brastow in guarding the gold were Chief of Police Jerome Meyers of Stockton and Wells, Fargo Messenger Billy Pridham. As soon as the three boxes of treasure were transferred, the stage rolled out of Caliente with the four guards aboard disguised as passengers. Once out of town, Hume broke open the arsenal he had brought along in a wooden chest—two double-barreled shotguns and a Henry repeating rifle to back up their individual Colt six-guns. As the *Chronicle* later observed, they were "duly prepared to salute any road agents," on the twenty-three-hour ride.

It is said by some that Hume had recognized a familiar face in Caliente and was, for that reason, doubly apprehensive. If so, the other man—Dick Fellows—probably recognized the lawman, too, and realized that the December 4 stage to Los Angeles was on no routine run. In any case, Dick Fellows (a man of many aliases, whose real name was Richard Perkins) determined to hold up the southbound stage. In time, Fellows would prove to be almost as prickly a thorn in the sides of Hume and Wells, Fargo as the masterful Black Bart, although historian

Joseph Henry Jackson has termed him California's most unsuccessful highwayman. Fellows was cursed by his poor horsemanship during all his illegal career. The Caliente stage affair was no exception, for the short, black-bearded bandit, rather likable in spite of his calling, had been born before his time—the era of the motorcar. Ludicrously, he started out on a hired horse to stick up Hume's stage but, almost immediately, was tossed on his head by the nag, which returned to the stable, leaving Dick unconscious. After he had limped back into town, Fellows stole a horse and decided to make the best of a bad day by robbing the northbound, instead of the southbound, stage. Perhaps his initial selection of a cranky mount saved Fellows' life, for he would have had a rough time had he taken on Hume and his friends, single-handed.

Like Black Bart, Dick Fellows preferred to underplay the role of badman. When the Bakersfield stage bore down on him, he called it to a halt almost casually. He might have been hailing a cab on Kearny Street. With consummate coolness, he drew a tiny pistol from one pocket. Cocking it nonchalantly, he ordered the driver, "Throw down the box!" Next, to the amazement of driver Dugan, he began whistling "The Arkansas Traveler." The San Francisco *Chronicle* termed it "a most creditable performance." Ideally, the paper should have called in its society columnist, as well as its music critic, for this knight of the road had been decked out in boots polished to a high sheen, a stovepipe hat—white—and a silk-faced overcoat. (It was hard even for Hume not to like Dick Fellows. He had won a full pardon from San Quentin in 1874, after serving barely half of an eight-year term for robbery and assault with intent to commit murder. After faking his conversion to Christianity, Fellows had organized a Sunday school and a Bible class at San Quentin and so convincingly oozed piety from every pore that Governor Newton Booth saw his duty as a Christian official and released him.)

Although Dick had chosen a particularly gentle horse to steal for the holdup, he had neglected to bring any tools from Caliente to use in opening the green Wells, Fargo lockbox. In the dark, he could not find even a proper boulder for lock bashing so he decided to carry the box away on horseback and open it at leisure. But his "borrowed" horse, choosing that moment to be thoroughly uncooperative, bolted and ran for home. There was nothing for it but to shoulder the box and make tracks before Hume, or others, should light on his trail. Fellows now grievously compounded his error. He struck out on a line that cut directly across the Southern Pacific Railroad track, then under construction. In the dark, Dick Fellows walked right off an 18-foot embankment leading into Tunnel Number Five. The fall broke his left leg above the ankle, and the heavy box crushed his left instep. At least, both breaks were in the same leg. When he regained consciousness, Dick managed to drag himself and the box to a thicket near Tehachapi Creek, where he refreshed himself with drinking water. From a Chinese workman's tent he stole an ax with which he opened the box and chopped out a pair of rude willow-fork crutches. Taking the $1,800 in loot, after burying the box, he bought food from a Chinese track worker and hobbled to the barn of the Fountain Ranch, where he stole a mount. Somehow, despite his filthy luck with horses, he managed to saddle and mount the creature from the pair of willow crutches.

By this time Hume was already on the case but not yet aware that his man was Fellows or that his quarry was now also a horse thief. Young Tommy Fountain, son of the victimized rancher, followed Fellows' trail easily because one hoof of the stolen horse temporarily bore a mule shoe. He set Hume and Kern County Deputy Edward Mahurin on the right track. Mahurin finally found Dick, laden with coin and greenbacks but armed with only his tiny, three-inch Ballard derringer. The injured bandit was hiding out, under the name Richard Kirtland, in an old adobe in the mountains near a sheep camp. Meanwhile, the *Expressman's Monthly,* aware of Hume's staggering case load, was trying to keep up his and his colleagues' morale with such items as (January, 1876): "Wells, Fargo & Company detectives are making vigorous efforts to ferret out the highwaymen who have made so many raids on their stages and boxes, of late." But the San Francisco *Chronicle* felt no such obligation to Wells, Fargo and exploded, "When it is considered that the stage was robbed by a man with a broken leg [it was not broken until after the holdup, of course] and with a little single-barreled pistol, it becomes ludicrous."

Hume met Mahurin in Bakersfield, where the Wells, Fargo detective brought suit in the name of the company to recover the money Dick had stolen. He attached all but $500. Dick insisted that he was innocent and therefore knew nothing of "the other $500." However, just before Hume left him, Fellows said, "Things are not working just right and I may send for you." Hume replied that he would be glad to come. Hardly had he arrived in San Francisco when word arrived that Fellows wanted him. He went to the Bakersfield Wells, Fargo office and had a cozy fire built in the fireplace, then got permission to transfer Fellows there from the jail. Dick confessed his guilt to Hume but insisted that Mahurin had taken *all* his money. Hume sent for the deputy and charged him with withholding the $500. The Kern County officer vehemently denied this but suggested that perhaps he had dropped the $500 somewhere on the trail. Disgusted, Hume let him make his search. He returned with $300, confident that Hume would be happy with a compromise. Instead, Hume got him dismissed from the sheriff's office.

On June 8, 1876, Dick Fellows pleaded guilty and was given eight years in the state prison. The jail in Bakersfield in which he was temporarily lodged was a makeshift structure of sturdy planks, about 12 feet square. When Jailer Reed opened the door to give Fellows his breakfast on the morning of June 9, he found him gone—new Kern County crutches and all—via a hole tunneled through the floor in one corner. The alarm was given, and Wells, Fargo added $200 to the reward of $300 already offered for Fellows by Sheriff W. R. Bower of Kern County.

For two uncomfortable days and nights Dick hid out in the Kern River bottom near town, then stole a horse from a Chinese. He somehow managed to ride it for a while but was soon captured and sent to San Quentin, where his education and interests won him a job as convict librarian. Hume received a long letter from the San Quentin library dated February 26, 1876. The prisoner had heard that ex-Deputy Mahurin intended to sue Wells, Fargo for the recovery of his share of Fellows' reward. Fellows was sure that Mahurin was merely trying to pressure Hume into letting him keep the money he had already hijacked. Wrote the con, as disgusted as Hume himself: "Without any spirit of revenge, I think it a shame that this double-eyed scoundrel, without even the redeeming feature of that little honesty said to exist among thieves, should not only go unwhipped by justice but retain what doubtless seems to him so handsome a reward for his treachery, and that, after being detected in it. . . ." Fellows then expressed regret over his escape from the Bakersfield jail, not only because it had "incurred a needless expense to others" and had rebroken his leg, but because of the ignominious circumstances of his recapture—"by a band of unscrupulous nincompoops who had the bad taste to divert from their legitimate calling as sheepherders to add to the distress of an unfortunate fellow-being who was only endeavoring to flee the country. As they crowded around me, each discussing his relative importance in effecting my capture, I could not help thinking (save the profane comparison) that, unless shepherds have woefully degenerated since Oriental times, the infant Jesus, Himself, would have met short shrift at their hands if Herod had had the foresight to offer a suitable reward."

Before Fellows asked Hume for his forgiveness, for allowing him to take up his valuable time, he advised the detective, "I do not think your Company ought to be very hard on me. I never have directed against them, particularly, any matured scheme for plunder . . . [but have tried] to live honestly within the pale of society and, if at any time compelled to trespass, to supply my immediate wants, I would aim at affluent corporations and never molest poor persons or private individuals. I do not say this complainingly but merely for the sake of a better understanding, and think that my whole record will attest to the truth of it."

This was not the last that Hume was to hear of the self-styled Robin Hood of California's express routes. Fellows was released from San Quentin when his term expired in May, 1881. Briefly, he tried to go straight by working for the Santa Cruz *Daily Echo,* and advertised himself as a teacher of Spanish. When he could enlist no pupils, he gave up the straight and narrow as a bad risk and returned to his old line of work, making roadside withdrawals from Wells, Fargo's accounts.

CHAPTER VII

---◆◄●►◆---

A CAUTIOUS COURTSHIP

IN A sense, Hume's victories over individual highwaymen were mere skirmishes in what seemed to him to be a widening war on the company. The more fat-pursed Wells, Fargo grew, the more it found itself the target of outlaws, despite the efforts of Hume and his associates. Tightened security and good cooperation by city and county law officers, special postal agents, and railroad detectives helped, but the issue was still in doubt during the 1870's. There were simply too many cases for the special officer and his men to cover, although Hume's chief aide, Jonathan Thacker, was developing into a skillful detective in his own right. Another would-be Hume was L. E. Thaw, Wells, Fargo's man in Colorado. Investigating the robbery of a Colorado Springs coach in 1875, he followed his man, A. W. Ellis (a crooked stage driver), through New Mexico, Arizona Territory, and Texas— some 2,500 miles of pursuit on muleback. Losing the trail, Thaw returned to Colorado and made a fresh start. He traveled by train to Kansas City, Arkansas, Texas, and Tennessee, and finally, with the help of a Reconstruction (Negro) sheriff, J. E. Ousley, he ran Ellis to earth in Bolivar County, Mississippi.

But an army of Humes, Thackers, and Thaws was necessary

to protect Wells, Fargo, whose money-packed express boxes proved irresistible to badmen. As early as the 1860's, Wells, Fargo's 150-odd offices from Portland to San Diego not only had monopolized express business on the Pacific Coast but were handling more mail in California than the U.S. Post Office. One reason that the Marysville *Daily Appeal* reversed itself early in 1876 to support Senator Stephen Spencer's bill for a state detective force was its awareness that Wells, Fargo had lost $87,000 to bandits in 1875 alone.

By the time California was preparing celebrations to mark the nation's centennial year, the situation had worsened and Hume worked at a furious clip to keep up with events. Wells, Fargo treasure receipts for the quarter ending June 30, 1876, were $17,600,000, compared to the first quarter's $15,786,000. With such pickings available, what retired road agent could resist getting back in harness? In January Hume had to investigate robberies of the Fiddletown and Georgetown stages, and in February, with the help of Steve Venard (as determined a crime fighter as he himself) and a Central Pacific Railroad detective, he arrested the men responsible for both. But he was immediately plagued with new robberies—of the Boise City, Idaho, and Camptonville, California, stages—and the murder at Jackson, California, of a stage robber who was planning to "sing" for him.

March brought more of the same: the Downieville stage was robbed for the sixth time in three months. In April it was the turn of Nevada's Columbus-Aurora stage and of the Forest Hill, California, Concord. So badly shaken was the driver of the Forest Hill stage that he swore to Hume that the bandit who got $1,300 from the box was 13 feet tall. When the Battle Mountain, Nevada, stage arrived at its terminal on May 16, it was lighter by some $2,200 of bullion. Rounding out an arduous summer for Hume were robberies of the Oroville, Laporte, Soledad, and Jackson-Latrobe stages in California and the Jacksonville coach in Oregon.

Inside jobs were not restricted to whip-cracking stage drivers atop the decks of careening Concords. In the February, 1876, robbery of the Kern Valley Bank in Bakersfield, Hume had to arrest cashier S. J. Lansing, who acted also as Wells, Fargo agent and deputy county treasurer. The next month, Wells, Fargo Agent J. W. Stevens of Fulton, California, absconded, leaving no other security for his unprocessed "loan" than a dazed wife and four children. Hume wondered why the company had hired Stevens in the first place when his boss, General Superintendent J. J. Valentine, described him to law enforcement officers—"He does not look anyone squarely in the face; has a poor education, as his conversation will indicate."

By and large, however, the record of the 976 employees of the company's 450 agencies, all west of the Rockies, was good. As the *Expressman's Monthly* observed, "[their] general reputation for fidelity is unimpeached." That year Wells, Fargo employees handled almost every ounce of the vast treasure of California's mines, transporting it over 3,000 miles of railroad, 6,080 miles of stage lines, 1,088 miles of inland waterways by steamboat, and 15,035 miles of ocean lanes by steamer.

The increasing loyalty of the firm's work force and even of men merely associated with Wells, Fargo as stage drivers, heartened Hume, particularly after a series of incidents in which courageous men stood up to bandits attempting to loot Wells, Fargo boxes. In one case, Messenger Thomas McGee, instead of surrendering to two bandits disguised in barley sacks who tried to hold up the Jackson stage on which he was riding shotgun, traded fire with them, saving the treasure box. The would-be robbers disappeared into the brush, humiliated and empty-handed but a lot luckier than the outlaw who tried the mettle of Wells, Fargo Messenger Phil Barnhart on a night run of the Hamilton-Pioche stage in Nevada. The bandit, absorbing the contents of both barrels of Barnhart's shotgun, never knew what hit him. And when the Shasta-Weaverville coach was stopped and robbed of its box, Wells, Fargo Messenger John McNemer had the driver pull up shortly after he had been ordered on. Returning to the scene of the crime, McNemer found

151

the bandit in the act of opening the green box with a pick. Mac's first shot knocked him over, and when the fellow got up and ran, the second barrel removed, once and for all, road agent Thomas Hunt from Hume's list of badmen.

Other good news for Hume included the failure of a novel attempt to stop the Chico, California, express wagon by tying a rope across the road to cripple the horse. The rope broke, and so did the bandits—into a run for the nearby hills. Better news yet was the report of Ramón Ruíz's capture. A small-scale version of California's almost legendary bandido, Tiburcio Vásquez, Ruíz was a four-time loser who had led gangs that had hit Wells, Fargo strongboxes three times in 1875, twice successfully. Yet another capture—that of Gumboot Charlie Tadman, who was hauled in for sticking up the Jackson-Latrobe stage— boosted Hume's morale. But as fast as lawmen put outlaws into state lodgings, more appeared to harass the stage lines of California and adjacent states. One of the most embarrassing holdups of the year occurred on November 4, when millionaire staging magnate Ben Holladay and his party were treated to a nonscheduled stop on a run of the California and Oregon Stage Line. The bandits ignored Holladay but took $1,100 from the box, slit open the postal pouches, and made off with the registered mail.

The Downieville-Marysville stage holdup of November 13, 1876, had a happy ending for Hume, but it was sixteen years in coming. The express box and the U.S. mailbags were rifled, the passengers were robbed, and one traveler was wounded. The state matched Wells, Fargo's standing reward of $300 for each of the two robbers, identified by Hume as Tom and Joe Brown (alias Tom and Joe Foster). The wounded passenger added another $500 to the pile. It was not until September 3, 1892, however, that Hume notified the governor, all U.S. postal authorities, and all "whom it might concern," that Wells, Fargo had paid off Charles L. Wilson, the son of a man from whom the bandits had stolen fresh horses in their flight of 1876. Wilson trailed the pair to Deep Hole Springs, Nevada, had a gun fight with them, shot Joe (who later died) and captured Tom, and delivered both to Hume in Chico in December, 1876. For some reason, payment of the rewards was delayed despite Hume's attempt to help by giving Wilson an affidavit verifying his long and expensive pursuit of the robbers. As late as September, 1892, only Wells, Fargo had paid up. Naturally such reluctance or tardiness to reward the allies of law enforcement officers did nothing to deter crime.

Stage holdups during 1877 held largely to established patterns, but the case of the Marysville-Downieville stage, robbed on July 31 by Ephraim H. White and George N. Rugg, gave the public a good look at one of Hume's special talents, tracking. The Marysville *Daily Appeal* covered the case and helped spread Hume's fame as a detective in the Central Valley. In the preliminary examination in Police Court, a coach passenger, Lawrence McCarroll, stole the audience's attention from Hume with his colorful testimony. He was unable to identify the holdup men because, he said, "My eyes are very bad. . . . I had on blue smoked glasses." Hume was amused, because the robbery had occurred at 4 A.M. McCarroll went on, describing the bandits' actions: "They invited us to get out, every last son of a bitch of us, to the last man. . . . It was about a quarter to four and a bright morning. I only saw two men. The man that did not do the talking had the driver covered with something; I don't know whether it was a fence rail or a shotgun."

When Hume followed him to the witness stand, he stated: "About 4 o'clock on the morning of the 31st, H. L. McCoy informed me of the robbery. In company with McCoy and George Hackett, I started for the scene of the robbery. At a point about half-way from the depot to the place of the robbery, I discovered two different boot tracks going in the direction of the robbery. I followed them almost continuously to the bridge spoken of by McCarroll. I saw them distinctly about the bridge; one was larger than the other. I saw the track of a box in the dust, about the size of a Wells, Fargo Company's box. I saw a great many of the smaller tracks about thirty feet beyond the track of the box. Close to the box track, I saw a great many of the larger tracks. From this locality, I followed both tracks down the lane to the levee, coming in the direction of town. I saw no more of the small tracks until I got to Eleventh Street. I took the measurement of the tracks. They were very distinct and perfect. Those coming this way were made after the stage had passed because they had stepped across the wheel tracks. The tracks going out were obliterated in many places by the stage tracks." Hume then described the boot tracks, including the number of nail impressions and the marks left in the dust by defects in the soles. He identified a court exhibit of a pair of boots taken from White, after his arrest, and demonstrated that they were identical to those that had made one pair of the tracks. He did the same with Rugg's smaller boots. The bootmaker followed him, then a passenger who identified a German five-groschen silver piece as having been stolen from him. Then Hume clinched the case by revealing that Rugg had stolen a Wells, Fargo box holding $13,700 from a stage at Red Buttes Station, Idaho, on July 9, 1871, but had escaped punishment by peaching (turning state's evidence) on his accomplices. This neatly killed his plea of never having been in trouble before. On Hume's testimony, Rugg and White were convicted and sent to San Quentin.

The same year saw the end of an old "friend" of Hume's, A. J. (Big Jack) Davis. An old Comstock miner, Davis had been mining recorder of the Flowery District, Nevada, but had turned to stage robbery to bolster his finances. He had had an enviable career in Six Mile Canyon, where his mill served both as a blind for his raiding and as a fine place to rework stolen bullion. Picked up in an 1867 robbery, Big Jack got off by bribing the jury. He next looted three Wells, Fargo shipments on the Reno-Virginia City run, then pioneered train robbery in the West, leading the gang that held up the Overland Express at Verdi, Nevada, on November 6, 1870. This exploit made headlines all over the country. Apprehended, he entered the Nevada State Prison on Christmas Day of 1870 to begin a ten-year sentence.

154

He came to Hume's attention there after the big break of 1871, in which he declined to join. In fact, he helped the authorities against his fellow cons, and won himself a pardon on February 16, 1875. But on September 3, 1877, Davis made the mistake of his life. He took on a pair of the gutsy new Wells, Fargo guards of whom Jim Hume was so proud.

The Eureka, Nevada, stage left for Tybo on Monday afternoon, with Jim Brown and Eugene Blair accompanying the driver. When the coach drew up at Willow Station, 40 miles south of Eureka, three masked men approached. One called out, "Eugene Blair, get off that stage and surrender!" Blair and his comrades thought that the Willow stationmen were just drunk and trying to play a joke on them. So the guard ignored the command. When it was peremptorily repeated, he started to climb down, uneasy. Just as his boots touched the ground, he was greeted with the discharge of two shotguns—one blast from the rear of the stage, the other from the corner of the stable. Both charges narrowly missed him, the powder blast of one warming his face. Although blinded by the flash and smoke, an angry Blair returned the fire. Suddenly he felt the muzzle of a gun pressed against his chest. He grabbed the barrel, tore the gun from the robber's grasp, and chucked it aside. Turning on the man, he pulled a trigger on his own double-barreled shotgun but found that he was trying to fire the barrel that had already been discharged. Now Brown, on the seat above, joined the fray. He gave Blair's opponent eight buckshot, mortally wounding him just before Blair again put his gun to the fellow's chest. Brown jumped down, but as he did so, he was painfully wounded in the ankle. After the two other robbers fired four more shots from their shotguns and revolvers, they fled into the darkness. Brown and Blair found the stationmen tied up in the brush; they had been threatened with instant death if either gave the alarm. Jack Davis was dying in the road. Although Davis was game to the last, refusing to name his accomplices, Hume did a little investigating and soon pinned the job on Bob and Bill Hamilton, with Tomás Lauria as an accessory. But he had to agree with the obituary in the Eureka *Republican*: "Davis has had *quite* a career."

The year 1878 brought Hume more of the same—holdups and embezzlements. He was in the Mother Lode in January when J. J. Valentine informed him that $1,400 had disappeared from the main office of Wells, Fargo in San Francisco. "The culpability rests between three clerks. We have investigated but to no effect, whatever," Valentine informed him. "As soon as you can leave Sonora without detriment, please come here and take the case in charge. Your experience, judgment and impartiality will enable us to reach a just conclusion and that conclusion shall be a binding decision." When he had cleared up that case, Valentine gave him time off for a vacation, and Hume went East to see his mother in Lima, Indiana, for the last time. (She died the following October 29.) He went well armed with letters of introduction which spread his fame eastward. Valentine wrote the superintendent of the Union Pacific Express Company of Omaha: "We take great pleasure in commending Mr. Hume to you as one of the best of men, whose services to our Company have been valuable." The general superintendent also gave him a letter of introduction addressed to "All Express Agents or Chiefs of Police," which ended, "Mr. Hume is a gentleman worthy of esteem and confidence, both personally and officially."

It was upon Hume's return from his Midwestern vacation that his vow of perennial bachelorhood began to weaken in response to the attractions of young Lida Munson. One humorous incident of their stormy courtship was published in both the *Daily Alta California* and the *Expressman's Monthly.* As early as 1860 the custom of Sunday steamer excursions to San Quentin Prison, on a San Pablo Bay peninsula of Marin County, had begun. Both society and middle class made the trips a habit. After a picnic the excursionists would stroll through the yard, the ladies alternately thrilled and horrified by the pale, hard faces of the cons they saw behind cell-door wickets. On a January, 1879, Sunday, Hume led a party of friends across San

Francisco Bay on such a visit. As the steamer touched the wharf at San Quentin Landing, in the lee of Mount Tamalpais, a friend on shore recognized Hume and hailed him. "Hello, Jim! Is that you? You do not seem to have anybody with you for the State's boarding house, this trip."

Hume laughed and called back, "Oh, yes I have!" And he grabbed the arm of his pretty companion, Miss Munson, who blushed and then laughed. The group roared at Hume's little joke, but Lida vowed revenge.

After a pleasant day at the penitentiary and on the bay, the group returned to the Embarcadero and, bound for their various residences uptown, took a streetcar from the Ferry Building. Lida saw her chance to even the score with Hume as he rose from his seat to get off the trolley at his hotel, the Cosmopolitan. In a voice that all could hear, Lida "whispered" to a companion, "I do not think that man should *ever* have been pardoned. He should have stayed in prison every day of his term." A red-faced Hume hurried inside the lobby, away from the gaze of the curious streetcar passengers.

Hume's romance with Lida Munson was completely unpremeditated and the first serious attachment of his fifty-one years of bachelorhood. When she was in San Francisco, Lida stayed at 810 McAllister Street with Mrs. Jennie McGlashan. Most of the year she lived in Truckee, high in the Sierra, where she taught in the grammar school. Luckily for Hume, Truckee was on the transcontinental Central Pacific Railroad line. Thoroughly inexperienced in matters of the heart, Jim Hume pressed his suit earnestly but clumsily. He wrote Lida, "The only aim I have in my few remaining years is to contribute something to the comfort and happiness of others and you, of all others, I feel this interest in."

Hume's family had complained of his infrequent letter writing; now Lida teased him unmercifully on the same score. When he did write, he was too embarrassed to commit endearments to paper; he usually closed with a "truly" or "very truly" and only occasionally summoned the nerve to salute her as "my *very* dear friend, Lida." Generally bantering or argumentative, Hume's love letters were even a little pathetic. In January, 1879, he wrote, "My 52d birthday. Pretty old, ain't I? Ought not to write to you for a *long time* but can't help it. . . . I know that you are cranky enough never to write again if I didn't. You say, 'As long as you can wield a pencil, I am not going to write to you except in answer to your letters. You shan't ever say I bore you with letters, etc., etc.' Now, ain't that pretty talk? The above should be sufficient reason for not writing you for a month or two. *Write, write,* Lida! Don't wait for letters. No sense in it." A few days later, morose, he was writing again. "I want to see you, Lida, terrible bad but can't, for I don't know how long."

Gossips in Truckee had a field day speculating on Lida's relationship with a man much older than herself. Hume was furious with them and cheered Lida when she told them off: "I am proud to be counted as a friend of Lida Munson. You have more sense than any of them. If any of your supposed or pretended friends say anything crooked about your trip to Frisco, why, stand away up and tell them the reasons why they act so infernally mean and dog-like. Tell them you are going again. . . . Now, don't fail to tell all those shysters everything and say, 'I am a'going with JB just as often as I can get a chance. . . .' There ain't an honest man, woman or child in Truckee but knows in their heart that our trip was entirely right and proper and if they were not envious of you for the real pleasure and happiness you enjoyed, they would meet you cordially and jubilate over it. Tell the She-Devils you are going again, the next vacation, and that you propose to come home purer than any of them. Damn them! Beg pardon for this language, but I can't look upon any person with any degree of allowance who would say or even think aught against you, Lida."

His assignments kept Hume from seeing enough of his beloved, and the course of their courtship was bumpy and prolonged. Unable to get to Truckee to visit her, he once wrote her a melancholy little note from San Francisco—"Have been in this office all of today and expect to spend most of the night in

Handsome, dynamic James B. Hume was a disgruntled young farmer and an unsuccessful prospector before he found his niche as a lawman in post-gold rush California. From the El Dorado County sheriff's office he went to Wells, Fargo & Company to be the chief of detectives and cut losses by robbery to a minimum. He served the express firm with unstinting loyalty from 1873 until his death in 1904.

Wells, Fargo Bank
History Room

Dominating most towns in the West was the Wells, Fargo agency, a combination bank and express office, whose steel-shuttered doors and steel-nerved guards ensured maximum security for company treasure in the brawling days of California's youth. Well preserved today is the Wells, Fargo building in the Mother Lode ghost town of Columbia.

Wells, Fargo Bank
History Room

The heart of Wells, Fargo's empire in the early West was the Express Department in the firm's San Francisco headquarters, the Parrott building on the northwest corner of Montgomery and California streets. The historic building was constructed of stone blocks cut in China and assembled on the site by coolies.

Wells, Fargo Bank
History Room

Jim Hume's first major beat as a lawman was the stage road linking California and Nevada. It was a major thoroughfare not only for travelers, but also for millions of dollars in Nevada bullion alone, that traveled its length under the hungry eyes of California's badmen.

Sutro Library

As under sheriff and sheriff of El Dorado County, Jim Hume had the responsibility of protecting the citizenry—whether Yankee, Indian, Chinese, Chilean, or Mexican—from the lawless elements that thronged to the rich diggings on both sides of the Sierras.

Sutro Library

While far fewer pistols are attributed to Wells, Fargo detective Jim Hume than to Billy the Kid, an arsenal of such weapons probably exists in the hands of collectors. This cut-down Colt, authentically Hume's, was surrendered to him by the slippery murderer and stage robber Charles Dorsey, alias Charles Thorn.

Wells, Fargo Bank
History Room

The predecessor of the Winchester rifle was the Henry, first used in the Civil War by Union soldiers. This particular Henry was Jim Hume's when he was under sheriff and sheriff of El Dorado County. In 1864, during the Bullion Bend stage robbery case, Hume sent his rifle to a colleague at Somerset House because the lawmen in the area had no long-range repeating rifles to use against the rebel band.

Wells, Fargo Bank
History Room

In the 1880's and 1890's Wells, Fargo depended on shotgun guards to protect its shipments of gold and silver. If these armed messengers failed, the job of recovery of the treasure and apprehension of the robbers fell to the three men who wore this silver badge—Jim Hume and his two assistants.

Bill Luther and *Wells, Fargo Bank History Room*

The most bizarre holdup in Western history occurred on a curve much like the one in this old photo—perhaps the very bend shown. On the Placerville-Carson City toll road, Confederate irregulars held up two stages in succession at a curve which came to be called Bullion Bend. The Bullion Bend robbery was Jim Hume's first big criminal case.

Wells, Fargo Bank History Room

The view eastward toward the summit of the Sierra Nevada, beyond Placerville. This was the road Hume and his men searched when they were on the trail of the DeTell gang in August, 1867. The telegram in the engraving is the original "grapevine" to which rumors came to be attributed.

Sutro Library

Before the arrival of the railroads, the main tie linking California to the states on the other side of the Sierra was the Pioneer Stage Company. Its coaches rolled along the rugged Sierra road between Hangtown (Placerville) and Nevada's silver boomtowns. Here the coach skirts Lake Tahoe, near which Jim Hume was wounded in his shootout with the DeTell gang.

Wells, Fargo Bank
History Room

Like Jim Hume himself, the lawmen with whom he worked looked more like successful Victorian businessmen than man hunters. Jonathan Thacker *(right)* was his right-hand man; Harry Morse was the aide who actually nabbed Black Bart. Ben Thorn *(center)* later turned from friend to enemy during a bitter controversy with Hume.

Wells, Fargo Bank
History Room

Dick Fellows was a road agent who was cursed with an allergy to horseflesh. Almost every time he mounted a nag—particularly when a getaway was imperative—he was badly thrown.

Dean Johnson

During the San Francisco Midwinter Fair of 1894, Wells, Fargo mascot Jack was persuaded to pose atop one of the historic green treasure boxes that Wells, Fargo used to transport coin and bullion over California's stagecoach routes.

*Wells, Fargo Bank
History Room*

No outlaw ever looked less a hardcase than Charles E. Boles, alias Black Bart. In fact, he actually resembled his nemesis, Wells, Fargo Detective Jim Hume. Well dressed, almost dapper, Bart carried himself like a successful businessman—which, in a manner of speaking, he was.

Redwood Empire Association

BEADLE'S

Dime
New York Library

COPYRIGHTED IN 1884, BY BEADLE & ADAMS.

Vol. XXII. Published Every Wednesday. *Beadle & Adams, Publishers,* 98 WILLIAM STREET, N. Y., February 27, 1884. Ten Cents a Copy. $5.00 a Year. No. 27

THE GOLD-DRAGON; or, THE CALIFORNIA-BLOODHOUND

A STORY OF Po-8, THE LONE HIGHWAYMAN.

BY WILLIAM H. MANNING.

During the 1880's Erastus Beadle, king of the dime novel publishers, temporarily abandoned Wild Bill Hickok and Buffalo Bill to salute Charles Bolton — Black Bart, the Po8—with a potboiler as absurd as it was badly written.

Wells, Fargo Bank
History Room

Black Bart's "territory" encompassed all California, from the Sierra Nevada to the Pacific. South of Willits, off Highway 101 in the redwood coast country, is Black Bart Rock, where the wily road agent lay in wait for an unsuspecting stagecoach.

Redwood Empire Association

Like most Pacific Coast periodicals, the San Francisco literary magazine *Wasp* anticipated that Black Bart would follow his release from prison in 1888 with a speedy return to the career of stage robbery that Jim Hume and Harry Morse had so rudely interrupted.

Wells, Fargo Bank History Room

WILL HE WOO HER AGAIN?

Black Bart's San Francisco hideout was the Webb House, a hotel in the Webb building at 37 Second Street near Mission Street.

Sutro Library

High forehead, points running well up into hair; large ears, standing well out from head; eyes light blue and deep set; nose rather prominent and broad at base; high cheek bones; heavy eyebrows; chin square and rather small; head large and long, (size 7½); two upper front teeth missing on right side of mouth; two lower teeth missing in center; small mole on left cheek bone; scar on top of forehead, right side; scar inside of left wrist; shield in India ink on right upper arm; two vaccine marks on right upper arm; forearms quite hairy; heavy tuft of hair on breast; gunshot wound opposite navel on right side; well muscled; has been troubled with throat disease, and voice seems somewhat impaired; is a person of great endurance, a thorough mountaineer, and a remarkable walker, and claims that he cannot be excelled in making quick transits over mountains and grades; when reading without glasses, holds paper off at arms length; is comparatively well educated, a general reader, and is well informed on current topics; cool, self-contained, a sententious talker, with waggish tendencies, and since his arrest has, upon several occasions, exhibited genuine wit, under most trying circumstances. Has made his head-quarters in San Francisco for past eight years; has made but few close friends, and those of first-class respectability; is neat and tidy in dress, highly respectable in appearance, and extremely proper and polite in behaviour, chaste in language, eschews profanity, and has never been known to gamble, other than buying pools on horse races and speculating in Mining Stocks.

He has acknowledged to having committed the following robberies.

1.
Stage from Sonora to Milton. July 26th, 1875. 4 miles from Copperopolis.—John Shine, driver.

2.
Stage from San Juan to Marysville, December 28th, 1875. 10 miles from San Juan.—Mike Hogan, Driver.

3.
Stage from Roseburg to Yreka. June 2d, 1876. 3 miles from Cottonwood.—A. C. Adams, driver.

4.
Stage from Point Arenas to Duncan's Mill. August 3d, 1877. between Fort Ross and Russian River.

5.
Stage from Quincy to Oroville, July 25th, 1878. 1 mile from Berry Creek.

6.
Stage from Laporte to Oroville, July 30th, 1878. 5 miles from Laporte.—D. E. Barry, driver.

7.
Stage from Cahto to Ukiah, October 2d, 1878, 12 miles from Ukiah.

8.
Stage from Covelo to Ukiah, October 3d, 1878. 10 miles from Potter Valley.

9.
Stage from Laporte to Oroville, June 21st, 1879. 3 miles from Forbestown.—Dave Quadlin, driver.

10.
Stage from Roseburg to Redding, October 25th, 1879. 2 miles from Bass Station.

11.
Stage from Alturas to Redding, October 27th, 1879. 12 miles above Millville.

12.
Stage from Point Arenas to Duncan's Mills, July 22d, 1880. 2½ miles from Henry's Station. M. K. McLennan, driver. Mr. W. J. Turner and wife, of San Francisco, passengers.

13.
Stage from Weaverville to Redding. September 1st, 1880, 1 mile from Last Chance.—Charles Cramer, driver. Took breakfast next morning at Mr. Atkinson's on Eagle Creek.

California historians and antiquarians disagree about the exact number of holdups Black Bart pulled off in his eight-year career of road agentry. But Jim Hume's official list of twenty-eight incidents, prepared for Wells, Fargo employees, is generally regarded as accurate.

Wells, Fargo Bank
History Room

14.
Stage from Roseburg to Yreka, September 16th, 1880, 1 mile from Oregon State Line.—Nort Eddings, driver.

15.
Stage from Redding to Roseburg, November 20th, 1880, 1 mile from Oregon State Line. Joe Mason, driver.

16.
Stage from Roseburg to Yreka, August 31st, 1881, 9½ miles from Yreka.—John Dulloway, driver.

17.
Stage from Yreka to Redding, October 8th, 1881, 3 miles from Bass Station.—Horace Williams, driver.

18.
Stage from Lakeview to Redding, October 11th, 1881, 2 miles from Round Mountain Post-office. Louis Brewster, driver.

19.
Stage from Downieville to Marysville, December 15th 1881, 4 miles from Dobbin's Ranch. George Sharpe, driver.

20.
Stage from North San Juan to Smartesville, December 27th, 1881.

21.
Stage from Ukiah to Cloverdale, January 26th, 1882, 6 miles from Cloverdale.—Harry Forse, driver.

22.
Stage from Little Lake to Ukiah, June 14th, 1882, 3 miles from Little Lake.—Thomas B. Forse, driver.

23.
Attempt to rob stage from Laporte to Oroville, July 13th, 1882, 9 miles from Strawberry. George Helms, driver. Geo. W. Hackett, Wells, Fargo & Co's messenger, fired at robber and put him to flight.

24.
Stage from Yreka to Redding, September 17th, 1882, 14 miles from Redding.—Horace Williams, driver.

25.
Stage from Lakeport to Cloverdale, November 24th, 1882, 6 miles from Cloverdale.—Ed. Crawford, driver.

26.
Stage from Lakeport to Cloverdale, April 12th, 1883, 5 miles from Cloverdale.—Connibeck, driver.

27.
Stage from Jackson to Ione City, June 23d, 1883, 4 miles from Jackson.—Clint Radcliffe, driver.

[In all the above mentioned robberies, he also robbed the U. S. Mail.]

28.
Stage from Sonora to Milton, November 3d, 1883, 3 miles from Copperopolis.—R. E. McConnell, driver.

Agents of Wells, Fargo & Co. in county towns, will hand copy to Sheriff, and preserve this in their office for future reference.

Respectfully,

JAS. B. HUME,
Special Officer WELLS, FARGO & Co.

J. B. HUME,
Special Officer.

OFFICE, ROOM 3, WELLS, FARGO & CO'S BUILDING,
Sansome and Halleck Streets.

RESIDENCE, 810 McAllister Street.

Wells, Fargo & Co's Express,

San Francisco, Nov. 26th, 1883.

To Agents of Wells, Fargo & Co.

Since the conviction and incarceration of CHARLES E. BOLES, *alias* CHARLES E. BOLTON, *alias* "BLACK BART, the Po 8," for robbing WELLS, FARGO & CO'S EXPRESS, numerous inquiries have been received from Sheriffs and other officers, inquiring as to the identity of BOLTON *alias* "BLACK BART." This inquiry has doubtless been occasioned by the statement of the prisoner when pleading guilty before the Court, to a particular robbery—that it was his first offence, and that he was not "BLACK BART." All officers will readily understand the reason of such a statement, viz: To excite judicial clemency. The man CHAS. E. BOLES *alias* BOLTON (of whom we herewith append photograph and description) is "Black Bart, the Po 8."

DESCRIPTION.

Received November 21st, 1883.

Number of Commitment—11,046.

Education—Liberal.

Nativity—New York.

Crime—Robbery.

Term—Six years.

County from—Calaveras.

Age—50 years.

Occupation—*Mining.*

Height, 5 feet 8 inches, in stockings.

Complexion—Light.

Color of Eyes—Blue.

Color of Hair—Iron Gray.

Heavy Mustache—Nearly white.

Heavy Imperial—Nearly white.

Size of Foot—No. 6.

Weight—160 lbs.

Size of Hat—7¼.

Does not use Tobacco in any form.

Does not use Intoxicating Liquors.

Does not use Opium.

Respectfully J. B.

Five days after Black Bart entered the gates of San Quentin Prison, James B. Hume issued a descriptive handbill which he distributed to law officers to clear up the confusion over Bart's identity.

Wells, Fargo Bank
History Room

The most embarrassing case for Wells, Fargo during Hume's long career was the flight of the company's cashier, Charles Banks, from San Francisco with more than $20,000 of the firm's money. Although Hume was never able to arrest Banks, he forced him to remain in exile on the island of Rarotonga until his death.

Wells, Fargo Bank
History Room

In 1887 Jim Hume told San Francisco reporters that "stage robbery is, comparatively speaking, a thing of the past, what with the extension of the railroads." But in 1866, when this rare photograph was taken at Cisco in California's Sierra Nevada, the situation was just the reverse. Trains were not yet being hit by raiders, whereas stages were constantly the targets of Western outlaws.

Wells, Fargo Bank
History Room

The Robin Hood guerrilla war, which Chris Evans and John Sontag waged against the monopolistic Southern Pacific Railroad, won even Jim Hume's grudging admiration.

Wells, Fargo Bank
History Room

The most remarkable outlaw in the history of the West was not the almost incredible Black Bart or the legendary Bill Hickok, but Chris Evans, who took on the Southern Pacific Railway, Wells, Fargo & Company, and an army of law officers and bounty hunters. Even after being wounded in the eye and arm, he escaped from jail to fight again.

Wells, Fargo Bank
History Room

Charles Dorsey, usually called Thorne (Thorn), was in a class with Dick Fellows, Sontag and Evans, and Black Bart. Murderer, stage robber, prison escapee, and rap beater, Dorsey was California's "compleat" criminal.

Wells, Fargo Bank
History Room

San Quentin Prison in Marin County was a familiar sight to Jim Hume, as both an El Dorado County law officer and Wells, Fargo's chief detective. Hume was married to Lida Munson at the prison, in the home of his friend Assistant Warden Charles Aull.

Wells, Fargo Bank
History Room

it. Am alone, now; all the others being out to supper (or dinner); all married men but me." Worse, Valentine sent Hume to Texas Hill, near Yuma, Arizona, early in February, 1879. Under a sky like a burnished brass canopy, he found a desolate outpost at which water, hauled from the Colorado River in railroad tank cars, sold for 5 cents a bucket. He had to sleep in a boxcar, lullabied by the braying of mules collected there to haul 100 freight wagons. He wrote Lida, "I think the whole thousand mules were laughing at the same time, all night." He described Texas Hill's amenities: "One eating tent and five gin mills patronized by tramps, cutthroats, assassins, Indians and idlers." Even Maricopa Wells, his next stop in the investigation, looked good to him. Absence should have made Hume's heart grow fonder, but instead he lapsed into the bickering that marred their courtship. "If you insist on taunting me about my old age, why, just go on. I've made up my mind to let you have your own way about it and shall not get offended about that or anything else." From Phoenix he wrote an addendum: "Oh, you girls! You are incomprehensible and past finding out. You would 'kill' a private citizen or a captain or anyone of my gender. Yes, 'antiquated' or 'ancient' is pretty strong but why don't you say just what you feel like saying? Something like this, that will fully express your thoughts—"My hoary headed old friend . . . !' Now, I expect you will be mad again, but if so, all right. I shan't get down on my bended knees again to fix up matters with you. You asked for an opinion and you have it."

By March 5 Hume was northbound out of Los Angeles, writing Lida of his good luck in Arizona. "Have been very busy and have had fair success. We got the stage robbers and recovered $2,000 of treasure. I know now the third man in the robbery. I expect to get him and $3,000 more treasure. He is in Mexico and I have sent a man there for him." His next bit of business, a forgery case in Marysville, turned out well, too, and he wrote Lida: "I know who the *artist* is and have sent the Sheriff to San Francisco for him and when arrested, I will be busy for some days in a preliminary hearing."

After another spat, Lida was remorseful, and Hume replied, "Your flag of truce is hailed with delight. I joyfully accept the reconciliation. . . . I presume to dictate; you *must* favor us with two days visit. . . . I fear you will provoke us by flying through and over [Sacramento] like the ducks, without even a flutter here. Lide, you must not disappoint me again. . . ." But it was a busy spring for Hume, with cases taking him to Roseville, Newcastle, San Francisco, home to Sacramento, then to Ventura and Newhall, near Los Angeles—but never to Truckee and Lida. At Cámulos Rancho, the setting of Helen Hunt Jackson's *Ramona,* Hume gathered a box of oranges for his true love and threw in some citrons good only, he advised her, for perfuming a trunk, a wardrobe, or a room. He described Cámulos as "the prettiest place on earth" but had to tear himself away to break a case. He reported his success to Lida: "Another case of a young man being crooked and for the sake of mother, father and relations. I let him off without punishment; he confessed and gave me the money. Tears and sobs, etc., etc., in abundance."

From the contrite wrongdoer in southern California, Hume hurried to Salt Lake City, planning to stop off en route in Truckee, to make peace with Lida. He had written what he admitted had been a pretty saucy letter on April Fool's Day and then had ruined a gift of flowers (plus oranges, watermelons, picnic tickets, railroad passes, and even arrows, for Lida was an archery fan) by scolding her in his paternalistic manner: "You go wild on the flowers I ordered and then act indiscreet with them. All you wanted of those flowers was to make someone envious of you. . . . Now, don't you know that ain't right? But you girls are mysterious and your ways are past finding out. I don't think I'll now send you anything unless you order it. My dear girl, how often have I told you? Now, you have made a dozen envious, and that seems to be the whole aim of you womenfolk."

Annoyed by his lecturing, Lida played coy and refused to come to the railroad station when Hume, aboard the overland

160

train, next reached Truckee, on the summit of the Sierra near the site of the Donner Party tragedy. Hume had had to hurry to her home to see her, then, at the warning blast of the whistle, had to run pell-mell back to the platform in the cold spring night, lit only by stars and the few kerosene lanterns, whose rays barely pierced the windows of the cabins by the tracks. He was grateful that the darkness and late hour hid him from the nosy children of Truckee as he huffed and puffed his way to the station, blowing clouds of foggy breath in the night air as he dashed. He threw himself aboard a car of the train just in the nick of time. He could have wrung Lida's neck, for she had urged him on with mischievous shouts of "Go it, old fellow! Don't break your shins on those rocks!" But, he swore, "I would have made the train even though I had to hire an engine to overtake it at Boca or Reno."

He meant it, for such was his sense of duty to Wells, Fargo. When a brakeman stopped the train to throw off a hobo, Hume made his way to his own seat. He could not resist embroidering on his adventure, and he began a letter—"No more visits at your home from passing trains! I heard you, still laughing, as I passed Boca. When I reached the train, I jumped on the first platform I saw . . . the baggage and express car." Then, according to Hume's fib, the brakeman had pulled the cord and roughly ordered him off. To which Hume, supposedly, had replied, "All right, you stop your damned train and I'll get off, and if you interfere with me there will be a vacancy in the brakeman business of this train!"

Jim Hume was lonelier than ever in Zion, as he waited for a Utah case to come to trial. As soon as he could, he hurried back to California, but business took him only as far as Marysville and Sacramento, not Truckee, so, with considerable embarrassment, he had to ask Lida a favor. "You no doubt, ere this, have discovered that I left my 'companion' [his revolver] on your lounge. Please have some *man* take out the cartridges, first, and then send it to me here, by express." As usual, Lida did not choose to do as she was told, and a disgruntled Hume had to dash off a note to her, saying, "Received the six-shooter. But why did you not have the cartridges taken out instead of firing them off?"

Incessant travel—plus separation from Lida—was fraying Hume's nerves. He caught a severe cold in the rough mining town of Bodie, east of the Sierra, and then was ordered to Arizona Territory, but not for his health. "Ye heathen gods!" he wrote Lida Munson, "how I dread it! Ah, Maricopa, mercury up to 112° at midnight!" When he managed to wriggle out of the trip by wiring such explicit instructions to Prescott that his presence there was not needed, he exulted, "God bless the telegraph and all night operators!" But he had to hurry to Wheatland for consultation with Sheriff Henry L. McCoy on a "horrible job," and summer turned into a blur of railroad timetables as investigations took him to San Francisco, Placerville, Kelsey, Garden Valley, Georgetown, Spanish Flat, and back to Placerville again. He took time to write, but his letters were most often chiding. When Lida, a temperance advocate, criticized one of his old cronies as "a poor, miserable, drunken wretch," he angrily retorted, "I'll be careful, hereafter, in speaking of any unfortunate friend of mine." He could be jealous, too, and in another letter scolded Lida: "I doubt the propriety of your running around with *young* men like Hollister. They are liable to become infatuated with you and die unhappy. I know from experience—except the 'die' part. You say I am getting morose, I growl at you. 'Tis a dog's delight to growl and bite, for God hath made them so.' "

Finally, Hume could no longer postpone the dreaded trip to Arizona. An August 8 stage holdup eight miles from Phoenix demanded his personal attention. "I start for that sanguinary region tomorrow morning," he wrote sadly. Arriving in Phoenix aboard a train in which the temperature had reached 112 degrees, although all windows and doors were left wide open, he found what looked like everyone in town sleeping outside on roofs, sidewalks, and in alleys. "It just beats anything I ever saw or thought of since I left Sunday school. Teach your Sunday school children to be good boys and girls or Arizona will be

162

their final position." Hume was glad to be called back to California but could not get to Truckee. He confided to Lida, "I feel now some hopes in the Nevada [County] case. Can't tell, though; am disappointed so often." He added, mournfully, "When at Colfax, I feel in shaking hands distance of you, and then can go no nearer."

Hume was worried about a matter that would have given few other lawmen pause. His sixth sense told him that the wrong man had been arrested for the murder of William Cummings on September 1, 1879. Sheriff William H. Montgomery wired him from Nevada City: "Can you come up? I feel sure I have the true business in the Cummings affair. I will pay your expenses." However, neither Montgomery nor anyone else heeded Hume's protests, and eventually the suspect, John Patterson, was hanged. Patterson's partner, the real murderer, Charles Dorsey—to Hume's disgust—was given only a life sentence because a juror in his trial, who had once been a Confederate with Quantrill, refused to let his fellow jurors give the death penalty to an ex-guerrilla who had served in Kansas during the Civil War. The Patterson case, and others in which the wrong men were punished, gnawed ceaselessly at Hume's conscience.

Investigating a Ukiah stage robbery in October, Hume was able to help local officers with the case of outlaw murderers Dr. John F. Wheeler and Sam Carr, alias Captain Jones, identifying the latter as a former con. "I hope to get those fellows," he wrote Lida, but before he could, he was drawn off the Mendocino County chase, when his most distinguished opponent, Black Bart, struck again. "The Po8 [as Bart called himself] is in Shasta County and although we lost nothing, I go. Mail lost 19 registered packages—probably a large amount." Bart eluded Hume on that occasion, and he resumed his fatiguing round of investigations. Crimes against Wells, Fargo took him to Lathrop, Johnsville, and Oroville in northern California, then to Darwin in the desert near Death Valley. As 1880 opened, he was dashing from San Francisco to San Jose to Santa Cruz and then back to San Francisco and north to Santa Rosa, inland to

163

Stockton, and home to Sacramento. The pace was killing, and it was hard for him to stay in Lida's good graces. But he wrote, stubbornly, "I understand, I think fully, your growing dislike for me but no ordinary act of yours or any seeming coolness shall ever estrange me from you. I am going to be your friend, anyhow!"

A steamer trip to Oregon to extradite Thomas Paul, the robber of the Ukiah stage, gave him a little rest, although most of the other passengers, largely drummers and actors, were seasick. When he arrived, he found that Paul had lit out. Hume caught him en route to Roseburg, where Paul cleverly gave him the slip and escaped into the hills. However, on February 2, 1880, Hume reported to Lida, "Got my man and will start down with him." Because the Ukiah holdup had taken place on the very day when he and Lida were enjoying the Nevada State Fair in Reno, he joked, "My negligence of the interests of the Company caused all of this trouble and expense. Ain't you sorry?" Rushing to the desert on a case, he prophesied, "As soon as I get through at Mohave, I will be wanted at Ukiah again to attend the trial of the Mendocino Outlaws." He was right, of course.

Of the defendant in the Ukiah holdup case, he wrote Lida, "This young man, Paul, is not an apostle of J.C. [Jesus Christ] He is a son of Timothy S. Paul, who has preached the word here for one year, a rip-roaring Methodist preacher." A confession from one of Paul's colleagues was followed by the outlaw's own. Sending Lida a picture of the twenty-three-year-old ex-schoolteacher, he wrote, "Nice looking boy, ain't he? I propose to give him 10 years in San Quentin to think over his youthful indiscretions."

Between trains and hearings and pursuits, Hume continued his quarrelsome wooing: "You know that you are the only person on the Coast that I would go out of my way to meet and that I would do your bidding at any time and at any reasonable sacrifice—and still you want to be *huffy*. . . . How you love to quarrel! I would not have your disposition for anything." Then, as if to pour salt in the wounds, he used stationery guaranteed to raise the blood pressure of his temperance-crusading sweet-heart—the Ukiah letterhead of "Whelan's Sample Rooms and Liquor House—Agent for Old Kentucky Bourbon Whiskies." His brash letters continued to irritate her: "I'll see you as soon as possible, when you can scold and quarrel as much as you choose. I can't fight on paper and I have no cause for ill feeling toward you. You know I have just doted on you for years and it is just *fun* for me to have you get cranky."

Perhaps some of Hume's own crankiness was due to his ex-hausting case load, advancing years, and slowly declining health. During the summer he hurried from Carson City, Nevada, to Folsom, Mormon Island, and Rattlesnake Bar, California, then back to Esmeralda County, Nevada. When he got back to Carson City, Hume admitted that he was "dusty, tired, worn-out and ill tempered." The strain of his job was telling on him more with each passing year. In the Pacific North-west, he dashed off a note: "Poor Paige—no chance for him. Is gone under. Don't drink, Lida, and don't swear. 'Tis danger-ous." After so many trips to bleak Arizona Territory, Oregon's green looked wonderful to him. He called Portland "a daisy of a city" and The Dalles "a little paradise."

In snowy Aurora, Nevada, for the October trial of highway-man Milton A. Sharp, he found lots of fellow Democrats, in-cluding that fall's election candidates. He wrote Lida, "We are a Solid South here; [William] Sharon's coin can't touch us!" On October 28 he told her, "I am certain of conviction unless some bad man has got a place on the jury." That evening, wit-nesses and attorneys conferred with Hume, and he told Lida that he was acting as their "usher." When the case was submitted to the jury, fifty people ("the really good element of this wicked community") stayed up to await the verdict. A friend on the jury managed to pass rolled-up notes out to Hume through the keyhole in the door of the jury room, and Jim learned that seven had voted for conviction on the first ballot; nine on the second. At midnight, ten were for conviction. "Then," he grumbled to

Lida, "this miserable sheriff's office locked up the doors to the Courtroom adjacent to the jury room and, from that time on, till 8 A.M., I got no report. But at 9 this morning, I was awakened in my chair in the rooms of the YMCA and informed that the jury had agreed on a verdict. I straightened up and sang in my full, melodious, voice that sentimental song that starts off this way—'Praise God from whom all blessings flow,' and then I closed the exercises with 'This is the way I long have sought.'"

Hume's facetious prayers were answered. The verdict was guilty. Hume reported with delight, "My little innocent heart leaped with joy as, Indian file, the 'wise, pure, conscientious' jury of 12 *Republican* persons were discharged and left the Courtroom."

Hume's joy was understandable. Milton A. Sharp had long plagued Wells, Fargo and was, in Hume's book, a nuisance second only to Black Bart. According to the dossier Hume prepared, Sharp did not smoke, chew, swear, or gamble; he devoted himself exclusively to the vice of robbery and had special success with Wells, Fargo's green strongboxes. With his partner, W.C. Jones (alias Frank Dow) he had held up six stages between May 15 and September 5, 1880, which beat even Black Bart's average—on a per-week reckoning. Four of the coaches had been on the Carson to Bodie run. In the last holdup, Sharp had had trouble. Wells, Fargo Guard Mike Tovey had shot and killed Jones, and Sharp, returning the fire, had disabled him. Hume's happiness turned abruptly to gloom when he learned that the outlaw had escaped from the Aurora jail on November 2. But Sharp was on the loose for only a week before Hume had the distinct pleasure of chaperoning him during a trip to Nevada State Prison, where he was expected to cool his heels for twenty years.

CHAPTER VIII

BLACK BART

IT was lucky for Wells, Fargo that Black Bart entered the ranks of the highwaymen no sooner than he did. Had he struck when Reelfoot Williams was pioneering road agentry in gold rush days, the company might have been hard pressed for funds with which to pay a special officer's salary. But it was two and a half decades later, in 1875, that Bart embarked on a new career during the twilight of stage robbery, an art form that was giving way to train robbery even when Hume arrived on the payroll in 1873.

Compared to the halcyon days of 1864, when shipments of silver bullion from Virginia City alone ran from $166,351 to $203,291.68 in a single week, the mid-seventies were lean, indeed. By the time Bart began making his heists, things were so bad that one stage driver, Sam Smith, was impelled to deliver the following alfresco address when he was held up near Milton in the Mother Lode region: "Gentlemen, I have been a driver, boy and man, going on twenty years. I never ditched a stage or growled at a passenger and, gentlemen, I assure you I have had some of the toughest outsiders that ever left Boston for a week's *chassez* in Yosemite. I have met gentlemen of your kind before and I defy any of them to come forward and say I ever treated them with contempt. On the other hand, it has been my aim to act toward highwaymen—excuse me, gentlemen, I mean road agents—with the distinguished consideration due their standing in society. Hence you will believe me when I say that I have nothing for you this morning. Sorry, gentlemen, but the truth of the matter is [that] Wells, Fargo and Company's boxes are young poorhouses on this road, just now, and you couldn't squeeze a picayune out of one of them to save your sweet neck from the gallows."

Black Bart was really Charles E. Boles, sometimes spelled Bolles, but in California he usually used the name Charles E. Bolton. According to the records subsequently compiled at San Quentin, he was born in New York between 1830 and 1832, but Hume was never sure if these dates were correct. Another story had it that he had been born in Norfolk, England, and had migrated to Alexandria township, Jefferson County, in upstate New York at the age of two, with his mother and father, John Boles, and had grown up on the family farm. According to Ernest G. Cook of the Watertown (New York) *Daily Times,* the Boles homestead of some 100 acres lay 4 miles north of the village of Plessis, toward Alexandria Bay, and across the road from the schoolhouse.

In the eight years after 1875, Bart robbed California coaches with the regularity of the Pacific tides. He struck twenty-nine times according to Jim Hume's final, revised, list of holdups, and failed only once to get booty. All the while he remained a shadow figure to Hume and other lawmen. When Jim wrote Lida in October, 1879, from Shasta County that he was on the trail of "the Po8" (Bart), he thought that the mysterious bandit was Frank Fox. Because Boles had no police record, Hume had no clue to connect him with Black Bart. Fox was purely a guess, and a wrong one. Hume so convinced himself that the one-eyed ex-Ohioan was Bart that he issued a wanted circular for him. (Luckily, he restricted it to sheriffs and police officers; otherwise he would have been greatly embarrassed by his bum steer.) He stated, "From information in my possession, I am pretty thoroughly satisfied that one FRANK FOX committed the following robberies, at two of which he left with the express box some doggerel signed 'Black Bart, the Po8.' " After listing the real Bart's holdups of 1877 and 1878, Hume ended his flyer by saying, "Please arrest the said FRANK FOX and telegraph the undersigned at Sacramento and [the] Sheriff at Ukiah. Any old convict who was serving at [the] same time with Fox will know him."

While Hume was dogging the wrong bandit, Bart was methodically looting treasure boxes. He never made a real killing, but he relieved the company of some $18,000 in all and caused much irritation and embarrassment. Since he usually robbed the mail sacks, too, Bart was also a burr in the U.S. Post Office Department's saddle blanket.

John Shine, on the box of the Sonora coach that left for Milton on July 26, 1875, was destined to be Black Bart's first target. In time, Shine would become a United States marshal, California state senator, and the recipient of a fine pocket watch from Wells, Fargo for saving a stageload of treasure from bandits in November 1876. But he did not play the hero that day. Four miles short of Copperopolis, as his team labored up Funk Hill from Reynolds Ferry and the Stanislaus River, he saw a masked figure dart out into the center of the dusty road from behind a large, rounded boulder. The bandit was polite— "Please throw down the box" was his command—impressively reinforced by the unblinking stare of a double-barreled shotgun.

Bart was well disguised in a soiled linen duster. His shoes were covered with heavy boot socks to hide his footprints, and over his head and face he wore a flour sack with two eye holes cut in it. When Shine fumbled with the box, the bandit tossed an order over his shoulder: "If he dares to shoot, give him a solid volley, boys!" Shine glanced at the hillside and, through the screening manzanita brush, thought that he saw at least a half-dozen rifle barrels aimed at him. He hustled along. Almost as soon as the metal box hit the dust, the highwayman attacked it, swiftly removing several bags of gold coins and a few express packages. When a frightened lady passenger tossed her purse out of the coach at his feet, the bandit picked it up, bowed, and returned it to her, politely demurring in a deep and resonant voice, "I don't wish your money, only [Wells, Fargo] boxes."

When the outlaw ordered him onward, Shine drove off, but he stopped a short way up the road as he saw the bandit disappear into the chaparral. The driver went back to collect the emptied treasure box, only to be badly startled when he saw the rifle barrels of the highwayman's confederates still leveled at him from roadside boulders. Nothing happened, however, as he stood rooted in place, and suspicion began to dawn. Approaching the guns gingerly, Shine discovered that they were sticks fastened in place as a ruse by the lone bandit. (Later a genuine shotgun was found there. For some reason, Bart had brought two guns and abandoned one.)

Perhaps Bart was a criminal with a subconscious desire to be caught. At any rate, he was soon strewing clues all over northern California, as if to make Special Officer Hume's work easier. On August 3, 1877, he stopped the Point Arena stagecoach on the Redwood Coast, en route to Duncan's Mills on the Russian River. Before he departed for parts unknown with $300 in coin and a $305.52 Grangers Bank of San Francisco check, which he was afraid to cash, he left a scrap of paper under a stone atop a tree stump, where it remained, despite the Sonoma coast's westerly breezes, until the law discovered it. Each line of the bandit's doggerel quatrain was written in a different hand, an attempt to bewilder any handwriting experts Hume might have consulted. Bart had added an enigmatic postscript, which read—"Driver, give my respects to our old friend, the other driver, but I really had a notion to hang my old disguise hat on his weather eye." But it was Bart's poesy that captured the imagination of press and public. Considering the hurried circumstances of its composition, Hume thought it pretty fair versifying:

170

I've labored long and hard for bred
For honor and for riches,
But on my corns too long you've tred
You fine haired Sons of Bitches.

It was signed "Black Bart, the Po8."

By the time he carried out his fifth robbery, in July, 1878, Black Bart was even more daring—or careless. As he sat alongside the road, the day before the holdup, timing the arrival of the coach at his ambuscade, he let the stage driver see him plainly. And immediately after the crime officers found more poetry awaiting them:

Here I lay me down to sleep
To await the coming morrow
Perhaps success, perhaps defeat
And everlasting sorrow.

I've labored long and hard for bred
For Honor and for riches,
But on my corns too long you've tred
You fine haired Sons of Bitches.

Let come what will, I'll try it on
My condition can't be worse
And if there's money in that box
'Tis munny in my purse.

By now, although he had no idea of his man's real identity, Hume had pieced together a pretty fair picture of Bart's working habits. He knew that he wore a No. 8 boot; that he always worked alone; that although he waved a shotgun in the faces of drivers and messengers, he never fired it. (Eventually Hume learned that Bart never even loaded it.) The detective knew that the outlaw always operated on foot, gambling that his pursuers would lose his light track before overtaking him with their horses. He won the gamble, every time, simply because he was a superb walker. Although he was about forty when he began operations and almost fifty when Hume's men put a stop to his career, Black Bart hiked and camped alone, carrying for long distances over rugged wilderness country a blanket roll containing the heavy tools of his trade—gun, ax, crowbar and, possibly, a small sledgehammer. On several occasions, Bart robbed two stages within twenty-four hours, but miles apart, and never once was in any real danger of being overtaken. He cut mailbags with a deft stroke that left a T-shaped slit at the top, near the lock, like a trademark. Hume guessed, correctly, that he had a modern shotgun which he had broken at the breech and hid in the center of his bedroll. He sensed, too, that Bart was not the type to hole up in an isolated hideout between robberies; in fact, while things were blowing over, the road agent preferred to assume a new identity and go to work as a laborer. At one point, for example, Hume rightly surmised that Black Bart was employed as a Mr. Martin at James Reader's ranch and sawmill on Shady Creek, near Sweetland in Nevada County, but he lacked proof. Or, thought Hume, Bart would lose himself in the crowds of San Francisco's busy streets. Again he was right. Bart loved city life and its amenities. In town he dressed elegantly, favoring a heavy derby, a stylish wide cravat with a diamond stickpin, a salt-and-pepper tweed suit, a cane, and a velvet-collared overcoat, and he was never suspected of being anything other than the prosperous mining man of his pose. He looked much more like a Wells, Fargo executive than a bandit and, in fact, bore a close resemblance to his indefatigable pursuer, Jim Hume.

Immediately before and after a holdup, Bart would ramble overland, posing as a hungry foot traveler looking for work. Many times he parked his dusty valise or innocent-looking bedroll on a ranch house porch and sat down to a meal. In return for such hospitality, he offered the isolated, lonesome and news-hungry ranchers his wit, conversation, and gentlemanly appreciation of the favor done him. He would entertain his hosts with tales of his Civil War career, promoting himself from top sergeant in the telling, saying that "the captain" did this or that.

Naturally, he never mentioned the wife and daughters he had abandoned in the Midwest.

For all the information Hume had in the Po8's dossier, he had absolutely no luck in trapping him. Nor had anyone else, even when Governor William Irwin matched Wells, Fargo's $300 reward for the bandit and the U.S. government chipped in another $200 because of Bart's reprehensible habit of reading (and spending) other people's mail. When Black Bart struck stages in Mendocino County twice in two days, he took a chance because the sheriff, J. R. Moore, was a good tracker and dogged his steps for 60 miles through rough country before giving up the pursuit. Bart had the knack for choosing holdup sites so skillfully that Hume never had any idea where he might strike next. From the coast the bandit would go to the Sierra foothills, then to northernmost California, then back to the coast.

Eventually Hume discovered some of Black Bart's rural hosts and pumped them for information. In Sonoma County he interviewed Elisha S. Shortridge, an ex-Hoosier like himself. The Redwood Valley farmer had found a suspicious-looking cache of a bedroll and a valise in the fall of 1880. From Mrs. Sydney H. McCrearey, a Potter Valley farmer's wife, Hume learned that a "gentleman tourist" had dropped by and accepted an invitation to lunch about the time of the Mendocino County holdups. Mrs. McCrearey's sixteen-year-old daughter had waited on the traveler and had been as fascinated as her mother by his obvious breeding, his jokes, and amusing conversation. Both noticed that their guest did not have the annoying and "filthy" tobacco habit of most wanderers, that he carried no liquor with him, and that he seemed completely contented with a second cup of coffee to top off his meal. Mrs. McCrearey told Hume that the blue-eyed stranger, who had complained of a sore throat, appeared to be down on his luck. His coat sleeve was clumsily darned with white thread, his shoes were split over the balls of his feet, and his gold watch chain was broken and held together with strips of leather. At least two of his front teeth were missing. His long slender hands showed no evidence of ever having performed manual labor. In Potter Valley Hume had found a mine of information about the handsome, neatly mustached gentleman who, he knew, was Black Bart, although Mrs. McCrearey insisted that he was an itinerant preacher.

In Shasta County, after the September, 1880, holdup of the Weaverville-Redding stage—during which Bart had asked driver Horace Williams to give his compliments to Hume—the Wells, Fargo detective questioned a rancher on Eagle Creek who had served breakfast to a stranger bound south to Tehama County, a man whose geniality and gap-teeth fit Mrs. McCrearey's description perfectly. He had been so personable that the rancher had pressed a box lunch on him when he left.

Only one of Black Bart's robbery attempts fizzled completely. His twenty-third stickup, of the Laporte-Oroville coach, was his third raid on that particular route and just too much for Wells, Fargo Messenger George W. Hackett. Bart's usual polite command—"Please throw out the box!"—some nine miles from Strawberry on July 13, 1882, was answered discourteously when Hackett raised his rifle and fired at the flour-sacked bandit. Bart jumped nimbly into the brush and ran for it. Hackett and driver George Helm pursued the bandit, but all they found was Bart's bloodstained and bullet-pierced hat. Hackett's shot was responsible for the "scar on top of forehead, right side" mentioned on Hume's rap sheet on Bart.

On Sunday, November 3, 1883, Black Bart's luck finally ran out. At 4 A.M. that morning Reason E. McConnell guided the Nevada Stage Company's Concord out of Sonora, bound for Milton and transshipment of San Francisco-bound express via the Stockton riverboats. At Tuttletown he picked up additional express for the Wells, Fargo box fastened under his seat. It soon contained $550 in gold coin, $65 in gold dust, and 228 ounces of amalgam from the Patterson Mine, worth about $4,200. At Reynolds Ferry on the Stanislaus, McConnell stopped at the hotel run by Grandma Rolleri. Her nineteen-year-old son Jimmy, the ferryman, easily bummed a ride with Mac, who was lonesome with no passengers aboard. Jimmy wanted to go hunting near Copperopolis. As they began the long climb up Funk Hill from the river bottom, the young man jumped off with his Henry rifle to see what he could scare up before reboarding the lumbering coach near the summit.

Just short of the hilltop a figure emerged from the manzanita and boulders on the left side of the road. He wore a linen duster and a sack mask and carried a shotgun at the ready. There was no doubt about it—he was Black Bart. Incredibly, he was holding up his twenty-eighth (and last) stage on the very same spot where he had held up his first, on July 26, 1875. Keeping his shotgun on McConnell's Adam's apple, the bandit asked in a voice so deep that it seemed to issue from the bunghole of a barrel, "Who was that man—the one who got off down below?" McConnell explained that he was only a friend, out hunting some stray cattle. "Get down from your seat," ordered Bart. "I've got to unfasten that box of yours." McConnell stalled, saying that he could not leave his seat—the brakes were weak, and the stagecoach might roll back down the grade. Annoyed, Bart said sharply, "The stage can't roll if you put rocks behind the wheels. Go ahead and do it."

McConnell retorted, "Why don't you?"

Surprisingly, the masked man did, chocking the wheels with heavy rocks from the side of the road. Then he snapped, "Now, get down and unhitch your horses. Run them up the road a ways. I'll be busy getting that box loose."

Driver McConnell was unarmed, so he did exactly as he was told. He heard the bandit hammering at the box, oblivious to the fact that Jimmy Rolleri was approaching. McConnell frantically signaled to the youth, and got him to circle the stage to join him without being seen. Both of them saw Bart straighten up and heft a sack of plunder. McConnell grabbed the Henry rifle from Rolleri and fired a shot. He missed. He fired again and missed. Jimmy then politely took back the gun, saying, "Here, let me shoot. I'll get him and I won't kill him, either." He fired.

175

Bart stumbled and almost fell. He dropped a handful of papers but kept a tight grip on the sack of loot as he dived into the underbrush.

At Copperopolis, McConnell reported the holdup, and soon Sheriff Ben K. Thorn of Calaveras County was at the robbery scene, with his deputies. There he was joined by Jim Hume and his chief lieutenant, Jonathan Thacker. In his haste, Bart had littered the landscape with clues: a black derby hat; two paper bags containing crackers and sugar from the grocery store in Angels Camp; a pair of field glasses, or opera glasses, and their leather case; a belt; a razor; a knotted handkerchief full of buckshot; three soiled linen shirt cuffs; and two empty flour sacks. Sheriff Thorn, assisted by Sheriff Tom Cunningham of San Joaquin County and Sheriff George McQuade of Tuolumne County, cast a dragnet and came up with an old hunter, named Martin, who that morning had seen a gray-whiskered gentleman walking to Jackson. The man had said he lived there. The walker exactly fitted Hume's description of the Po8. In Angels Camp the local storekeeper, Mrs. Crawford, gave a similar description of her customer of the week before. Finally, Jimmy Rolleri offered the information that a graying gentleman had aroused suspicion when he had stayed at the family's hotel a week before the holdup because he insisted on having a key to lock his room. Hotel rooms simply were not locked in the California foothills in the 1880's—unless the roomer had something to hide. Rolleri was now sure that the bandit he had winged on November 3, was his grandmother's mysterious lodger.

In his office, Sheriff Thorn gave his collection of clues a closer inspection. He emptied the shot out of the soiled handkerchief, and although the lead pellets told him nothing, he caught his breath when he saw faint lettering on the kerchief. It was not a name but a laundry code number. Thorn read the cryptic mark —F.X.0.7, almost washed out of the linen. He turned it over to Hume, who passed it on to the man he had hired, six months back, to do nothing but get the goods on Black Bart. He was Harry Morse—Henry Nicholson Morse, ex-sheriff of Alameda

County—who remarked, "The first worthwhile clue we've uncovered yet. It won't be an easy job but maybe we'll be lucky." Morse learned precisely how difficult it would be when he found that there were ninety-one laundries in San Francisco. But he set out to visit every last one of them.

Eight days of checking laundries brought Morse only disappointment and protesting feet. But at last he walked into Ferguson & Bigg's California Laundry at 113 Stevenson Street. Ferguson recognized the mark and directed Morse to one of the laundry's agencies, a tobacco shop run by Thomas C. Ware at 316 Post Street. Ware said that the F.X.0.7 was his mark, all right. He consulted his records and said that its owner was Charles E. Bolton, a mining man. Morse, quickly assuming the role of a mining man himself, told Ware that he wanted to meet Bolton to talk business. He added, lamely, that he had heard that Bolton sometimes came to the tobacconist's shop to drop off his laundry. When Morse asked Ware if he knew Bolton personally, he answered, "Why, certainly, I know Mr. Bolton well. He is in the city now, just arrived from his mine two days ago and if you will call later, you will probably meet him here, for he is an old acquaintance of mine and makes this his headquarters when in the city."

Morse hurried to police headquarters and got a plainclothes friend of Hume's, Captain Appleton W. Stone, to watch Bolton's hotel, the Webb House, at 37 Second Street. Still reluctant to take Ware into his confidence, Morse returned to the tobacco shop and asked the proprietor if he would walk with him to Bolton's hotel in the hope that they might meet him en route. Apparently Ware never suspected that a trap was being laid for his friend. Later, smarting under the label of decoy, he wrote to a newspaper, "When he asked me if I could spare a few moments from my business, I consented and we started down the street together." Everything went beautifully for Morse, dismally for Bart. A block from the Webb House, Ware suddenly stopped. The tobacconist and laundry agent explained what happened: "He [Bolton] spoke to me before I noticed him

177

and I then hailed him and told him the gentleman wished to see him; then, turning to the stranger, I said, 'I don't know your name, sir.' 'Hamilton is my name,' said he. I then introduced Mr. Bolton and they walked down the street together and I returned to my business, not dreaming of the trap that had been set."

Morse, alias Hamilton, eyed his companion as they walked and made small talk. Yes, in spite of the walking stick and handsome attire, he did fit Hume's description of Black Bart— almost five feet, eight inches in height, straight as a stake, with muscular shoulders, a flowing gray mustache, prominent cheek bones, and deep-set blue eyes. He bowler was natty, his heavy gold watch was suspended from a gold chain, and a diamond ring reflected the light of Bush Street. "One would have taken him for a gentleman who had made a fortune and was enjoying it," said Morse later. "He looked anything but a robber. [But] I knew he was the man I wanted, from the description."

Morse had not had time to alert Jim Hume and now decided to give him a real surprise. Telling Bolton that he wanted him to meet a business acquaintance, he steered him down Bush Street to Montgomery and then to California and Sansome, where he led him to Hume's upstairs office in the Wells, Fargo building. Bolton knew the building, of course, but did not bat an eye as he confronted his old adversary for the first time. Hume shook hands and offered him a seat. If Bolton's heart was in his mouth, he gave no sign. However, Hume noticed small beads of perspiration gathering on his forehead as he put polite questions to him. When he asked Bolton where his mining property was located, he got only evasive or confusing answers, such as "In Nevada, on the California line." The Wells, Fargo detective continued to probe as Bolton, wiping his brow, showed increasing signs of nervousness. Morse noticed that Bolton's hand was injured and, remembering Jimmy Rolleri's snapped shot, called Hume's attention to the wound. "You've hurt yourself. What happened?" Hume asked. Now Bolton became angry. He said that he had hurt himself getting off a train at Truckee. Hume closed in; was his mine near Truckee?

Indignantly, Bolton prepared to leave Hume's office, saying that he would answer no more questions. "I am a gentleman and I don't know who you are. I want to know what this inquiry is all about." Hume replied, reassuringly, that if he would just answer a few questions, he would soon know what the matter was about.

While Morse tried to placate Bolton, Hume slipped into an adjoining room and sent for Captain Stone. When the San Francisco police officer arrived, he identified himself to Bolton and then led them all outside. He whistled for a hack, and the four rode to the Webb House. As the detectives started to ransack the large trunk and three valises in his room, Bart angrily demanded, "What right have you to search these things?" The detectives did not bother to answer. Of the three suits in the trunk, one fit the description of that worn by the Funk Hill robber, according to Reason McConnell. Next, Morse found a handkerchief in a bundle of soiled linen ready for laundering. It bore the F.X.O.7 mark and was perfumed with the same scent Hume had noted, faintly, on the Funk Hill kerchief. In another satchel was an unfinished letter in the hand of the Po8, and in a Bible the detectives found a slip of paper with a faint, penciled inscription that read, "This precious Bible is presented to Charles E. Boles, First Sergeant, Company B, 116th Illinois Volunteer Infantry, by his wife as New Years gift—God gives us hearts to which His . . . faith to believe. Decatur, Illinois, 1865."

This was enough for Hume. He had Captain Stone place Bolton under arrest. When he feigned astonishment and asked why he was being detained, Hume answered, "Because you're Black Bart."

Bolton then tightened his lips and said nothing more until the desk sergeant, booking him, asked his name. Instead of giving Bolton, or Boles, he snapped, "T. Z. Spalding." Although during subsequent questioning Hume got nowhere, he at least found

Bart's hostility gone, his coolness returned. When he gave him his lost derby to try on, the robber patted it down in place and said, blithely, "Why, gentlemen, it fits very well, doesn't it? And it is a very good hat. Perhaps you would allow me to buy it from you?" He stubbornly denied all guilt in the Wells, Fargo robberies. When asked about the handkerchief, he argued, "What of it? I am not the only one whose things bear this mark. Others have their washing done at the same place." Then he changed his tack, "Why, somebody may have stolen the handkerchief from me. I may have lost it and someone else found it. What do you take me for, a stage robber?"

Hume kept the arrest quiet for the moment. With the cooperation of the San Francisco Police Department, he sent Bolton to Stockton and Milton for identification. Hume could go only as far as Clinton Station in Alameda County with him, because urgent business called him south to Bakersfield. But he turned Bart over to Morse, Thacker, and Stone there, knowing that he would be in good hands. Morse had already wired Sheriff Thorn of Calaveras County to meet the boat at Stockton and to bring the hunter, Martin, to see if he could identify Bolton as Black Bart. The prisoner, who was not in irons, enjoyed the boat ride across San Francisco Bay and up the San Joaquin River. In fact, Morse described him as being "full of fun" on the passage. He was delighted with the crowd waiting for a look at him on the Stockton wharf. Thorn kept Martin back and did not let him see Bart as he was escorted ashore. He then asked his witness to pick the bandit out of the crowd of 100 people, and Martin went to the robber like a yellow jacket to a watermelon. Jabbing a finger at him, Martin shouted, "That's the man! That's him!"

Next, Thorn took Bart to a photographer's studio to have his picture taken, over his violent protests. "You have no right to do this! You have no right! I have done nothing!" But his sense of humor returned as the photographer ducked under his black hood and leveled his lens at him. "Will that thing go off?" quipped Bart. Then he added, wryly, "I would like to go off, myself."

After Bart had spent the night safe in the Stockton jail, the lawmen drove him to Milton, where he remarked to them, "Look, the whole town has turned out to meet me. I guess they'll know me when they see me again." He stood silent as Reason McConnell walked up to him.

The driver stared at him but finally admitted, "I can't be certain. The man who held me up had a flour sack over his head. Maybe if he spoke I could recognize the voice." Morse asked his charge a few innocent questions. Suddenly, McConnell interrupted. "That's enough. I could recognize that voice, anytime."

In spite of his reiterated protests of innocence, Bart was taken to the Calaveras County jail in San Andreas. Here he was amused when the crowd, momentarily, took *him* for the San Francisco peace officer and Morse for Black Bart. But Morse straightened things out and locked him in a cell while he went out to dinner. He returned and began his interrogation at 7 P.M. Five hours later he was still at it without having got a thing for his pains, except Civil War reminiscences, including a tale of how Bart had been wounded in battle, and a large assortment of Biblical quotations. However, the tense five hours he had spent denying his guilt had weakened him and a tired Bart began to crack. Hedging, and still affirming his innocence, he asked what benefit would accrue to a stage robber if he should acknowledge his crime. Morse could say only that he thought the necessity of proving, laboriously, a long career of robbery would influence a jury toward severity, whereas a confession and restitution would doubtless mitigate a sentence. Bart was not satisfied; he asked if a clean breast of everything could not clear a man of charges altogether. Morse shook his head. "No, but if the man were convicted of every crime," he reminded his prisoner, "it would mean life imprisonment."

That just about did it. Bart was almost—but not quite—ready to call it quits. He damned the unreliability of witnesses: "These men may all come up to testify, just as you say. Men are apt to commit perjury and courts are apt to be prejudiced, and whether a man is guilty or not, he has to suffer the consequences." He then reached into the air to pull out a case to support his argument—an innocent man accused by all the witnesses. "I know, of my own knowledge, that he didn't do it."

Finally, around midnight on November 15, 1883, his brow furrowed with worry, Bart blurted, "I want you to know that I'm not going to San Quentin Prison! I'll die first!" Around 12:30 A.M., with Bart at sixes and sevens, Morse called in Stone and Thorn and told them that Back Bart had decided to confess and reveal the whereabouts of the Funk Hill loot. The power of suggestion worked. Bart got to his feet and said to Morse, "Well, let's go after it." On the 20-mile ride to moonlit Funk Hill, Bart confessed in great detail, although at first he confined his revelations to the period prior to 1879 in the belief that the statute of limitations freed him from all culpability for these crimes. But finally he admitted having pulled off the last robbery on the very site of his first, lamenting, "And when I started out that morning, I had a presentiment that it would, indeed, be my last."

Bart told them how he had walked the route of the coach first, in order to find the ideal holdup site and how he had set up "sleeping camps," cutting grass for a comfortable mattress under his blankets. He had lived on a light diet of crackers and coffee, dousing his fire by daylight to hide the smoke, while spying out the coach's routine and schedule with field glasses. He told the officers that he had had to go a mile to the nearest water and, sometimes, had hiked the two miles to the Stanislaus River for better drinking water. By chatting with acquaintances in Tuttletown and elsewhere, he had gathered a good idea of the value of the express shipment. He told the lawmen of observing another man, with a scarf over his face, whom he took to be a competitor. "I thought, what a good joke it would be to let the stranger capture the treasure and then for me to rob him and if he did not have at least $500, I might turn him over to the authorities and get the reward."

When the officers asked him why he had taken the name Black Bart, he explained that he had read it in a novel and had liked it. The story was *The Case of Summerfield,* a potboiler by a San Francisco attorney, William H. Rhodes, who used the nom de plume of Caxton. The story had appeared in the Sacramento *Union* in the summer of 1871.

Then Bart told them of his visits to San Francisco, of eating in William Pike's New York Bakery on Kearny Street, near police headquarters, a rendezvous for detectives, some of whom, like Dave Scannell—"a devilish good fellow"—were his friends. He told them of having reported his overcoat stolen from the Commercial Hotel, where he had been living. Detectives William S. Jones and Dan Coffey had recovered it, and Bart claimed that he had tipped them for their trouble. When Morse asked if he had never feared that he might give himself away, Bart answered, "Why, no, they didn't know who I was. I never associated with any but good people and not one of them ever dreamed what my business was." (According to Gertrude Atherton, Bart also posed as "Mr. Samson," a favorite customer in bookseller Alec Robertson's shop.)

At 6:45 A.M. Black Bart led Morse and Stone to a shady cove tucked under a large shelving rock, from which he had watched the stage road which skirted a conical hill there, near Tuttletown. Showing them the loot, he then reconstructed his dog-tired run for life. Lugging 15 pounds of treasure, he had had to hide the sack only a quarter of a mile from the holdup, in a hollow log, over which he kicked dirt and leaves. "A ten-year-old could have captured me," he told them. After catching his breath, he had fled, pell-mell, down one side of the ravine and up the other, bypassing Angels Camp and throwing away his shotgun and all other ballast. He kept only the cash he had taken and did not really stop walking, except for brief rests, until he was almost in Sacramento, 100 miles away. Much of the distance he covered was over very rough country. Stealing a hat from a cabin to replace his derby, he had walked into the capital on the Tuesday following his Saturday morning holdup, got a shave, ordered a suit of clothes, and bought a ticket to Reno. He had loafed about the Nevada town for a few days and then returned to Sacramento and the tailor before going on to San Francisco. He took one last precaution there, spending the first night in an Embarcadero lodging house before settling down in his regular Webb House room.

Harry Morse wired Wells, Fargo's Division Superintendent Leonard F. Rowell, "Black Bart throws up the sponge. Stone, Thorn and myself have received the stolen treasure. Inform Thacker." On November 16, in Judge P. H. Kean's court, Charles E. Boles entered a guilty plea only to the November 3 holdup. He was held for trial in superior court but waived a jury trial and pleaded guilty before Judge C. V. Gottschalk the next day. (According to the Sonora *Union Democrat,* he denied being Black Bart but admitted having pulled off the recent Funk Hill robbery, suggesting that it was his first offense.) It was said that he smiled with relief, glad the ordeal was over, when the judge sentenced him to six years in San Quentin. Certainly, the Calaveras *Weekly Citizen* was right in reporting, "He seemed rather pleased with the sentence." Thanks to the Goodwin Act, Black Bart's six years were to metamorphose into barely four years and two months with the time-off credits he was to earn for good—indeed, exemplary—behavior.

On Wednesday, November 21, 1883, only eighteen days after the robbery, Bart entered San Quentin Prison, still insisting, for some reason, that his name was Bolton, not Boles. He immediately settled down as a model prisoner while the press concocted a Black Bart of legend. Reporters dug up aliases that had never existed—Barlow, Barton, Fleming—and chose to believe that he was not from New York, as he had told Hume, but was the black sheep of the famous Samuel Bowles family of Springfield, Massachusetts. They had him rising to the rank of captain in the War of the Rebellion while fighting alongside General Phil Sheridan, and they gave a Bulwer-Lytton novel credit for his Black Bart alias. Of course, the myth took hold and grew as reporters waxed eloquent: "All who meet the man come away inspired with the liveliest feelings of astonishment that he should have embraced such a career. He is well educated and converses fluently and intelligently on all ordinary topics."

The press grossly inflated the reward offered for Bart by multiplying the $800 "package" offered by Wells, Fargo, Uncle Sam, and the State of California by the number of crimes (so far) pinned on him—twenty-three—and came up with a figure of $18,400! The San Francisco *Call,* a little more responsible than the other papers, pointed out that Hume got his salary and nothing else and that Morse got his pay, the $800 reward, and one-fourth of the value of the recovered booty.

Suspicious of the speed with which Hume had wound up the Black Bart case, the papers hinted at a deal between the Wells, Fargo detective and the bandit—perhaps a copped plea, a confession, and full restitution in exchange for a light sentence. The San Francisco *Examiner,* particularly, was piqued at Hume for keeping the initial arrest of Bart so quiet, and it was jealous of the *Call* for its scoop, although it derided the story as "laughable." Next, it cried, "The credit of capture and conviction would seem to belong to Thorn and Thacker instead of to Hume and Morse and, doubtless, both men are sorry they trusted the latter to the extent of letting them have the handkerchief by which they gained so much advertising."

The *Call* was all over the case, definitely outreporting the *Examiner.* Wiring Boles' old hometown of Decatur, Illinois, the *Call* learned that he had served in the Illinois Volunteers "with much bravery." The paper confirmed, in short, the biography that Hume had pieced together for Bart—that either from gold fever or the equally virulent Illinois shakes (malarial ague), Boles had set out for California in 1849 but had had to winter in Missouri, not reaching the coast with his brother David until 1850. They had mined on the North Fork of the American River and in various diggings in Butte, El Dorado, Tuolumne, Shasta, and Trinity counties before returning East, to New York. They returned to California, where the future bandit's brother died and was buried in Yerba Buenea Cemetery in San Francisco as David Bowles on July 9, 1852. Charles had drifted back to the Midwest in 1854, settled in Decatur, married, and enlisted in the Union Army on August 13, 1862.

Mustering on September 6, 1862, Boles had served in Company B, 116th Illinois Volunteer Infantry until June 7, 1865, when he was discharged near Washington, D.C., as a first sergeant. Boles was commissioned a second lieutenant but never served in that rank, probably because of the war's end. (The 1886 report of the adjutant general of Illinois actually listed him as a first lieutenant but, under "Remarks," added the phrase "Commission Cancelled.") Boles had started for the front, via Memphis, from Camp Macon, the old Decatur fairgrounds, on November 2. His baptism in battle came at Chickasaw Bayou on the Yazoo River in Mississippi. Soon after, Company B was torn up badly in the Battle of Arkansas Post, January 10-11, 1863, which left only twenty-five men fit for duty. Boles was severely wounded in his right side in action at Dallas, Georgia, on May 26, 1864, and hospitalized. But he later returned to his unit, which went on to fight at Vicksburg, Chattanooga, Kenesaw Mountain, and Atlanta.

After receiving his discharge, Boles left his wife, Mary (or May), and daughters in either New Oregon, Iowa, or, according to Hume, Oregon, Illinois, in order to work in the mines of Idaho and Montana. In 1867 he wrote May that he was coming home but failed to do so. Again, from Helena on April 4, 1869, he sent her a note, announcing his purchase of a mining claim for $260 in gold dust. "Now," he said, "it all depends on how it pays, about my coming home this fall." Apparently, it did not pay. He sent a last letter to Mary on August 25, 1871, from Silver Bow, Montana, then migrated to Salt Lake City. After a few years in Utah, he returned to California. Some say that he taught school there, either in Sierra County or in Concord, Contra Costa County. Legend, rather than history, has him losing a teaching post because of his addiction to gambling. Meanwhile, his wife had sacrificed her home in order to raise money to make a search for her vanished husband. By 1874, when Boles was, possibly, teaching in California, she and her daughters were near the brink of poverty, eking out a living by taking in sewing.

The Black Bart story finally grew cold as he became a faceless number—11,046—in San Quentin Prison and he dropped out of the news. While "inside," he kept his nose clean and made few friends among the cons. Although his wife years later told the *Chronicle* that his friends there were Dr. Rich and Pharmacist Fuller, Hume said the vicious Charles Thorne, alias Dorsey, was his closest pal in prison.

The *Examiner,* its editorial nose still out of joint, tried to pick a quarrel with Hume and almost succeeded. It high-handedly accused him and his firm of defeating the proper ends of justice. "What is the result of this perversion of justice?" asked the editors. "A few detectives divide a few thousand dollars and instill into the dime novel-charged heads of ten thousand youths of this city the idea that one has but to be a bold and successful robber to be able to force the united detective talent of the Coast to intercede with the judges to obtain light sentences and to get two column notices in the papers. . . . Whether Charles Bolton, who was sentenced, is Black Bart remains to be proved. If he is, then the law has been tampered with. . . . The only tenable explanation of such a miscarriage of justice is that Bart's prosecutors made a bargain with him whereby he received a light sentence and they the $4,000 which he had hid in the woods near Copperopolis." Hume, like Morse, declined to spar with the *Examiner,* although he denied the story categorically. Four years later, when Black Bart was released from San Quentin, the Sonora *Union Democrat* revived the charge: "Bolton's light sentence, followed so closely by his giving up the stolen treasure, leads many to the supposition that he made some kind of a compromise with the officers." Hume never said so, but just as likely is the explanation that the lawmen, fearing a not-guilty verdict in a case based entirely on circumstantial evidence—for no witness ever saw Black Bart's face during a holdup—decided to let Boles cop a plea in order to have him put away at least for four years.

Reward there was, but it was manifestly modest. As Sheriff Tom Cunningham reminded the public, the reward had *not* been multiplied by the number of holdups. On December 4, 1883, Wells, Fargo Superintendent G. T. Rowell sent Reason McConnell $105 in coin as a portion of his share of the reward, upon the recommendation of Hume and Thacker, although Morse was entitled to the full $800 and got it.

On January 10, 1884, about two months after entering San Quentin, Black Bart wrote McConnell a letter which showed that he had not lost his sense of humor: "You will please pardon me for this long delay in acknowledging your 'kind compliments' so hastily sent me on the 3d of November last, but rest assured, my dear sir, that you are remembered and with nothing but the most friendly feelings as a man having done your whole duty to your employer, yourself, and to the community at large. I have often admired your qualities as a driver and only regret that I am unable to compliment you on your marksmanship. I would like to hear from you, however, if consistent with your wishes and, my dear sir, you have my best wishes for an unmolested, prosperous, and happy drive through life. I am, dear sir, yours in haste, B.B. P.S. But in not quite so much a hurry as on the former occasion."

Black Bart was a free man again on January 21, 1888. According to a *Chronicle* reporter, as of July, 1887, he had not received a single visitor while in prison. But other accounts had both Joaquin Miller and Ambrose Bierce visiting him, and Bierce may have used incidents from Bart's career in the story he titled "My Favorite Murder." Legend has Bart turning teacher, or a Sunday schoolteacher, in "Q," instructing his fellow cons in "moral uprightness," but the *Chronicle*'s anonymous reporter who visited the pen and wrote a story, "Prison Celebrities," placed Bart in the prison dispensary as a pharmacist. "Black Bart has gained the respect of the doctor and apothecary by close attendance to his duties and has become sufficiently acquainted with the art of compounding prescriptions to enable him to take a position in a drug store." In fact, when the reporter asked him what career he would follow after his release from prison, Boles replied that he thought he would settle down somewhere as a drug clerk.

Black Bart told the reporters who met him after his release that prison life had not hurt him. But he had aged in the four years; he had become slightly deaf and needed glasses for reading. His spirit was broken, too, if the letter he wrote his wife (and which she sent to Hume, to show that Boles still cared for his family) was an honest one. "Dear Family: I am completely demoralized and feel like getting entirely out of reach of everybody for a few months and see what effect that will have. Oh, my dear family, how little you know of the terrible ordeal I have passed through and how few of what the world calls good men are worth the giant powder it would take to blow them into eternity. Thousands that under your every-day life you would call good, nice, men are—until the circumstances change to give them a chance to show their real character. I have reference now to those that have charge of our Public Institutions. For instance, you might go about them as a visitor and meet men there that you would think the very essence of official purity. But go into the Hospital and see there what they are doing for those that need their care and you will find 99, yes 99 in every 100, that would not turn his hand over to save a prisoner's life!"

When a reporter asked Bart if he intended to resume his highway career, he answered with a vehement no. Another inquired if he might write more poetry, and he replied, smiling, "Young man, didn't you hear me say I would commit no more crimes?" This quip suggested a poem to Ambrose Bierce, author of the "Prattle" column in the San Francisco *Examiner*. The poem, titled "Black Bart, Po8," was published in his volume of poetry called *Black Beetles in Amber*. Bierce's gag line came in the sixth stanza:

> What's that?—You ne'er again will rob a stage?
> What! did you do so? Faith, and I didn't know it.
> Was *that* what threw poor Themis in a rage?
> I thought you were convicted as a poet!

Another of Bart's letters that Mary Boles forwarded to Hume as proof of his fondness for his family suggested, when one read between the lines, that Bart had no intention of ever returning home: "Oh, my constant and loving Mary and my children, I did hope and had good reason for hoping to be able to come to you and end all this terrible uncertainty but it seems it will end only in my life. Although I am 'Free' and in fair health, I am most miserable. My dear family, I wish you would give me up forever and be happy for I feel I shall be a burthen to you as I live, no matter where I am. My loving family, I would willingly sacrifice my life to enjoy your loving company for a single week as I once was, but Heaven knows it is an utter impossibility. I love you but I fear you will not believe me and I know the world will scoff at the idea."

In still another letter that came to Hume's hands, Bart praised his wife for her wonderful constancy and affection, then wrote: "All other relations are like 'ropes of sand'. . . . How I do hope you may retain your health until I can come home to you. . . . I hope you will not think or attribute my not coming home to any lack of desire on my part, or lack of affection for any of you . . . I do regret not being able to come to you. The clouds look dark and gloomy and the real struggle of life is at hand, and I must meet it and fight it out. Let come what will, I must see my own loved Mary and our loving children once more. When that time comes, then and not until then, can I expect the first ray of sunlight to enter my poor bleeding, desolate, heart."

Black Bart roomed at the Nevada House in San Francisco for the first two or three weeks after his release, and Hume kept a wary eye on him. On Monday, January 23, 1888, the *Examiner* "Personals" column carried an item that read: "Black Bart will hear something to his advantage by sending his address to M.R., Box 29, this office." The notice appeared only once. It might have been inserted by Bart's mysterious sister—the "rope of sand"—to whom he had referred bitterly in a letter to his wife: "Only think of a once-loving sister, only a few miles away, and

190

never bestowed a line, or likely a thought, on her once-loved brother, simply because he was in trouble and in need of a sister's sympathy." Some attributed the cryptic item to Bart's mythical mistress. Or it may have been planted by Hearst, himself, in search of a story.

Bart turned down an offer of a theatrical engagement from the manager of the Oakwood Theater and Dietz Opera House and pompously remarked to Mary, in a letter that was printed in the Hannibal paper: "I cannot, of course, lend myself to any dime museum racket." Hume took this sample of Bart's outraged sense of decency with a grain of salt. And he refused to "buy" the romanticized image of Black Bart fabricated by the press, believing that he was basically a fraud who, with the help of irresponsible papers, was Robin Hood-winking a gullible public. Even when a newspaper started out to criticize Bart, as did the Stockton *Independent* on January 3, 1888 (for his lack of "sand"—*i.e.,* nerve), it usually ended up by patting him on the head: "There was nothing coarse or brutal about Bart; on the contrary, he was one of the most amiable rogues that ever 'stood up' a stage or rifled a treasure box."

When an *Examiner* reporter asked Hume whether he thought Boles might turn into Bart again, the detective answered, "Oh, I don't know or care very much, because he can't hurt us, as every sheriff and constable in the state has his photograph and he can't make a living at this business. It may be some of his admirers may take him into business with them as a good drawing card or, as you call it, 'a display ad.' "

When another *Examiner* man began an interview with Hume by throwing him a leading question, "How about Black Bart? He was rather above the ordinary run of convicts—something of a gentleman, despite his manner of gaining a livelihood?" Hume was reported to have answered tartly: "In the popular mind, Black Bart as he so romantically styled himself, has come to be regarded as a sort of modern Robin Hood, a stage robber of 'heroic mould,' a gallant freelance who never robbed the passengers or the poor but confined his attentions entirely to

191

wealthy corporations such as Wells, Fargo & Company. This is a delusion. He is, in fact, the meanest and most pusillanimous thief in the entire catalogue for, by his own statement, he made all his large hauls from the mail which he always rifled and from which, excepting his last robbery, he always obtained more than from the Express and, by so doing, he robbed the most needy, those who—to save a small express charge—used the mails as a means of transmitting their money. From these hard earnings Black Bart, with his boasted magnanimity, realized his largest revenue. When the express is robbed, the shippers are reimbursed as soon as the amount is known; but for the people who intrust their money to the United States mail, in the event of a robbery, there is no redress. Their loss is irrevocable. The Government never repays them or makes the slightest effort to recover the money or discover the offender."

"Moreover," went on Hume, "aside from his criminal manner of obtaining a livelihood, his career has been entirely and completely despicable. The outlines were given to the press at the time of his arrest but the details have only been learned since his imprisonment. Twenty years ago, he left a wife and two daughters in the East and came west, first to Idaho and thence to Montana. From Montana, he dropped all communication with his family, substituting the name of Bolton for his true name of Boles and, during the ensuing fifteen years, never sent one word to relieve the uncertainty of his faithful wife. While he dwelt in idleness and comfort upon the proceeds of his crimes, she was left in poverty to endure all the misery of hope-deferred and heart-breaking uncertainty, striving continually to obtain some trace of him, living or dead, traveling for miles to see any one coming from Montana in the vain hope that they might know something of the wanderer. And when misfortune and disgrace made his whereabouts known to all the world, her devotion remained unshaken, as no one can doubt who reads the letters written by her to the heartless scoundrel in his well merited prison cell. Whenever you feel carried away with admiration for the brilliant exploits of Black Bart, pause and reflect upon the sneaking and cowardly career of C. E. Boles."

The dogged reporter persisted, "Well, don't you consider Black Bart the brave man of 'the road?' " Hume snorted. "I have never known him to be tried but once, which was on July 13, 1882, when he tried to stop the stage going from Laporte to Oroville, on which George Hackett was the shotgun messenger. There was $23,000 in the Wells, Fargo & Company's box. Black Bart got in front of the lead horses, his usual style of proceeding, and ordered a halt but George opened on him at great disadvantage, because he didn't want to kill a good horse, and the brave Black Bart dusted like a whirlwind for the brush on the side of the road, with his loaded [sic] double-barreled shotgun in his hand, with two scalp wounds from Hackett's buckshot on the top of his head—merely flesh wounds—while both barrels of Hackett's gun were empty."

One day, early in February, 1888, Black Bart vanished from San Francisco. Hume collected reports on him as he made his way southward through the San Joaquin Valley—Modesto, Merced, Madera and, finally, Visalia, where his trail petered out. In March Hume received a package from a Visalia hotel-keeper containing a valise left in his hotel room by a Mr. Moore, who had registered on February 28 and then disappeared. In the bag Hume found two neckties, a glass of currant jelly, pickles, a pound of coffee, a can of tongue and another of corned beef, crackers, sugar—and two pairs of cuffs bearing the laundry mark F.X.O.7.

Hume could not help suspecting Bart when three stages were held up by a lone bandit in July and November, 1888. He thought he detected Bart's style in these operations, whereas he was sure four robberies in Santa Barbara and San Luis Obispo counties were the work of another loner. But he was not completely convinced of Bart's guilt, and when he issued a last circular on him, on November 14, 1888, he was cautious in his statement: "We have reason to believe that the robberies described above were committed by C. E. Boles, alias C. E. Bolton, alias Black Bart, the Po8. We have not sufficient evidence to warrant a conviction or arrest, but are desirous of locating this man. Make careful inquiries, get your local officers interested. *Do not arrest,* but wire any information obtained at once, to the undersigned." The press was not as cautious as Hume. The *Chronicle* ran a headline—"BOLD BLACK BART. The Poet Robber Again at Work. Three Stages Surrender to His Shotgun." Other papers bid for readers with such banners as "IS BLACK BART ON THE ROAD AGAIN?" and the *Wasp* printed a cartoon showing Bart flirting with a damsel (Wells, Fargo), over the caption "Will He Woo Her Again?"

It was not long before a newspaper in the mining country turned up a new effort by the Poet Laureate of Road Agentry:

> So here I've stood while wind and rain
> Have set the trees a'sobbin'
> And risked my life for that damned stage
> That wasn't worth the robbin'.

Although it was signed "Black Bart, the Po8," Hume labeled it a hoax when he examined the handwriting. (As late as 1946 the New York *World-Telegram* was printing brand-new Bart verse, which the bandit certainly never saw in his life.) The story that accompanied the poem described "Professor Charles E. Bowles," the Sierra County schoolmaster, as having stuck up his first stage with a stick instead of a gun. (To his surprise, Bart had been taken seriously.) A story in the Watertown (New York) *Daily Times* improved on this by having Bart hold up a railroad train with the help of a line of fence posts togged out in hats and coats to simulate a gang of bandits.

About this time a tale grew up which has never died—that, to keep Bart from robbing any more express boxes, Wells, Fargo put him on the company payroll. Hume and other company officials consistently denied the truth of the story, but it persisted. When a *Chronicle* reporter asked him flatly if it were not true

194

that he had pensioned off Black Bart, Hume, shook his head sadly, and patiently replied, "I am astonished at your asking such a question. If it were so, don't you think he would have been only too glad to say in his letter to his wife that he was working, instead of writing in such a despondent strain?" If the unlikely yarn *were* true, Hume wasted considerable time and money in circulating his 1888 flyer on Bart. According to one version of the tale, Boles lived in Oakland but worked in the Ferry Building on San Francisco's Embarcadero, where Hume could keep an eye on him.

To give circulation another little boost, Hearst decided to stir the ashes of the old *Examiner*-Hume controversy over the Black Bart story. And he chose the Sunday supplement, which sold about 7,000 copies more than the daily paper, in which to do it. The stage was set for the feature by a short item datelined Lakeport, November 30. Supposedly written by an *Examiner* stringer in Lake County, it reported that recently "a man supposed to be 'Black Bart' came east from Willits through the mountains to Gravelly Valley. . . ." The identification was attributed to George Vann, a rancher who had seen Bart, years before at the McCreary ranch. The item had all the vagueness of hearsay and might very well have been a pure plant on the part of Hearst.

Headlined "HUME IS CONTRADICTED. How a Great Detective Made a Reputation," the Sunday, December 2, 1888, feature was given a prominent four-column spread. Hearst—already a master of the faked interview and the phony story—lead off with a purported telegram from his special correspondent, Martin, which read: "Have seen the man of whom I spoke. Am under absolute obligation to conceal whereabouts." Supposedly, Hearst had replied to this cryptic wire by ordering his man to spare no expense to get a story. Martin claimed that Black Bart had not returned to a life of crime, and he was determined to have the ex-bandit verify this. According to the *Examiner,* he took a train to an undisclosed destination, then rode for some 25 miles on a borrowed horse in order to reach a mountain

195

ranch (perhaps Vann's). En route, Martin was rescued by a stranger—a superb horseman—as he forded a creek and almost drowned. (According to the story, his horse *was* drowned.) The stranger—surprise—turned out to be none other than Black Bart. He was reluctant to talk, but when Martin showed him a newspaper story in which Hume was reported to have sworn that Boles was up to his old tricks, the sometime road agent replied, "To speak plainly, I don't think it exactly a square deal for the papers to keep hammering away at a man after everything is over." He termed the Hume story "A little truth and a pretty strong dose of lie" and launched into a story of his own, modestly speaking of himself in the third person:

"Detective Hume makes a great many mistakes in his pretended 'Life of Black Bart' [the November 28 story in the *Chronicle*], some through sheer ignorance and some evidently from motives not wholly creditable. He takes some pains to abuse C. E. Boles, calling him a pusillanimous wretch and declaring that there is nothing honorable about him. Let Mr. Hume's opinion be what it may, the fact remains that Black Bart never gained a man's confidence to betray it, never swindled a person in trade, and never plundered working people by taking what they produced, sheltering himself behind laws made to legalize theft. He robbed Wells, Fargo and Company without pretending that stage robbery was a perfectly legal and commendable occupation. He took the chances of being shot and at least was frank in his method of obtaining other people's property. . . . All the thieves in San Quentin are not wearing stripes. The biggest robbers are not on the road with shotguns, but they make every man who works stand and deliver." This line of comment sounded more like Hearst than either Martin or Bart; the publisher was in his early, liberal, muckraking and antimonopoly period—about 180 degrees around from his eventual stance as a conservative.

Hearst and Martin—or Bart—picked up a few minor errors in Hume's dossier on Bart and made good use of them. "Hume says that Boles left his wife and children at a town in Illinois

[Oregon, in Ogle County, Illinois]. . . . He didn't. He joined his family in Iowa and tried farming there until he found that it meant only starvation, and then he went West. His wife was a smart, capable, woman who could earn a living by dressmaking. . . . It was agreed between him and his wife that he should go back to the mines and try to make a stake."

According to Martin's purported interview, Mrs. Boles was well fixed. Bart said that he sent money home to her, and his propertied father had also looked out for her. Although she had not managed to save any money, his wife was in comfortable circumstances, not in poverty. And when Bart's father died, some of his money had gone to Mary Boles. According to the *Examiner* scoop, trouble arose only when her brother Johnson swindled her out of her property and took a female companion into the house, while Bart was languishing in San Quentin. As for Hume's claim that Bart had written a villainous letter to his son-in-law in order to produce a desired rupture between his family and himself, the *Examiner* was blunt to the point of libel: "That is a lie!" According to Martin. Bart wrote an indignant letter to his swindling brother-in-law, who in turn sent the letter to Warden Shirley at San Quentin, asking him if prisoners were permitted to write abusive letters to law-abiding folk. Shirley had then turned the letter over to Hume's close friend Captain Charles Aull, who, in the words of Hearst's correspondent, "was practically running the prison."

Bart was reported as saying, "Now I can tell you why Hume, Aull, and the rest of that crowd are so bitter against Bart. When he first went to prison, they were all very friendly. The detectives had been getting a great deal of cheap glory on his account and he was useful to them." According to Martin's purported interview with Boles, Hume had had a private talk with Bart in which he said, "Now, this thing is all over and nothing that you say can make any difference to you, but you can help me out. I have on my books a long list of robberies that nobody has been arrested for. You can admit to me that you committed them and I can cross them all off." When Bart had supposedly refused, Hume

197

was said to have pleaded, "What difference does it make to you? All I want is to clear up my books and square myself. If you will say that you did them and can make my record clear, it will help me with the Company." But Bart would admit having pulled off only the last stage robbery. Still, said Martin, "Hume and the rest of the crowd were very friendly after that. They conceived the great idea of inducing Bart to write a book about himself, giving the history of his life and exploits. They were to superintend the job and, of course, they were to be cracked up as the greatest detectives that ever lived. They made the proposition to Bart and he scornfully rejected it. They were then not so friendly."

Next, Martin and Hearst insinuated that Hume, Aull and, presumably, Harry Morse were thieves: "The detectives and Captain Aull were very anxious to get hold of Bart's diamonds and jewelry and they tried all ways to get them." Perhaps the mysterious Martin was a woman, for the reporter now, in typical *Examiner* fashion, played on the readers' heartstrings. Bart, said Martin, had destroyed all clues to his identity except a Bible with an inscription in it from his dear mother and had taken to the road because of the lack of charity on California ranches. When on the bum, he had stopped at a ranch house to ask if he might join the family at dinner. Instead of inviting him in, the rancher brought out a tin plate of scraps for him. Bart gave them to the dog, and his host snapped, "Isn't it good enough for you?"

"No, I do not think such hospitality good enough for anybody," was Bart's reply. When the rancher said that he did not believe in encouraging tramps, Bart swore a solemn vow— "This is the first time I ever asked anybody to give me anything and it will be the last. Hereafter, when I want anything, I shall demand it and take it."

After a farfetched account of Bart's stealing a horse, making a nose bridle out of a reata, and cutting a candle in his room to suggest that he had been reading by it all night while he was really robbing a stage, the feature story ended with what were supposed to be Bart's parting words for Wells, Fargo's detective: "He [Bart] never promised Mr. Hume or anybody else to do or refrain from doing anything whatever. . . . He is under obligation to none of that crowd and he cares very little for their advice."

Doubtless, Hearst expected Hume to explode in rage. The detective rose beautifully to the bait, firing off a letter that led to another *Examiner* story, on December 3, titled "MR. HUME GETS ANGRY." Stormed the detective, "It is a thorough falsehood, made up of distorted and villainous lies and the man who wrote it is a low, malignant, contemptible man. . . . That interview was the boldest of inventions and was invented by a sneak too cowardly to sign his name in order to vilify me."

Regarding Bart's pious unwillingness to admit to a bunch of robberies he had not committed, Hume had this to say: "That is as ingenious a lie as the rest. The facts of the confession are just these—After Black Bart's conviction, I told him in the presence of Ben Thorn of Calaveras County, who is an honest man, and will testify to the truth of what I say, and one other person, that I had him in my book charged with twenty-one robberies. I asked him to tell me which he had committed in order that I might see if there were any other stage robbers to look for. 'You don't intend to use them against me?' he asked. 'No,' I answered. 'We are done with you.' Then he confessed to the twenty-one robberies and seven more. Later, in San Quentin, he confessed to another, making twenty-nine in all. I never said a word about his helping me out, for I needed no helping out."

"The tale or book which the article states Black Bart was asked to write, in order to puff up the detectives who captured him is another unadulterated lie. A book was never mentioned and I hardly think was even thought of," asserted Hume. As for stealing Bart's sparkler: "Among the proceeds of one of Bart's robberies was a valuable diamond ring, the rejected one of two from which a Plumas County merchant had chosen a bethrothal ring. When returning the rejected ring, a clerk marked on the package 'Value $100.' The ring fell into the hands of Black Bart. When Boles was convicted, this merchant, who is a personal friend, wrote me about the ring, saying that it cost in reality $200 and offering to repay the $100 that the Company had given him for his loss, if the ring was recovered and returned to him. I asked Bart about a diamond ring he had had, but he denied that it was the one. This ring was then in the possession of an Oakland man. I asked him about it, saying that he ought not to wear a stolen ring, but he would not admit that Bart lied, and I dropped the matter. That's all there is to our trying to steal Bart's diamond."

Hume knew well that the story of Bart's stealing a horse, while a candle, as decoy, sputtered in his room, was a fake. "I talked a good deal with Bart and I never heard of his traveling on a horse. He always did his work on foot. He told me that he had no equal in climbing over mountains, and could easily make fifty miles a day." (Hume could also have cited the blunder Martin—or Bart—made in mentioning the Bible signed by Boles' mother; it was actually inscribed by his wife.)

Hume's strong language damned the *originator* of the story, not the reporter, Martin, who probably had written it from someone else's dictation. Rumor had it that Harry Morse was behind the *Examiner* stories, but Hume stated publicly that he did not think Morse was involved. (However, Morse and Thacker quarreled over the reward for Black Bart, which made good copy for Hearst.) Hume closed the interview by saying, "Before you go, I want to say to you again that the anonymous scoundrel who directed that attack against me is a vile miscreant, a cowardly, contemptible cur. I say it again and I live at 1466 Eighth Street, Oakland, and my office is Room 28, over Wells, Fargo & Company's—and I'm always in!" The reporter ended the article with one word—"Wow!"

Hearst was delighted, of course. He answered Hume's letter in an editorial, also printed on December 3, which he headed "KEEP COOL, MR. HUME." It read as follows:

"Mr. Hume, the head detective of Wells, Fargo & Company, seems to be very angry because the *Examiner* has given Black Bart's version of some matters in which both were interested. Mr.

Hume loses his temper, applies bad names to the correspondent who wrote what Black Bart said, and accuses the reporter of malignant designs upon his (Mr. Hume's) well-earned reputation. Mr. Hume's criticism on the reporter for not signing his article is childish. It is not the custom in newspaper offices to allow signatures to news matter.

"The great detective should remember that he had his say about Black Bart and said some very hard things about the famous robber. It is only fair to let Mr. Boles have his say.

"And, moreover, Mr. Hume should remember that the *Examiner* exists to give the news, hires men to collect it, and gives more interesting news than any other paper. It can be safely asserted that Mr. Hume, himsef, was more interested in the *Examiner's* report of what Black Bart said than he was in anything else that appeared in the San Francisco papers yesterday.

"It does not follow that the *Examiner* indorses Black Bart or that its correspondent is responsibe for any misstatements made by that interesting and much-missed person.

"Mr. Hume should cool down."

When the *Chronicle* sent a man to Oakland to interview Hume about the *Examiner's* story, he found the detective still furious. "The article is a tissue of falsehoods from beginning to end. The man who wrote it is a dirty, contemptible, lying cur," Hume declared, for an opener. When the reporter asked him what it was in particular in the story that he objected to, the detective answered, "I object to all of it. In the first place, the writer of the article never saw Black Bart and the twaddle it contained was therefore manufactured out of whole cloth. Secondly, it was written solely to injure my reputation as a private citizen and as a detective. Isn't that enough?"

The reporter changed the subject. "It is your belief that Black Bart is not in the state?"

"It certainly is," answered Hume. "The last time I heard of Black Bart was on November 23, immediately after the Ukiah-Eureka stage robbery. I have reason to believe that he has since left California."

"What, in your opinion, could have inspired the writing of the article?" asked the journalist.

"I do not know," said Hume, "unless it was animosity toward a man who never injured the author. But it is a dime novel story which will delude no one. Why, Black Bart himself, as accomplished a scoundrel as he is, wouldn't have stooped to anything so low."

On December 6, 1888, the *Chronicle* ran a brief item on the recent holdup of the Mendocino-Ingram stage, stating, "Special Officer Hume of Wells, Fargo & Company says that the man was Black Bart, without a doubt. The robbery was just in his style and he had robbed the stage in the same place a number of years ago." That same day, an *Examiner* story appeared, too, reporting that Hume had no doubts, now, that the "lone highwayman" was his old antagonist, Black Bart. But less than a week later, on the eleventh, Hearst exploded another of his yarns in Hume's face, with the headline "IT IS NOT BLACK BART." The story began: "A derrick would not have been strong enough to pull the great detective minds, and especially Detective Hume, from the pet theory that Bart was taking undue liberties with Wells, Fargo & Company treasure boxes, but the express company's Vidocq is coming around slowly in indicating that anybody but Bart is the present lone robber."

Why was Hearst suddenly so sure that Bart was not the guilty party? Because, said the *Examiner,* Wells, Fargo had placed Boles on its payroll upon his release from San Quentin. His only duties were to not rob any more of its express shipments. According to this story, Bart had told a friend, "I'm a detective, myself, now. I've just received my first month's salary." The *Examiner* added, "They would have preferred to make the payments daily, their head detective to be the paymaster, but Bart did not like Hume nor did he like the idea of being tied down to drawing his salary piecemeal." Bart, it reported, preferred to wander all over the state, collecting his $125 per month at any nearby Wells, Fargo agency. And instead of returning to robbery, he had resumed gold mining, reopening an old shaft with a friend.

But why was Hume so sure that Bart *was* holding up stages again? The Monarch of the Dailies had an answer for that question, too: "When Bart ceased to send his daily mail to the express company, and on the recurrence of bold stage robberies, Detective Hume began to get fidgety and, as time rolled on and no highwayman could be arrested, the express company's Hawkshaw declared openly that Bart was at his old tricks again."

But *did* Hume really suspect Bart? Possibly. He refused to tell reporters anything specific about his investigations, insinuating that it was because Bart was an inveterate reader of newspapers and he did not want to forewarn him. However, he definitely told a *Chronicle* reporter on December 3, 1888, that "Black Bart is a slippery man, and one hardly knows what to think [about him]. It is certain, however, that he is the lone stage robber, notwithstanding the statements to the contrary attributed to him. . . . Extra efforts are being made to bring 'the greatest road agent the world has ever seen' to justice."

Even Hume's brother-in-law, Samuel P. Williams, in Indiana, wrote him to say, "Your old customer, BB, may still be roaming your mountains." But Mrs. Mary Boles, writing from her home at 117 Market Street in Hannibal, Missouri, advised the *Chronicle* on December 5 that "Everyone of us here believe today that Hume and Company are after an innocent man, now." She said that Hume's story was seamed with base falsehood. She admitted that her husband had, once, written unkind words, but to her sister-in-law (not her brother-in-law, son-in-law, or herself, as West Coast papers had garbled it) when she had cheated her out of her Hannibal home. "I presume he did say some pretty sharp things to her, and she certainly deserved it, for as bad as he has done, he would scorn to stoop to the deed she has to account for." She reminded the paper that her husband had been as friendly in San Quentin with Dr. Rich and the druggist, Mr. Fuller, as with the murderer Dorsey: "He has told us over and over again that, while God gave him breath, he would never lift his hand to do a dishonorable act to disgrace us further; and we know he refused to write a history of his life while at San Quentin, which probably would have been a source of quite a good sum of money in the end, simply, as he said, because he had done enough to make us unhappy and, for the future, if let alone, he would do all in his power to aid us and not disgrace us further."

Mary Boles sent excerpts from Bart's letters to the *Chronicle* to show that he was a doting family man and father, despite his having written her that it was utterly impossible for him to return home. Bart mentioned that Hume kept tabs on his goings and comings at his ramshackle Sixth Street lodgings in San Francisco: "I have made no effort to avoid them, or anyone else's yet—but when I do, Mr. Detective will find his hands full to keep track of me. Not that I care for anything, only his contemptible annoyance by his constant presence." Bart apparently feared a frame-up, too, for he added, "I know, too, if they can they will put up a job on me if I remain among them, thinking that [by] my having served a term it will be easy to fasten the second on me. But I don't propose to allow them to succeed in anything they can concert against me." Hume noted that, buried in the letter, was Bart's good-bye to his family—"I am completely demoralized and feel like getting entirely out of reach of everybody for a few months." The "few months" stretched eventually to years, for Bart disappeared entirely.

Although the new "lone bandit" was traveling on horseback, Hume thought (or pretended to think) that his technique was practically identical with Bart's. He told the *Chronicle* again that he was sure the man was Bart, and when a reporter asked him why, he would say only, "I would not care to show Mr. Bart my hand, as he, by his actions, does not seem imbued with very much confidence regarding myself. Any hint from me might cause him to alter all his plans."

Finally, it dawned on the press that the intuitive Hume was not after Bart but another San Quentin alumnus, J. A. Wright, alias John A. Garvin, who had held up five stages in 1876 and 1877, always alone. Sent up for fifteen years in 1877, Garvin had been transferred from San Quentin to Folsom in 1880 and discharged on October 1, 1886. One reason Hume suspected him was that he had applied for a pardon or commutation of sentence while in Folsom and had been turned down. He had blamed his failure on Wells, Fargo influence on the authorities and had cried out, "Damn them! I'll make those sons of bitches suffer dearly for that, yet!" The *Examiner* noted that Wright's comings and goings since his release tallied well with the pattern of stage robberies and added, "Who will be the first to catch him is what is worrying the stealthy Detective [Hume]."

When a reporter asked Hume, point-blank, if his suspicions were not on Wright rather than Bart, the detective hedged: "I may have intimated it; Wright is a great stage robber and quite likely to be the man we want. But I have not had any circulars sent around regarding him." Soon the story began to spread that Hume was drawing attention to Bart in order to lull Wright into carelessness.

John J. McComb, in charge of San Quentin's commissary, reported that Hume had come to the prison to question him about Wright and to check his dental records as a positive means of identification (another example of Hume's use of advanced detection techniques). Said McComb, "It wouldn't surprise me to learn that Hume knows exactly where Bart is, and has been, since his release."

Hume tried to straighten Hearst out in the Bart vs. Wright controversy, explaining, "I feel that Bart and this individual [currently robbing stages] are not one and the same. Their methods of proceeding are entirely different. He uses a pistol as an intimidator while Black Bart used a gun [a shotgun] in his work. He did not believe in the efficacy of a pistol to frighten stage drivers while he had the greatest confidence in a double barreled shotgun. . . . Finally, when last seen, on April 6th (1888), he was leaving the state and bound for the [Far] East."

But Hearst, news-hungry as always, merely changed the subject and teased Hume toward another outburst. He sent a reporter to ask Hume if Bart's letters, made public by his wife, had not changed his opinion of the road agent. "There, you're all mixed up to start with," Hume told the journalist, "and I can see plainly if I don't explain the matter, you're sure to misrepresent me—as usual. The statement made was that he wrote an abusive letter to his son-in-law. I do not doubt but what his letters to his wife were always pleasant and kind; there is no reason why they should not have been. But if anyone thinks that a man who lets his wife struggle along in poverty for years while he lives comfortably off our express boxes, without so much as letting her know where he is, even, is acting as a husband should toward his wife, why, we differ in opinion, that's all."

Gradually, most Californians came to believe that Black Bart had drifted on. It was said that he had gone to Australia, to China, to Japan, to Mexico, to Indian Territory (Oklahoma). One report identified him as "a peaceful tiller of the soil in Nevada," and Hume once had to wire the sheriff at Cripple Creek, Colorado, that Bart was not wanted in California. Hattie Reader claimed that he returned to her father's ranch at Sweetland in 1900. Hume's thoughts on the matter were not quoted, but in 1897 Thacker stated that Bart had gone from California to Utah, Montana, and Hailey, Idaho, where he had some business. "Anyhow, he was as straight as a string. Finally, he made a bee line for Vancouver and boarded the steamer *Empress of China* for Japan. He is in that country now."

Still, Black Bart might have returned to the States, although when Hume sent Thacker to check on an Olathe, Kansas, robber who confessed that he was Bart, his aide found him to be one H. L. Gorton. Thacker reported that Gorton looked about as much like Black Bart "as a bird's nest is like a mile post."

Francis Reno, described as "the famous detective" by the *Chronicle*'s Sunday supplement in 1909, claimed to have met Bart a few years earlier in Mexico City, where he was using the alias Jim Clarkson. But Reno, who had named Bart as the robber of the Milton stage in 1886, when he was snug in his San Quentin cell, was hardly a reliable informant.

As early as 1892 Mrs. Mary Boles was listing herself in the Hannibal, Missouri, City Directory as "Widow of Charles E. Boles," but that did not prove that Bart was really dead—at least not to Hume. In 1909, when Mrs. Rose Schwoerer was a young girl waiting tables at Frank Mitcheler's Murphys Hotel in Murphys, California, her boss told the cook and waitresses one evening that the little gray-haired man, partly bald, who was dining with them was the famous Black Bart. In any case, Boles seemed to have dropped off the face of the earth, and what finally became of him is not known.

When San Quentin inmate "Johnny Behind the Rocks" (John M. Brannan) wrote a song, he included both Jim Hume and Black Bart in its stanzas:

> Now there is old Jim Ivy
> Who thought he was a chief
> But he has proved himself to be
> A petty, mean old thief.
>
> When he was at the lower gate
> He used to pass his time
> In giving points to old Jim Hume
> Of Wells and Fargo's line.
>
> Yet still there is another
> Who well did play his part
> He's known throughout the country
> As highwayman Black Bart.
>
> He robbed the mountain stages
> To him it was a pleasure
> He seemed to dream of nothing else
> But Wells, and Fargo's, treasure.

Whether Boles ever dreamed of Wells, Fargo boxes in his last years or not, Hume had closed the books on him by about 1900. (The *last* word on Bart—quite apocryphal—was an unsubstantiated story, in a New York paper, that carried his obituary in 1917.) Hume never felt it necessary to revise or update the report on Black Bart he had deposited in Wells, Fargo's archives soon after the highwayman's arrest:

"He is a person of great endurance, a thorough mountaineer, a remarkable walker, and claims he cannot be excelled in making quick transits over mountains and grades; when reading without glasses [he] holds paper off at arm's length; is comparatively well educated, a general reader, and is well informed on current topics; a cool, self-contained talker with waggish tendencies; and since his arrest has, upon several occasions, exhibited genuine wit under most trying circumstances. Has made his headquarters in San Francisco for the past eight years; has made but few close friends and those of first class respectability; is neat and tidy in dress, highly respectable in appearance and extremely proper and polite in behavior, chaste in language, eschews profanity and has never been known to gamble other than buying pools on horse races and speculating in mining stocks."

This estimate of Bart, made before his failings as a husband and father were revealed and affected Hume's ultimate opinion, might well stand as a proper evaluation of California's most curious—and competent—Dick Turpin of all time.

CHAPTER IX

———— ◆◄◆►◆ ————

FROM TUCSON TO RAROTONGA

DURING the years that Jim Hume had been trailing the ultra elusive Black Bart, he had, of course, also been investigating scores of other Wells, Fargo cases. As 1881 rolled around, for example, he was busy in Nevada and Arizona. He described Tombstone, to be made famous later that year by the Earp-Clanton shoot-out at the OK Corral: "Six thousand population. Five thousand are bad. One thousand of these are known outlaws." He searched the desert for the man he wanted, but the culprit gave him the slip, and Jim had to leave a posse in the field to find him, as he hurried on to assignments in Colusa, California, then in Nevada, and Shasta, California. He had hoped to stop at Truckee for a visit but had not even found time to write. He begged Lida, "Let up on me this time for my seeming neglect in not writing and don't swear that you will never speak to me again." He filled her in on his current case, without revealing company secrets: "I am not making much headway in catching the villain but have the testimony to convict him when he is caught. Have found his accomplice and recovered a portion of the treasure and may arrest him this after-

209

noon. The only thing that deters me is a wife and four children, including a daughter 16 years of age."

From Sacramento Hume then started on another voyage to Oregon. The rough passage up the coast sent most of his fellow passengers to the rail and proved wearing to Hume, too, who was not getting any younger. After the next leg of the journey, by steamer up the Columbia River, he "enjoyed" a jolting 40-mile stage ride to Pendleton, site of the trial he had to attend. To his delight, he found Pendleton a charming town, full of comparatively wealthy Indians who rode about on fine horses every Sunday, with their squaws tricked out elegantly in woolen dresses beautifully worked with beads. One Indian, he learned, owned 2,700 head of horses. The detective found the Villard House lodgings comfortable and the countryside surrounding the town quite handsome. It was a well-developed area except for 30,000 acres of Indian reservation that bordered the town. " 'Twill be busted, some day," he mused, "and the land sold, and then Pendleton will be a terribly nice place." He wrote Lida, "Every man on the jury is first class. I have no fear about the result."

Late in June Hume sailed for San Francisco, arriving in plenty of time to welcome that accident-prone horseman Dick Fellows back into action after his release from prison. Fellows had robbed the San Luis Obispo-Soledad stage on July 19 but got only $10; then he went north and held up the Duncan's Mills-Point Arena coach near the Russian River. This time he did even worse. There was nothing in the Wells, Fargo box but a single letter—and *it* was in Chinese. At this point Fellows must have seriously considered having another stab at teaching.

The moment Hume was informed of the second robbery he telegraphed for a man to wait for him at the scene of the crime with saddle horses for a fast pursuit. Unaccountably, the man left the horses and his gun at the Duncan's Mills livery stable and walked to the holdup site, two miles out of town. There he awaited Hume's arrival by the regular stage. As he sat by the side of the road, an acquaintance rode up and asked him what he was doing there. He explained that he was waiting for Jim Hume, the Wells, Fargo detective. As soon as the horseman rode out of sight, a masked man rushed out of a nearby hiding place and demanded angrily, "What in hell are you interfering in my business for?" The startled and unarmed gentleman could not even answer but stared stupidly as the bandit—none other than Dick Fellows—disappeared into the redwood forest. As soon as Hume came along, he sent the stage back to town for a posse. Within an hour he had eight or ten horsemen on Fellows' tracks, but a thick coastal fog sagged down over the redwoods, and Hume lost the trail in the gloom.

Fellows, wanting to give Jim Hume a wide berth, shifted his operations southward again. Between July, 1881, and January, 1882, he robbed three stages in the San Luis Obispo area. He failed in a fourth attempt, although he fired several shots at the driver. Hume was now so burdened with cases that he had to delegate Fellows to his friend Captain Charles Aull, whom he had persuaded to leave the state prison for a tour of Wells, Fargo detective duty. Dick was captured, but he escaped. Found hiding in a cabin near Los Gatos, he was rearrested and thrown into the San Jose jail on February 4, 1882.

Meanwhile, Hume had been in the Southwest again, poking about Tucson, Tombstone, and Benson. A box of bullion worth $1,900 had disappeared from the Benson railroad depot. Hume knew the thief and was shadowing him in Tucson, but he did not have enough evidence to make an arrest. (Hume hated to have cases dismissed for lack of evidence and was scrupulous in his preparations.) He bided his time, counting on an informer he had hired to bring in the needed proof: "I have a friendly thief with him all the time and have been expecting he will 'fall down' [confess], but my patience may give out before he quits. I may leave the business in the hands of Bob Paul. I am tired of the country and anxious to see San Francisco." Once again, Lida was scolding him for letting his Wells, Fargo work get in the way of correspondence, and he retorted, a bit hotly, "Sorry that you are unable to make a *little* allowance for my not writing you oftener. Can't you imagine . . . ? Well, I won't try to write it, but will give you a 'medicine talk' when I see you again."

Hume had one extremely embarrassing experience in Arizona, which he was, understandably, loath to mention but which made the papers anyway. The Tombstone *Epitaph* on January 9, 1882, ran a column with the subhead "Sandy Bob's Up-Stage Stopped Last Night. The Robbers Reap a Light Harvest. Wells, Fargo's Chief Detective Stood up with the Rest." On the Benson coach's night run from Benson to Tombstone, Hume had dropped his guard completely and gone to sleep because he knew the coach carried no treasure. However, when it was just out of Contention, halfway to Tombstone, it was ambushed by two robbers. The nine passengers, all men, put up no resistance, although the bandits were amateurish Mexicans. As the stage was stopped, Hume awoke and thought he saw four bandits. At the robbers' orders the stage driver was holding the lead horses in their tracks. One of the outlaws poked a mean-looking shotgun barrel through the coach's window, and the detective, fearful of starting a fight in which passengers might get killed, surrendered his two fine pistols. Hume could not identify the two masked men, but one was tall and dressed in tight clothes while the short fellow wore a gunny sack over his clothing, to disguise it. Hume had no choice but to let them get away with $75 and three revolvers. Through its Tombstone agent, Wells, Fargo offered a $300 reward for the capture of the two men although the firm had suffered nothing more than a loss of face.

Perhaps Hume had been distracted, as well as sleepy, when he allowed himself to be robbed. For at this time self-conscious Jim Hume was finally trying to summon the courage to propose to Lida. After apologizing for not seeing her—"I don't know that you would be alone and don't fully realize but you might have company more satisfactory . . . [who] might not shake easily . . ."—the overwrought Hume poured out his heart: "I have concluded to await train time and go my way to wait and wait and wait to hear from you at Auburn. You don't know and

212

I can never tell you the interest I feel in your welfare and happiness. If it was in my power, you should have your own way in everything and should never have an unpleasant thought and should never want for anything to make your whole life a Christmas, a Thanksgiving. But, you know, 'Man proposes and God disposes,' and He don't stand in with me very solid. But you are the best friend I have and when I seem sullen and mean and cranky and unsatisfactory and irreligious and profane, etc., etc., you must remember that you are not the cause and that I can't always explain, and that had it not been for your restraining influence, I should have been a wreck, years ago. . . . Now, you will have no excuse for not writing. You said you would *never* write again until you heard from me and I was rather inclined to believe it. You are too good and I am ashamed of myself in the matter. You have forgiven me long ago and it is folly to refer to such things. Now, write—and don't be saving of your ink and paper. My right (and left) arm is a little shaky today and I can't account for it—but you will discover that my writing is not as artistic as usual."

Anyway, added Hume, who dashed off his notes to Lida with the stub of a pencil, "writing in ink is not my forte, you know." For some reason, though, he stopped short of a proposal, and no wedding plans emerged for almost two years.

Hume buried himself in his work again, relieving Aull of the Dick Fellows case in San Jose. The next day Dick was captured while hiding in a cabin near Los Gatos. At the request of Sheriff Williams, Hume let Fellows—now something of a celebrity—remain in the San Jose jail over the weekend. Even Hume was surprised when 700 people paid Dick a visit. The prisoner took it all in his stride. Then Hume escorted him to San Francisco and held him until the sheriff of Santa Barbara County could take him into custody. Fellows had made a full and voluntary confession to Hume, so the detective was immediately suspicious when the bandit demanded a preliminary examination. He tagged along to Santa Barbara, to keep an eye on Fellows, figuring that the slippery road agent was buying time by asking for a jury trial. And Hume knew all too well how Fellows would put that time to use—arranging an escape. Sure enough, shortly after being sentenced to life in Folsom State Prison, Fellows made his third escape from the law. When the jailer brought his breakfast, Fellows overpowered him, saying between clenched teeth as they struggled, "It is life or death with me, and I am going to get your revolver!" He did get it but did not use it on the guard. Two or three blocks from the jail Dick stole a grazing horse and tried to ride off, bareback. As unskillful a horseman as ever, Fellows was thrown once again and recaptured. Hume could not linger to see what Dick's next trick might be; on the day of Fellows' sentencing, he caught a 4 A.M. train for Texas and the town he called "Hell Paso."

From Texas Hume hurried to Reno, in May, checking on the movements of a robber named Curtis, who used the alias W. Dalin. Learning that the man had bought a ticket for Omaha, Hume telegraphed Ogden to hold the culprit, then wired Thacker to join him in Reno. As usual, he had far too many cases under way to handle them all personally. For a while he considered taking himself off the Curtis affair in order to proceed to Aurora, Nevada, on another case, but he decided to stick with Curtis. He could not help crowing a little when he wrote Lida, "I will have a *dead case* on Curtis and feel quite well pleased at getting him."

Back in California on a railroad case, he wrote Lida, "We have had a good success. Only one of the [five] train wreckers is now at large and I think we will get him." (And he enclosed a picture of the wanted man.) Then Hume's heart sank. General Superintendent Valentine had ordered him to Arizona again. Hume protested that he was needed in Auburn, and an interested associate, Charlie Jones, got Valentine's ear and convinced him that Hume simply could not be spared. When Valentine canceled his marching orders, Hume chortled, "Charlie and I had 'put up the job,' for I had learned from Tracy what Mr. Valentine's plans were. Ain't Charlie a good fellow?" It was not a trick played merely to escape Arizona, an area Hume detested.

His presence in California was essential. The next day he left Auburn for the scene of the train wreck with a topographer to execute a large diagram of the site that would be used as evidence in the upcoming trial.

Hume was distracted from the train wreckers' trial by the robbery of the North San Juan stage in September (curiously, $600 was taken, but $29,000 in bullion was left behind) and the halting of the Sonora-Milton stage for the nth time. Again, Hume wished that he could be in two places at once. Heading, at last, for Auburn and the train wreckers' trial, he wired Aull to take the new Sonora case. He joked to Lida; "I feared you might see in the papers an account of this robbery and, in your simplicity, you might conclude that I had chopped and gone to Tuolumne, or that I had divided and would be part in Auburn and the other part in Tuolumne, and that when you concluded to write, you would be at a loss where to send your letter. I will be in Auburn, and don't you forget it! And don't forget that the time between letters from you seems intermidable. (I guess that last word is not spelled right, but you know what it means.)"

July found Hume back in the Southwest, but this time he was not riding boxcars and drinking tank car water. For a change, he was living in comfort in the plush new Montezuma Hotel at Las Vegas Hot Springs, New Mexico. Probably, Hume had been sent there for his health by Wells, Fargo General Manager J. J. Valentine. But although he wrote Lida that it was "a love of a place, 6,500 feet above the level of the sea, and full of Eastern people," he soon was restless and then bored. He wired Valentine that his presence in the resort hotel was "altogether uncalled for" and asked, and received, permission to visit his relatives in Lima, Indiana.

When Hume returned to his office in September, he found a letter from the Wells, Fargo agent in Bodie, a town in the desert country east of the Sierra as famous for its badmen as Tombstone. "Your black-eyed girl, Tilly Schwisher, skipped out a few days since with a Johnny Ralls, from Belleville, a sport formerly of Mason Valley. . . . It is possible that the [Patrick]

Reddy outfit brought some influence to bear upon this man, Ralls, to take her out of the country. She is very much attached to Ralls, who is a young man and a lucky sport, who gives her all the money she wants. Hence, she might be influenced to abandon our cause in this suit against Rogers. Try and hunt her up. Probably you can fix her." This cryptic message, about a witness Jim hoped would testify in an upcoming case, suggests the kind of courtroom cloak-and-dagger work which was a secret but essential part of Hume's job. And he took infinite pains to have conclusive evidence and the proper witnesses on hand when Wells, Fargo set out to prosecute a malefactor.

In February 1883, Wells, Fargo Messenger Aaron Y. Ross defended his railway express car at Montello, Nevada, from a holdup gang and emerged a hero. His shipment was only $600, but next door in the postal car was $500,000 in currency. Although shot through the hand and hit in the groin by a spent ball, Ross stood his ground, and the robbers finally gave up their assault, which had included attempts to set the car on fire. Jim delegated the case to Thacker, who nabbed the whole gang in the wilds of Utah only five days after the holdup attempt. Meanwhile, Hume had again been posted to his personal Siberia— Arizona. This time, he found himself in Separ, a blot on the map about 40 miles from Deming, New Mexico. He growled to Lida, "I can't tell you how long I shall be detained in this God forsaken country." It was not too long. On February 26 he had the pleasure of escorting hero Aaron Ross around San Jose. When a San Jose *Mercury* reporter interviewed the 6-foot 4-inch, 250-pound express messenger, he found him still wearing the suit he had worn during the siege. The bullet holes were now neatly darned. As Ross left the room with Hume after the interview, the reporter heard the detective say to a local friend, "Ross and I have been looking around and I told him if he saw a farm he wanted, to let you know and we'd buy it for him."

After working in Los Angeles and San Francisco in May and June, 1883, Hume had to go to Winnemucca by train and then by stage to Boise and Idaho City. This investigative jaunt required Jim to ride for fifty-three hours on an outside coach seat, with only a six-hour break for sleep. He recovered the money in the Idaho stage robbery but did not catch the bandits. Perhaps his fifty-six years were slowing him down. He decided, if no clues turned up soon, that he would abandon the case and return home via Portland, Roseburg, and Redding, although he dreaded the long hours of stage travel ahead. Typically, his plans were changed for him. He got no farther than Pendleton before two holdups required his attention, one near town, the other between Roseburg, Oregon, and Redding, California. Glumly, he wrote Lida, "No telling, now, when I can leave Oregon."

Although the big news of 1883 was Black Bart's capture, Wells, Fargo's crime frontier was, increasingly, Arizona and New Mexico, rather than California. There, in December, Hume was involved in another of the curious efforts that he considered as much a part of his duty as the relentless pursuit of the guilty or the gathering of court testimony. He wrote Lida from Deming, New Mexico, "I have succeeded in demonstrating that a number of bad men who were suspected are innocent of this. I am making some headway towards the right ones but it is slow work." Hume always feared that someday he might imprison the wrong man. He bent over backward in this respect, combining a dedication to detail in his investigations with a willingness to stand up and spiritedly defend criminals who were not guilty of the particular crime with which they were charged. Around the holidays he was working hard to convince the people of Arizona, via articles in the *Daily Citizen*, that the gang that had robbed a train at Gage Station was not the same one that had raided Bisbee. He learned that the latter gang had ridden into San Simon, 78 miles from Gage, and had been told of the Gage holdup by the station agent. They had even remarked, jokingly, "We want you to bear witness that we had no hand in the robbery. If the rewards are sufficient, we might take a hand in capturing the robbers, as we are well fixed for that kind of business." To prove the innocence of this crew, Hume took Southern

Pacific Railroad Detective Len Harris and a section boss and wiper from San Simon and had the latter pair identify O. W. (Red) Sample and Tex Willis in Lordsburg as two of the gang that was in San Simon at the time of the Gage holdup. Hume announced flatly, "The train robbers are still at large and the rewards offered by the railroad company and the express company still stand and hold good, and the amounts offered will be paid to any party or parties who may capture the robbers." As usual, Hume proved to be right. The actual wreckers and robbers of the SP train at Gage Station on November 24, 1883, were George Cleveland, Mitch Lee, Frank Taggart, and Kit Joy. After being arrested, they broke jail but were retaken, and Cleveland was killed. Lee and Taggart were lynched, and Joy, when his shattered leg was amputated, was sent to the territorial prison at Santa Fe just a year and a day after he had helped wreck the train and kill the engineer.

On Christmas Day Hume was in Arizona, far from Lida and lonely, but he and the Southern Pacific's detective, Len Harris, were the holiday guests of Robert H. Paul, Sheriff of Pima County, and his family in Tucson. They enjoyed a superb dinner of roast beef and mashed potatoes, with white gravy, boiled turnips and beets, celery, coleslaw (Hume wrote "cold slough— is that right?"), cake, pie, cold custard, and claret. On this occasion, at least, Arizona was a pleasant place to be. Naturally, Jim bragged about Lida's cooking to the Pauls, but he also had to admit to her, "It came nearer being one of your dinners than anything I have seen." The day after Christmas Hume joined Paul and Harris on a vacation trip to Hermosillo and Guaymas, in Sonora, Mexico. But he was desperately lonely for Lida and complained, "No letter from you, *for months!* What is the matter? I am in splendid health but damn this country and people!" In the past he warned his girl to keep the Wells, Fargo matters that he mentioned in his letters strictly confidential, but now he was loath to tell her about his detective work for fear of boring her—"I would write something of my movements and doings but I fully realize that the subject does not interest you."

At the end of February, 1884, Hume was investigating a curious, double-holdup attempt against a single stagecoach on Funk Hill, the spot that had proved so irresistible to Black Bart. In fact, the press now referred to the vulnerable site as a "toll-station for road agents." Because the bandits had been unable to open the bolted-down treasure box, the Sonora *Union Democrat* chided them as nonprofessionals and as "Black Bart's unworthy successors." The paper predicted that, with Hume and Sheriff Ben K. Thorn on their trail, "the State Prison will have more recruits from the wilds of Calaveras." But Hume's heart was not in the case; it was elsewhere. After almost five years of courtship, he had finally mustered the courage to propose to Lida, and on April 28, 1884, they were married at the San Quentin Prison home of their good friend Charles Aull, who was now deputy warden.

Hume was not free to enjoy domestic life for long. As early as May he was on the road again, closing the case of a Yreka-Redding stage robbery with the arrest of the two culprits. In October both Thacker and he were embroiled in one of the petty arguments endemic to California law enforcement. The Mendocino City constable, envious of their fame and local publicity, insisted that *he*—not the detectives—deserved the credit for recovering the silver stolen in the Cloverdale-Mendocino City holdup. He insinuated that Hume and his aide had loafed about Ukiah and Boonville and concluded, "The silver might have been lying there still, if other parties had not been interested in Wells, Fargo and Uncle Sam to the extent of getting their money and mail." Normally, Hume, a pretty fair verbal in-fighter himself, enjoyed these little scuffles. But newly married and happier than he had ever been in his life, he ignored the jealous constable and let the teapot typhoon blow itself out. However, in December he was moved to throw a few brickbats at state prison officials. Noting escapes from both San Quentin and Folsom prisons, he said, for publication, that, as far as he was concerned, "considering escapes and pardons, it is more work to keep road agents in prison than to catch them."

Hume was exaggerative. Escapes, pardons, and paroles were exceptions, rather than the rule, and the general public was made aware of Hume's remarkable record of law enforcement as a result of the special report he prepared, with Thacker's help, and submitted to Vice-President and General Manager J. J. Valentine of Wells, Fargo on December 19, 1884. When the document was published in 1885, it immediately caught the attention of the local press and public, and soon it was being studied by law enforcement men and other interested persons all over the country. Its title was a resonant one—*Report of Jas. B. Hume and Jno. N. Thacker, Special Officers, Wells, Fargo & Co.'s Express, Covering a Period of Fourteen Years, Giving Losses by Train Robbers, Stage Robbers, and Burglaries, and a Full Description and Record of All Noted Criminals Convicted of Offenses Against Wells, Fargo & Company Since November 5th, 1870.* Known as the "Robbers Record," it listed 313 stage robberies in the fourteen years ending November 5, 1884, and 34 attempts that had misfired. Burglaries totaled 23. There were only 8 train robbery attempts, half of which had failed. The heyday of the railroad bandit still lay about a decade away. Hume's most impressive statistic was the high number of convictions—206 for stage robbery, 20 for train robbery, and 14 for burglary.

Remarkably, only two Wells, Fargo guards had been killed and six wounded during the period under study. However, four stage drivers had been killed, and four others wounded; four passengers, too, had been killed and two seriously wounded by stray bullets. On the other hand, Hume reported, Wells, Fargo guards had killed five bandits, five more had been killed while resisting arrest, and seven had been lynched. (He did not neglect statistics on horseflesh, either, and the public learned that seven horses had been killed "in the line of duty" and thirteen rustled by bandits.) The big losses, of course, were neither human nor equine, but monetary—$415,312.55 stolen from Wells, Fargo's coffers. In addition, the company had paid out $73,451 in rewards, $22,367 in lawyers' fees and other legal costs, and

$90,079 in various other expenses attendant upon the arrest and conviction of bandits. Finally, almost fifteen years of salaries (largely his own and Thacker's) added $326,517, which brought the firm's total "war" expenses to just under a cool million—$927,726.55!

Hume was well aware that one reason for the continuing high losses was the hostility of those who viewed Wells, Fargo as a bloated yet pinchpenny corporation which, reluctantly, had given Reason McConnell a mere $100 and Jimmy Rolleri a cheap gun for their help in ending Black Bart's career. Also circulating were false stories of fat purses awarded to company detectives while cooperative citizens collected chicken feed. The press sometimes fed the public's resentment. On one occasion Hume read in the Tuolumne *Independent* of Sonora an item picked up and reprinted from the Oakdale *Wheat-Grower:* "It seems to us that, by fair treatment, the Company could gain the sympathy and aid of the people who live in the vicinity of the stage road and thus make stage robbery a more dangerous pastime." Nor was this mere newspaper talk; Hume knew of the Milton man who had been asked what he would do if he saw a stage being robbed of its express box. The man had answered, "Why, I'd turn my back and walk away."

Hume's "Robbers Report" was a powerful public relations restorative for all the skeptics who would see no good in Wells, Fargo. The papers filled columns with excerpts from the document and also followed up with interviews with the company's chief detective. A San Francisco *Call* reporter on February 5, 1885, was proud of the way he got Hume to open up. Said the newsman, "After a little conversational fencing, the Wells, Fargo man surrendered at discretion—a thing he has never been known to do in a physical conflict." One of the things Hume tried to do in his interviews was clear up generally held misconceptions concerning crime detection. "There is a tremendous amount of fiction in the yarns that are told about detectives and particularly as to the marvelous disguises they are supposed to adopt," he reminded the newspaper-reading public: "During

221

the twenty-four or five years that I have devoted to robber hunting, I have never once assumed a disguise and have never known an attempt at disguise on the part of a well-known officer that did not prove a failure. There are times when a coat collar will be turned up, a hat pulled down, a handkerchief held at the nose to conceal one's features for a few moments, but this idea is simply absurd that one's appearance, manners, movements and voice can be so altered as to escape detection for a considerable time. A thief-taker's identity may, of course, be concealed from those who do not know him well, but the fact that he is a disguised man will soon become apparent to everyone and will hinder his efforts to obtain information by making everyone suspicious of him, especially those persons of the criminal class amongst whom he expects to find his game. My business as a Special Officer of this Company is thoroughly legitimate and appeals directly to the sympathetic assistance of every respectable citizen and, therefore, by an attempt to conceal my identity, I would lose many more chances than I could possibly gain.

"Our service consists of three Special Officers and a varying number of guards or, as we call them, shotgun messengers. These latter travel over the lines that offer the greatest temptations to highwaymen and are, every one of them, stayers. We may temporarily employ an extra messenger who turns out to be made of poor stuff, but all the regular guards are men of thorough courage and prompt action and robbers are always careful to steer clear of any stage on which they suppose one of those men may be riding. In all my experience, there has never been an occasion when a regular shotgun messenger showed the white feather no matter what the odds against him or the promise of danger might be. They are the kind of men you can depend on if you get in a fix, with the certainty that they will pull you through or stay by you to the last.

"In the great majority of stage robberies, we can pretty soon get a clue to the party or parties who have done the job and, frequently, can name them at once, but there are cases where they escape detection for a long while—this being almost invariably where their apparent respectability prevents suspicion from resting on them. A marked instance of this was the man Boles, or 'Black Bart' as he is more generally known. That chap ran his course as a highwayman for eight years, during which time he robbed, single-handed, no less than twenty-nine stages. He was, without exception, the most singular stage robber I have ever known, for he had none of the vices common to such men, kept free from accomplices, lived very quietly until the proceeds of his last steal were gone and then made another haul to meet his expenses for the next few months. In fact, he systematized stage robbery better than any of his predecessors and carried out his plans so carefully and, at the same time, so boldly as to make detection almost impossible. Although so long a time passed before we could place him, still, his style was such that we knew every one of his robberies was committed by the same man. Instead of standing at the side of the road as stage robbers almost always do, he'd step out directly in front of the horses and call a halt, at the same time stooping to conceal his height and holding his arms well up before his face. Then again, he always wore a long linen duster to hide his clothes and never used the profane language that all robbers indulge in to intimidate the drivers and the passengers."

In April, 1885, Hume was more amused than annoyed when the burglars of the Princeton office of Wells, Fargo had the nerve to advertise in the "Personals" column of the San Francisco *Chronicle*: "Valuable Papers. Papers and Notes. We are willing to negotiate. Suggest a method by which it can be accomplished." Hume responded via the same column: "Give full list of what you have; can't comply without some guaranty of good faith on your part." After the foolish thieves sent him some of the Wells, Fargo letterhead from the Princeton office, Hume laid a trap for them with the help of San Francisco's captain of detectives, Isaiah Lees, whose men made the arrests of Thomas P. Wilson and James Martin.

While Jim was in the field in 1885—Albuquerque, Kansas

223

City, Council Bluffs, Tucson, New Orleans—his wife kept up a steady stream of affectionate letters. Once the two were married, they were lovebirds for life, and all traces of bickering disappeared from their correspondence. Mostly, Lida reported on young Sam Hume, born on June 14, 1885. Also, she expressed concern for her husband's health. "I do think, Jim Hume," she wrote, "that in justice to yourself and *family,* you ought to take a little rest. . . . You know what you have always said about that hard Idaho trip and now you are doing the same thing again and tiring yourself out so that you won't get rested up for the rest of your natural life. . . . I want you to keep well and strong and cheerful and happy, and to live a thousand years." After his son's arrival, Hume was sorely tempted to ease up, despite his strong sense of duty toward Wells, Fargo. The San Francisco *Daily Post* observed the doting father and described Sam's birth as "the proudest event in Mr. Hume's adventurous life. . . . He is so engrossed with the first addition to his family that his many friends in the office say that a report of the escape of Black Bart would hardly cause him a ripple of excitement."

However, Hume found it impossible to slow down, even with the growing weight of years and added responsibilities at home. Fortunately, 1886 was a good year for Hume—with one enormous exception. In the annual report of criminal activities that he submitted to his superiors, he cited only fifteen successful stage robberies in eighteen attempts, plus eight office burglaries. (Of the former, nine occurred in California, two in Arizona Territory, and one each in Montana, Oregon, Nebraska, and New Mexico Territory.) Hume reported that the burglars had made off with only $319.31, the road agents had netted $1,500 in California and $1,100 outside the state, but he had recovered all but $235 of the California loot.

That year, however, Hume was shocked and deeply disillusioned by the conduct of one of his fellow employees. On November 1, 1886, the trusted cashier of Wells, Fargo's express department, Charles Wells Banks, vanished after starting out on a supposed fishing trip to the Russian River, just north of San Francisco. It was not a case of foul play, for Hume quickly discovered that his associate had embezzled more than $20,000. As he dug deeper into the case, it began to look more like $100,000. On the eighth Hume issued a $1,000 reward for Banks' arrest and delivery to any jail in the United States, promising, in addition, 25 percent of any recovered money.

Banks was a forty-seven-year-old Englishman who had been naturalized in 1867. He was hardly "the criminal type." About 5 feet 9 inches, and 145 pounds, with thick, curly, black hair lightly dusted with gray, he was prepossessing in appearance, although Hume's description (doubtless influenced by his contempt for Banks' treachery) did not indicate this. According to Hume, the embezzler had a flat nose, large at the nostrils and turned up at the tip, and flanked by a pair of small, gray, cold eyes. But Hume had to admit that Banks was a neat dresser, in spite of his use of tobacco and snuff. Banks had served in the New York Volunteers in the Civil War and fought at Sabine Pass in Texas. At the Battle of Pleasant Hill he had been wounded. With a leg smashed by a Rebel rifle ball, Banks had taken a military discharge and accepted a civilian post as a quartermaster clerk in New Orleans. Later, he was chief clerk in the Freedman's Bureau in Washington, D.C., and a customs inspector in New York before migrating to San Francisco in 1871. He was a Republican, a Knight Templar, and a member of the exclusive Union and Bohemian clubs. Science was his hobby, and Banks, a member of the Microscopic Society of San Francisco, possessed one of the first oil-immersed instruments on the Pacific Coast.

During his Wells, Fargo career Banks had seemed to be the epitome of dependability, but gradually Hume found that there was a lot more to Banks' flight than impulse. Quietly, some time before, the embezzler had sold his extensive scientific library and had sent his wife East on a long shopping trip and holiday. Then, just before his disappearance, he had shaved off his beard. The detective learned, too, that science had not been

Banks' sole hobby—he owned a vineyard and a gravel pit, as well as a house in Oakland and a sailboat. And, Banks had been a familiar speculator on the San Francisco Stock Market. Rumor had it that the embezzler had not only kept mistresses but was a regular patron of local brothels, ultimately investing in the ancient business himself and setting up a "house" conveniently near his Wells, Fargo office. Before he was through, Hume was more familiar with Banks' habits and character than he was with his own. The fugitive emerged as a bon vivant who liked to tip servants lavishly, who always bought the best and never questioned a tradesman's price. Openhanded and vain, Banks was, as well, a connoisseur of French cooking and a judge of wines and liquors. Hume even had to concede, "He has a streak of kindliness." The detective's information led General Manager J. J. Valentine to write to the company's New York agent to explain why Banks had gone wrong and had had to run: "As usual in such cases, we have found out, after he is gone, that he has been leading a profligate life, maintaining a mistress as well as a wife, for years past, and you will readily understand what that implies." With the horse gone, the company firmly locked the barn door by requiring all employees called upon to handle money to bond themselves or to resign. Valentine learned a lesson from Charley Banks—"Long service and confidence are not necessarily a protection to the Company."

Though Hume had the full cooperation of Fannie A. Banks, abandoned by her husband, he could not get his hands on the thief. He discovered, in an interview with Captain John Berude of the barkentine *City of Papeete,* that Banks had sailed in the vessel, on November 1, to Tahiti via Australia, posing as a well-heeled invalid, John Scard, traveling to the Society Islands for his health—in a sense, true enough. Scard had enjoyed the trip, tipped the sailors at the crossing of the equator, and had taken the captain buggy riding from his rented cottage in Tahiti. Berude could hardly believe Hume; his passenger had, after all, been "real nice—and he could drink wine and coffee like a gentleman." He had let the captain take care of his money until he sailed on the steamer *Janet Nicoll* for Auckland, New Zealand, and, presumably, Australia and Europe—just six hours ahead of the arrival of the *Raiatea,* bearing Hume's "wanted" posters. Just before he sailed, on December 11, Banks gave Berude a vial of morphine, saying, "I guess that I won't need this now and you might as well put it in your medicine chest." When, some time later, a box of seeds arrived in San Francisco, bound for a Mr. Scard in Rarotonga, Hume traced his man. He apparently sent an agent on a lumber ship to Tahiti and then, via chartered schooner, to Rarotonga. Again, probably in 1892, he sent a second deputy, presumably auditor Edwin B. Riddell. But by then Banks was either the prince consort of Queen Makea of the Cook Islands or married to her daughter. In any case, she would not allow extradition of her charming, wealthy, and trusted (!) adviser and new kinsman.

Hume's strategy was to isolate Banks on his atoll by broadcasting reward circulars in Australia and New Zealand, making the embezzler's haven a prison. The plan worked. If Wells, Fargo never recovered its money, Charles Banks did not really enjoy his dishonest gains for long. He fell out of favor with Queen Makea and had to move to the neighboring isle of Aitutaki, and Hume learned from a Captain McCoy in April, 1884, that the once-sociable Banks was miserable and broke. Said the captain, "His reputation is well known through the South Seas and he can get no position of trust. . . . The existence the embezzler ekes out is a poor one. He is an exile from home, an outcast of society, and dead to the world." Information on Banks' last years is virtually nonexistent, but according to tradition, he went blind around the turn of the century and lingered on until 1915, when he died and was buried in the Mission Cemetery on Rarotonga.

With a loving wife and baby at home, Hume was coming to hate the incessant travel his work demanded. In the spring of 1887, dashing by train from Topeka to Pueblo and Las Vegas, he wrote Lida, "I am wild to be with you again and hope *no* business will keep me away so long again. . . . I never realize how I love you and prize you and worship you till I am absent for a few days." In Tucson at the end of May, he was ill, exhausted, and dispirited from having turned up no clues concerning a month-old train robbery. The whole year proved dismal for Hume. September was the worst month, for Lida nearly died after delivery of a stillborn baby.

Stage robbery survived in vestigial fashion after Black Bart's curtain calls. When innocent-pleading George Henderson was given fifty years in prison for robbing the Oroville-Quincy stage, he ranted, "I only hope I live long enough to get a whack at Jim Hume!" A San Francisco *Examiner* reporter asked Hume if he did not think Henderson's sentence was a bit severe. "Not in the least," replied Hume: "While it is more than is usually given for this class of crime, I think it just the right medicine and not a grain too much. He robbed the United States Mail at the same time and had he been tried in the United States Court, the Judge would have had no alternative but to send him up for life. He can serve this sentence in twenty-nine years and two months if he behaves himself, and it is not a day too much. It was shown in the trial that he had not only robbed the mail and express but also the driver and an old, white-headed, citizen over 70 years of age, taking the last cent he had in the world. When he was on the witness stand, he swore he was in Oakland, a hundred miles away, at the time the robbery was committed and induced several of his own ilk to perjure themselves by corroborating his testimony. No, sir, he did not get a day more than he deserved and I predict there will be no more stage robberies in Butte County while Judge [Leon D.] Freer is on the bench."

Because Henderson had robbed some mail sacks, the reporter asked Hume if the government worked in harmony with him in apprehending such stage robbers as Henderson. He got a surprising answer: "Oh, yes, with the most perfect harmony. There has never been the slightest clashing. [But] since I have been with Wells, Fargo and Company, the express has been robbed 353 times and I judge the mail has been robbed on about 200 of these occasions, and I have never known of the Government paying out a cent to detect the robbers, nor have I known of a United States officer going out to investigate, excepting perhaps on one or two occasions, years ago. If the 'boys' would confine themselves to the mail, and let Wells, Fargo and Company alone, they would have a comparatively safe and probably more lucrative calling. Black Bart told me that in his first twenty-seven robberies he realized more from the mails than from the express.

"Still," added Hume, "stage robbing is, comparatively speaking, a thing of the past. What with the extension of the railroads, closing down of many of the mines and adoption of the money order system, there are no longer sufficient inducements for the higher grade of criminal talent to engage in the business. There are a few stage routes on which considerable treasure is still carried, but as they are guarded by shotgun messengers with established reputations and having carefully selected graveyards, the alleged 'knights of the road' are very diffident about molesting them. Occasionally, however, some miserable petty larceny offender stops the stage in some of our out-of-the-way country routes, finds the box empty, is captured, confesses and is forwarded to the home for the vicious-minded individuals, at San Quentin or Folsom. But the loss to the Company, from fifteen robberies during last year, amounted to less than $300. This, of course, leaves a very narrow margin for the robbers."

One of the these belated stage holdups supplied Hume with what the Sacramento *Record-Union* termed "An Interesting Case of Skillful Detective Work." In an October 21, 1887, holdup of the Redding stage en route to Bieber, a bandit shot and killed a passenger, George S. Henderson, riding alongside the driver. Hume was puzzled that this up-bound stage had been chosen as a target; anyone familiar with local affairs knew that pickings were best on stages bound *for* Redding. Also, the bandit had ignored the heavy going of the Churn Creek Grade and, instead, pulled off his stickup on a slight downslope where the team was at a trot. Hume knew that only one other outbound stage had ever been held up on that route—that one by the half-breed Stonewall Jackson Arthur—so he guessed that the culprit was either an Indian or an amateur road agent. Putting the puzzle together piece by piece, Hume learned that three men, Ed Beck, Lee Sykes, and Leslie Jones, had been working for rancher A. M. Goodenough, cutting and hauling wood. Three days before the holdup-murder, Sykes had left Goodenough's employ, and about ten days later Beck showed Jones and Clara Wright, Mrs. Goodenough's nurse, a letter from Sykes, ostensibly mailed from Silver City, Idaho. Jones and Beck also left Goodenough's, in November. In March, 1888, Jones wrote his old employer to tell him that in Redding Beck had torn down three of Hume's reward posters for the unknown killer of Henderson and had boasted, beerily, "I know who killed Henderson and I harbored him in Goodenough's barn the first four nights after the murder!" He had then clammed up. Jones had asked a Fresno County officer to question Beck, but the lawman told him that he had seen a Redding telegram advising officers of the arrest, in Oregon, of Henderson's murderer. So Jones dropped the matter.

Goodenough was not satisfield, however, and he wrote Hume on March 16 to offer him what information he had in exchange for the entire reward. Hume sent him a wanted poster and told him that if his information were reliable, he would assist him at his own expense and take no part of the Wells, Fargo reward. Goodenough's account was so vague, however, that Hume went to his ranch to investigate and also had an interview with Jones, from whom he learned that Sykes had borrowed Beck's pistol. But he could not locate Sykes, although he questioned his relatives in Live Oak, California. Hume was sure that Beck was involved and knew the whereabouts of Sykes, almost certainly the murderer. He was afraid to arrest Beck because that would cause Sykes to go underground. Instead, he worked out a plan, crossing his fingers as he did so, that involved his getting a warrant for Beck's arrest for having stolen a watch from a friend. Next, Hume sent it to Fresno Officer C. W. Fraser, who used a little stratagem of his own, and subpoenaed Beck as a witness in a horse-stealing case. Beck came into Fresno and was soon tossing down drinks; in a boozy daze, he found himself whisked quietly aboard a northbound train by Fraser. On receiving Fraser's wire, Hume met the train at Lathrop. He interrogated Beck in Sacramento and learned that the fellow had fed Sykes while he was hiding in the brush near Goodenough's on October 18, 19, and 20, 1887. After the holdup and murder he had fed him for four nights more in the barn. When he described Sykes' coat and pants, the last time he had seen him, as being of the same material as his own vest, he was "persuaded" by Hume to sacrifice it in the name of justice. The detective cut it into pieces, which he sent to law officers in Kern County, where he thought Sykes (alias W. R. Short and Bob James) was hiding out.

Once again, to his chagrin, Hume came up against a non-cooperative law officer. District Attorney Edward Sweeney of Redding refused to swear out a complaint charging Sykes with murder so Hume could obtain a warrant. His reason was that another suspect, John Curtis, was to be arraigned the following day for the crime. Hume hurried to Shasta County with Beck. By the time he arrived, he learned that an indictment had been found against Curtis, but both Sweeney and Sheriff W. E. Hopping came around to Hume's way of thinking when he got Beck to talk. Hume made an unsuccessful personal search of Bakersfield but pinned his hopes on the city's Fourth of July festivities, which he thought might lure Sykes out of hiding. Hume asked local officers to be particularly watchful on the Fourth, but they failed him, for he later learned that Sykes had, indeed, paraded the streets of Bakersfield, drunk but unnoticed, on the national holiday.

The case seemed stymied until August 2, when a man brought a saddle and a valise into the Wells, Fargo office in Bakersfield. He wanted to ship them to Hildreth. The agent did not like the look of the big six-shooter on the fellow's belt and half-suspected him of the robbery of the Hildreth-Madera stage, which had just occurred. Then his heart pounded violently as the man took his coat out of the valise before shipping it. The patterned material exactly matched the swatch Hume had sent him. The agent called the sheriff and a constable, who disarmed and arrested the man. Hume was far away, in Chicago, but he wired instructions to California, and Sheriff Hopping took Sykes to the Redding jail after Beck had been transferred, at Hume's suggestion, to the Tehama County jail in Red Bluff. Wells, Fargo's chief detective hurried to California to question them, arriving in San Francisco on August 9. That night Beck broke out of jail. Still, with Hume's testimony, there was enough evidence to hold Sykes to answer in a preliminary hearing, and the DA eventually charged him with murder.

By September 15, thanks largely to his excellent descriptive circulars which made no hideout safe, Hume had Beck back in custody. His flyer on Thomas Edward Beck is typical of Hume's capsule-biography circulars: "Twenty-four years of age, about five-feet ten inches tall, quite stoop shouldered, features thin, especially his nose; light blue eyes, light colored hair, thin, light colored moustache; quite dull-looking. At the time of his escape, he wore a 6 3/4 soft black hat, a single breasted blue flannel shirt, old blue overalls, a pair of No. 7 half-dressed laced shoes, and a common white merino undershirt and drawers. Beck chews tobacco and smokes cigarettes to excess; gets hopelessly drunk whenever he has money and the opportunity to buy liquor. When drunk he is very loquacious and braggadocio but, in reality he is harmless as a sheep. In the community where he is best known, he is regarded as honest and truthful but weak and easily influenced. He is a fair underground miner, a good woodchopper, and handles a four-horse freight team fairly well. He knows nothing of tramping as a profession, has had no experience in 'beating' his way on trains or 'sparring' for food. He had no money when he escaped and it is believed by his family and friends that he will seek employment at mining or farm work, or wood business, instead of 'beating' his way a great distance out of the country. He is decidedly *gawky* in appearance, seems to be constitutionally incapable of maintaining an erect position. When idle or talking, *must* have something to lean against or loll upon and if there are no supports near at hand, he will squat down upon his haunches and employ his hands whittling. Even when sitting in a chair, or on a stool or bench, this tendency will develop itself, for he will spread himself onto an adjoining wall or door or drop his elbows upon his knees. When sober, there is nothing in his appearance to indicate that he is other than a pleasant, obliging, inoffensive fellow."

Hume put Beck in the Sacramento jail, and on October 6 Sykes pleaded guilty. He hoped to escape death with his plea and a show of contrition; it worked, and he was given a life sentence. At last, Hume could relax after devoting forty days to the case, traveling 6,000 miles, and spending $300 beyond his expense account allowance. Said the Sacramento *Record-Union* in its story, headlined "MURDER WILL OUT": "While the primary reward will be paid to others, Mr. Hume, alone, is entitled to all credit which may attach to the successful result of the case for, without his energy, skill and discretion, the murderer of Henderson would, in all probability, never have been brought to justice. As it is, it forms one of the most interesting cases of detective pursuit that has occurred on the Coast."

Once again, however, a successful case left a bad taste in Hume's mouth because of the jealousy of other lawmen. The California Associated Press distributed a copyrighted story that began, "The arrest and conviction of Sykes was due to the untiring efforts of Detective J. B. Hume of Wells, Fargo and Company, who has spared no efforts in bringing to justice the perpetrator of the crime." It did *not* mention the sorry hassle in which Hume found himself after the Red Bluff *News* printed a letter Beck had sent him when he had agreed to surrender. It gave the reason for his jailbreak of August 9, 1888. Beck had feared for his life because he would not peach the way Tehama County's sheriff wanted him to—that is, to swear that Hume had "put up" the Sykes investigation. The Tehama County officers, Beck had written, had promised to release him with enough money to get out of the county *if* he would testify against their suspect, Curtis. If not, they had hinted, he would leave Tehama County in a box. For once, Beck had been smart enough to turn down free drinks, offered him by the deputies. He had been held incommunicado, without a hearing, a trial, or an attorney, and had had to saw his way out in order to contact the two men he trusted, Sheriff Hopping of Shasta County and Jim Hume.

Hume felt obliged to hand the letter over to the local press, and the Red Bluff paper ran the story under the banner headline "SERIOUS CHARGES AGAINST THE SHERIFF'S OFFICE—A FEARFUL CONSPIRACY." Convinced by Hume's notarized affidavits confirming Beck's charges, and the fact that local deputies had bribed a horse thief to testify falsely against Curtis, in exchange for his freedom, the *Daily News* was led to quote Beck: "I was in danger of my life all the time I was there and that is the reason I escaped. I am willing to go up there with you [Hume] anytime, but I do not want to go with any other officer. I want a written guarantee from you that I will be back home safe as you took me away. I do not want to run away. . . . All I want to do is to keep out of those Tehama fellows' way."

With California stage holdups netting only an average of $20 each by 1887, only fools could be expected to pursue careers as road agents, and Hume increasingly directed his energy toward discouraging train robbery, which was already becoming a criminal vogue. In April, 1887, Train No. 20 was stopped by a red light and a barricade of ties near lonely Papago Station, not far from Tucson. Failing to persuade one of Hume's disciples, Wells, Fargo Messenger C. F. Smith, to open the express car door, even after a volley had left eleven bullet holes in the chocolate-colored car, the outlaws forced the engineer to light the fuse of a stick of giant powder (dynamite). Smith understandably reconsidered and surrendered his stronghold. As the bandits pinched out the sputtering fuse, he threw $5,000 in gold, of his total treasure of $8,000, into the cylindrical, clay-burning stove in the car. The robbers uncoupled all the other cars and had the locomotive pull the combination express-mail-baggage car six miles away, to loot it at leisure, but they overlooked the money in the stove. The newspapers compared them for their coolness and efficiency to Frank and Jesse James or Sam Bass.

Hume was closemouthed about the case, although he was sure that some or all of the robbers involved were railroad men because of their expert knowledge of train operations and the language they had used. All he could tell the press, however, was that he was confident that the gang would be taken, because not a single train robber on the coast had, so far, escaped capture and trial. "I am always willing to give you any news," he concluded, "but this is a matter that we do not want published yet." In his San Francisco office, far from the scene, he worked hard on the Papago case. When four of the robbers were eventually caught in Tucson, he revealed to reporters the clue that had led to the breaking of the case—a letter that had been accidentally dropped in Isaac Rosenthal's "misfit clothing" (secondhand) parlor in San Francisco. Given to Detective James Bee, who thought it a hoax, it finally wound up in Hume's hands. It read: "WJF. All ok with Lou but he says he must make a 'coon' of himself [don blackface]. The blacker the better in this case. He will either have to have a wig or dye that red hair some way. He can clean himself up before he gets to Nogales and he must get on the engine instead of bag'e car. He will get further instructions on train. Please be at your office at 6K [o'clock] as I go to supper." The postscript, in a different hand, read, "Red—you must blacken up and get on the engine, not in the baggage car; get yourself up as a darky so they won't know you.— A.H."

Following the Papago case came a rash of similar heists—four during May, June, and July, 1887, alone. The Flatonia, Texas, holdup was a particularly brutal affair. It began with a man in tramp's clothing climbing over the coal of the tender into the engine cab. He then produced a revolver, impressing the engineer with the fact that he was not really a box car tourist. At a bridge marked by the campfire of his confederates, he forced the engineer to stop the train. When Messenger Frank Folger threw away the keys to his safe, the bandits pistol-whipped him and tortured him by slitting his ears with pocket knives until they recovered the keys. The masked men attacked sleeping travelers in their bunks and beat up a Mexican Army lieutenant and a woman passenger, while their leader, whom they addressed as Captain Dick, calmly sucked on a piece of hard candy. Hume hurried to Texas and ordered Thacker there, too, from Tucson.

The press applauded the bombast of Governor Lawrence S. Ross of Texas, who threatened to ballast trans-Texas trains with Rangers. Ready to authorize commissions for 390 new Texas Rangers, he declared, "Train robbery is to be a fighting business and attended with almost certainty of failure and detection. There will be five to ten well-armed fighting men on each train." Hume received such political manifestos philosophically, and continued to pursue his tried methods of investigation. The case did not end neatly, but it was largely wrapped up by October, when Ed Reeves was wounded in a gunfight and captured. Two others were killed and three jailed, two of whom confessed. Hume's guess had been good; all of them were ex-Southern Pacific railroaders. Reeves was thought by Thacker and Hume to be Captain Dick, but Texas lawmen preferred to believe that they finally wrote finis to that alias when they killed Brack Cornett in 1888.

The August 11, 1887, holdup of the Southern Overland on the Cienega Cut near Papago, Arizona Territory, was another rough affair. The engineer applied the air brakes when he saw a red light and heard the popping of track torpedoes, but only to slow down, not to stop. The waiting bandits then filled the cab with lead, but still the engineer did not halt the train. However, the switch that the robbers had opened did the trick, dumping the locomotive on its side and throwing engineer and fireman down the embankment. The U.S. mail messenger came out meekly, but the Wells, Fargo messenger, again C. F. Smith, refused. The robbers, wearing linen dusters and black cloth masks, blew a hole in the door and boosted the mail messenger inside, to persuade Smith to surrender. He did so, reluctantly, feeling that the odds were just too much for him with four bandits toting Winchesters, pistols and explosives and threatening to blow the express car to smithereens, if necessary. As Smith emerged, one of the outlaws bashed him on the head with a pistol, snarling, "You son of a bitch, you won't play us any more tricks by hiding the money in the stove!" Hume was on the case, pronto, convinced that it was the work of the April thieves. He would admit to the press only a loss of $3,500, but the San Francisco *Chronicle* guessed that it was closer to $20,000 since the robbers had left behind a heavy sack of 800 Mexican dollars, and had not touched the mail. The bandits were as ill-tempered as the Papago gang, if not the very same men. They swore at the conductor and threatened to kill him. "You are the man we want! You have been saying that your train could not be held up. We'll show you!" When the fireman finally clambered up the bank of the cut, down which he had been thrown, a bandit fired a shot at him, which tore away part of his mustache, and harangued him, "You son of a bitch, aren't you dead yet? Why didn't you stop the train when I told you?"

The sheriff led a posse out of Benson, and it was joined by a party of soldiers from L Troop, 4th Cavalry. Two of the gang's hideouts, caves in the rugged Rincón Mountains and near Mountain Springs and the San Pedro River were discovered. Hume had Thacker join another posse and SP Detective Len Harris, with two Yuma Indian trackers, led a third. Finally, Wyatt Earp's brother Virgil joined the hunt, too. Thacker got one suspect arrested in Los Angeles, but presumably, the gang was the same one that had pulled the Papago job and that was broken up in October, 1887.

Meanwhile, two more Texas trains had been held up, at Benbrook and near El Paso, on September 20 and October 14. The October robbers did not have the good fortune of their predecessors. They dynamited the express car and shouted to Wells, Fargo Messenger J. Ernest Smith, "Die, damn you!" This Smith was made of even sterner stuff than the doughty C. J. Smith. He put out the lights and laid his pistol just inside the express car door, then emerged with his hands up. He was ordered back inside to relight the lamps. Grabbing his pistol, he shot the bandit prodding him, who got off two wild shots, then fell dead. Smith then exchanged fire with the other robber until he broke and ran as the messenger switched from pistol to shotgun. But he must have been badly wounded, for at sunrise his body was found only 50 yards away.

El Paso's citizens gave Smith a new suit of clothes and raised $100 for a medal for him. Wells, Fargo congratulated him and rewarded him with $2,000. The Southern Pacific contributed $250 and the U.S. government $200 more for protecting the mails. The State of Texas threw in $1,000, and the San Francisco *Chronicle* cheered Smith's work: "If his example were followed, train robbing would soon be a thing of the past."

The killing of the two bandits by Wells, Fargo Messenger Smith did not result in the expected decrease in train robberies. Hume was kept as busy as ever in 1888, pasting clippings in his voluminous scrapbook library to document holdups in Arkansas, Indian Territory, Missouri, Arizona and Mexico. On February 23, at Stein's Pass, near Pantano and Papago, that loneliest stretch of lonely Arizona Territory, bandits posing as tramps again stopped a locomotive. Hume headed for Stein's Pass and sent Thacker to join Len Harris of the Southern Pacific in a pursuit into the Sierra Madre of Mexico. Hume told Wells, Fargo, "They will certainly be caught. I will remain in the region a few days longer. Have made some important investigations in Albuquerque and Chihuahua." Thacker and Harris returned to the United States from Janos before U.S. Marshal Meade's posse was arrested for trespassing into Mexico and escorted back across the border. But Hume's old pal in Arizona, Sheriff Robert H. Paul, led Mexican Army troops to the train robbers' hideout, and the bandits were killed by the soldiers on March 16, 1888.

When a train was stopped on the Sonora Railroad near Nogales on May 11, Hume sent Thacker to join Paul and his

Apache scouts. He then told the San Francisco press, "These Apache trailers that Mr. Paul speaks of are wonderful people. They assisted very materially in tracking the Stein's Pass robbers to the place where they were killed. When they once get on the track of a man, they never get off of it. On following a blind trail, they generally travel on foot but where the trail is fresh, they can follow it riding on horseback, the animal going at full speed. They have the keenest eyesight of any people I ever came across. Why, they could track a fly over a looking glass." The Apaches did not disappoint their publicist; on May 14 Thacker wired Hume that he had two Americans and two Mexicans under arrest at Nogales.

In spite of the wearying routine of incessant travel, combined with declining health—Hume had had to give up claret, beer, and meat, presumably because of a gouty foot—these were very happy years for him. His wife wrote her friend Mrs. Charles Aull on April 26, 1888, the fourth anniversary of their wedding at Aull's San Quentin cottage, "It would be folly for me to attempt to tell you how happy we are and are always going to be. It seemed to me, then, madness to think that I could ever make Jim H. happy. . . . [But] I ventured and I have the blessed consequence of knowing, past all doubting, that these have been the happiest years of his life."

Hume himself was never so happy as when he was engrossed by an intriguing criminal puzzle, such as the robbery that occurred in July, 1888. A package of $1,000 had been looted between Carbondale, Kansas, and Torch, Ohio, the bills being replaced with cut-up strips of a Sacramento daily. "It is an *exceedingly* intricate case," he wrote Lida on July 14, "and is spread over a vast extent of country [it took him to Columbus, Chicago, Kansas City, and Cincinnati] and I can't have any satisfactory investigation made by any other than myself." His first step was to clear the Carbondale agent of suspicion. "I discovered how the 'funny business' had been performed on the envelope and satisfied the management that the theft was committed *after* the package left Carbondale. They had their suspicions so firmly set on the Carbondale office that they were loath to quit but did so, finally, but quite reluctantly. They, of course, were quite chagrined at having entirely overlooked the true condition of the envelope." Hume demonstrated that the envelope had been cut neatly at the end, the seal loosened, and a buttonhook used to draw out the string that had been passed through the bills by the packer to ensure safe shipment. Then the bills were extracted and replaced with the bundle of newspaper clippings, carefully cut to bill size. He wrote Lida, "I am determined to win this case, if possible, so don't complain if I take ample time. . . . I certainly have located the theft on the right man, Jno. A. Sheets. I haven't the least misgiving about it and you know I am generally right. . . . I have a 'spot' [a tail] on Sheets and will continue it til he uses [some] currency." (Hume could identify the bills by the perforations where the string had been threaded through.) Despite all his efforts, Hume was unable to bring Sheets or anyone else to justice in the case. Later he remarked to Cincinnati reporters, "It was the slickest job ever done; yes, sir, the slickest job ever done in the world," and told them that the guilty party had confessed but had been saved from prosecution by the influence of powerful relatives.

Having tangled with William Randolph Hearst, Hume decided to take on Governor Robert W. Waterman in his next letter-writing campaign. He always tried to protect his sources and to reward "friends" (even criminals) who tipped him to information during his investigations. Thus he decided to support the El Dorado County district attorney when he suggested to the governor that one of the accomplices in the murder of a farmer named Lowell was entitled to a pardon because of his complete cooperation with law enforcement officials. Hume's letter to the governor, of November 26, 1888, makes clear his feelings about his personal brand of justice, whatever custom or tradition might dictate: "Personally, the matter does not interest me in the least for I have never seen the condemned men nor any of their friends and upon general principles the crime is one which deserves

FROM TUCSON TO RAROTONGA

the full penalty of the law, but the practice of according mercy to the man who first confesses and expresses a willingness to aid in bringing to justice his confederates in crime is one from which no departure should ever be made. I have had thirty years experience in dealing with criminal classes and I can safely say that the custom of granting immunity from the full penalty of the law to the first of a number of offenders who shall confess and testify against his co-conspirators does more to prevent crime and deter criminals than all the shrievalties [sheriffs' offices], constabularies, and police departments in the civilized world."

To do away with this precious bit of leverage against criminals, argued Hume, was to discard the law officer's most effective weapon. "This fear that some one of their number will be induced to turn traitor for the sake of clearing himself is the strongest restraining influence of which we have any knowledge." He then reminded the governor of the Troy Dye case, in which a murderer was hanged in Sacramento after being promised that his life would be spared if he confessed, which he did. "In my opinion, his execution was the most shameful thing which can be produced in the court annals on this Coast and officers of the law have not yet recovered from the disastrous results of the failure of the District Attorney and other officials to keep the promise made to the man to secure his confession. . . . That promise should have been sacredly kept although the whole State clamored for his blood!"

Hume continued, "The statutues of the several states wisely provide that, when two or more people are included in the same indictment, the Court may, on motion of the District Attorney, direct one of them to be discharged that he may be used as a witness for the people, and this discharge is, in effect, an acquittal. Why should not [William] Drager [the man in question], who confessed before indictments were found, receive the same clemency? . . . In commuting Drager's sentence to imprisonment for life, the ends of justice would be served and Your Excellency will be only abiding by a practice of the law and courts upon which we must be able confidently to rely if we are to successfully prosecute our business of bringing malefactors to justice and suppressing crime." He suggested that the governor poll Chief of Police Crowley and Captain of Detectives Lees, of San Francisco, Sheriff Cunningham and Sheriff Thorn of San Joaquin and Calaveras counties, and Warden Aull of Folsom. "I have not interviewed any of these gentlemen upon this subject," wrote Hume, "but I have no doubt that they, and indeed all experienced officers upon this Coast, will sustain me in the point I have taken, and would unite with me in urging upon Your Excellency the necessity of commuting Drager's sentence to imprisonment for life." Hume's plea was convincing, but it was not strong enough to cause Governor Waterman to meddle in judicial matters, as he saw it, and he took no action to spare Drager.

Hume's mind was diverted from this defeat by the holdup of the Central Pacific train in the Sierra Nevada snowsheds on Christmas Eve, 1888. Two masked men, who had got on the roof of the express car at the Clipper Gap water stop, let themselves down on rope ladders and broke in the transom windows over the express car doors. After covering the messengers with pistols, they gained entry, filled grain sacks with money packages, and in five minutes dropped off the train and vanished without being seen by the brakeman in the caboose as the train lumbered up a heavy grade. Hume declined to say how much was stolen, so the *Chronicle* gave itself considerable leeway in estimating the haul at between $15,000 and $60,000. Hume cut short his Christmas Day celebrations and started for Clipper Gap in the afternoon with Thacker; they were joined there by Len Harris and other law officers, causing the *Chronicle* to predict, "By morning, the woods about New England Mills will be full of detectives." Before he could get deep into the case, Hume was sent to Dallas, where he had six Wells, Fargo men fired for incompetence. Writing home about the shake-up, he confided to Lida that the chief of police and detectives of Dallas were "clever gentlemen but not very bright officers." Texas provided more trouble for Hume when the Brownwood agent robbed the company and skipped the country.

Back in California in January, Hume resumed his investigation of the Clipper Gap case. He wrote Lida from Sacramento, "I have found a man who says the Clipper Gap train robbers stopped with him in his cabin four miles from New England Mills from December 18th until the 29th." He learned that the robbers had had the ironwork of their Jacob's ladders made in Grass Valley and that they had persuaded their Sierra host to buy the necessary rope at New England Mills and to lend them an ax. Hume's informant was willing to talk because he felt that the thieves had treated him shabbily, giving him only $30. Hume was on the track of one of the men in Reno, and said of his witness, "If he stands by his first story, we will commence an investigation by visiting his cabin." Before Hume could follow through, he was sent to Boston in pursuit of a San Jose check forger. By the time he brought back his man, in July, Thacker had already made the arrest of Clipper Gap robber H. L. Gordon. Gordon confessed on August 20, while lodged in the Auburn jail, to having pulled off the tricky holdup with his brother George.

CHAPTER X

THE SOUTHERN PACIFIC WAR

JIM HUME could have retired, famous, after closing the books on Black Bart—notwithstanding Boles' mysterious disappearance—but retirement was anathema to him. He had the instinct for work of a Clydesdale and he stayed in harness until he took to his deathbed, in 1904. His last *great* case—really a series of connected cases—brought him frustration. For one thing, his duties, which included transcontinental junkets to the East on company business, were so demanding that he could not devote himself wholeheartedly to it but had to delegate much responsibility to Jonathan Thacker and others. Worse than that, Hume found himself on the wrong side in this particular instance.

Wells, Fargo's detective became involved in the great undeclared civil war of the 1890's in California. One antagonist was the Southern Pacific Railroad, which, literally, ran the State of California from capitol dome to crossroads chamber of commerce. (By 1900, railroads controlled one-sixth of the country's wealth.) Wells, Fargo, like most businesses, became a virtual satellite of this powerful monopoly. Facing the battalions of politicians and business sycophants that the mighty SP could muster was a rabble in arms, consisting of a San Joaquin Valley alliance of farmers and small businessmen and reformers such as capitalist Adolph Sutro and writer Frank Norris, who, together, damned the railroad with an epithet that stuck—"the Octopus."

The Southern Pacific had antagonized small entrepreneurs by deliberately bypassing towns like Stockton and Visalia, which did not kowtow and setting up stations like Lathrop and Goshen, which it attempted to build into commercial rivals. The small farmers hated the railroad, not only for its cruelly high rate structure, especially on short hauls, but because it had lured many of them as squatters onto land adjacent to the right-of-way by offering them a guarantee of "privilege of purchase" of the properties at $2.50 to $5 an acre when the railroad's patents should be approved. But when that time came around, the price turned out to be more like $35 an acre; when the squatters could not pay, deputies ruthlessly booted the farmers and ranchers off the land they had so laboriously improved. Facing ruin, the small settlers—derisively called sandlappers by the railroad—fought back by forming the Settlers Land League to contest the decisions of the Government Land Office. They had little or no success, and it appeared that even the federal government stood in awe of the Southern Pacific Railroad.

The first salvo in the hot war between the SP and the public was fired on May 11, 1880, by a special deputy, W. J. Crow, who shot four farmers in about four minutes. The Octopus lost its deadliest gunslinger within the hour, however, when he was ambushed on his way home. But the death of four of its leaders at Mussel Slough, near Hanford, southwest of Fresno, and the jailing of seventeen others thoroughly cowed the Settlers Land League. So much so that the next battle in the SP war did not occur for nine years, when the farmers received aid from strange allies—outlaws.

On February 22, 1889, Southern Pacific No. 19 was cutting through an early evening gloom intensified by patches of tule fog when the engineer was forced to bring the locomotive to a stop near Pixley, about 30 miles southeast of Mussel Slough. Two masked men then transferred their attention from the cab to the express car, ordering Wells, Fargo Messenger J. R. Kelly to open the doors and throw out the treasure box. The Irishman was made of the same stuff as the shotgun messengers Hume had described in 1885—"They are the kind of men you can depend on if you get in a fix, with the certainty that they will pull you through or stay by you to the last"—and he refused to obey. The bandits then proceeded to ignite a dynamite bomb, which lifted the car right off the tracks and shook the bejesus out of Kelly. They shot a member of the train crew and a deputy, who was a passenger, but the messenger, dazed by the shock and concussion of the explosion, still refused to budge. He finally gave in when the outlaws threatened to shoot the engineer and fireman if he did not cooperate. Kelly kicked the treasure box out the door onto the cinders, and the masked man made off with it.

Posses formed and galloped bravely off up Deer Creek and toward the Temblor Range of the coastal mountains. But they found that even with the dangling bait of handsome rewards, the San Joaquin Valley public was not willing to help the law in behalf of the hated SP. The trail grew cold; a closemouthed Hume was reluctant to provide the press with a solid figure for the embarrassing loss, which newsmen quoted at figures anywhere from $500 to $5,000. The case was written off, for the moment, as unsolved.

Less than a year after the Washington's Birthday upset, two masked bandits struck Train No. 19 near Goshen, about 25 miles south of the first holdup. They used the same technique, crawling over the coal in the tender of the southbound night train to reach the cab and pulling pistols on the engineer and fireman. The Wells, Fargo messenger on January 20, 1890, was not of Kelly's fiber, and Hume could issue no words of praise. The guard meekly complied with the robbers' command to surrender the express shipment. After shooting a tramp who made the mistake of running away from the stalled train, the robbers

247

disappeared into the night. Sheriff's deputies and railroad detectives scoured the area but again got near-zero cooperation from the citizenry and had to abandon the pursuit. The boodle, amounting to $20,000, according to rumor—for Hume again was mum—stayed lost.

Just a little more than a year later, on February 6, 1891, it was SP No. 17's turn, at Alila, a ghost town whistle-stop today, about a quarter of a mile south of Earlimart. When the masked men ordered Wells, Fargo Messenger C. C. Haswell to open up, he told them to go to hell. Then he doused his light and prepared to shoot through the grating at the bottom of a door. One of the robbers anticipated him, however, and fired his shotgun through the hole. Haswell ducked back in time and suffered only a scalp wound from a single buckshot. Although he could not see well, for blood was cascading down his face, he fired his revolver through the grid and heard a man cry out, "Oh, my God!" Haswell then crawled to the opposite door and put a few pistol balls through its grating to discourage any bandits on that side of the car. Perhaps a dozen shots were fired, in all, before the bandits gave it up as a bad job and left, emptyhanded. Haswell was the hero of the hour. It turned out to be the shortest hour on record, however, for he found himself accused of having killed the fireman. Meanwhile, the sheriffs of Kern and Tulare counties galloped about over California's wide central valley in vain pursuit of the phantom raiders. Hume rushed to Alila on the special train carrying the coroner's jury investigating the shooting of the fireman (Haswell was acquitted), but he had no more luck than the local officers, because of the valley's conspiracy of silence, worthy of Sicily itself.

The trail again led toward the Coast Range but petered out near the hamlet of Huron. There, between Visalia and Paso Robles, the lawmen finally got a lead. Since it was their first, they can perhaps be forgiven for overreacting. Someone reported seeing three strangers loafing around on the day before the holdup. Someone else then reminded the law that some of the Dalton brothers, cousins of the Younger brothers and more distant kin of Frank and Jessie James, were resident in California. Littleton Dalton had a spread near Clovis, right in the San Joaquin Valley, and William Dalton had a ranch near Paso Robles. Both were more or less respectable ranchers, but their visiting brothers, Bob and Grattan, were already becoming as notorious in California as they were in their native Indian Territory haunts.

Grat Dalton was placed under citizen's arrest. He made no objection, acting as innocent as an infant. After being quizzed at the sheriff's office, he was allowed to go. Bob hid out in brother Bill's attic and, possibly, in the Sierra, then skipped to Oklahoma. When some stirrups were found in an abandoned camp of the Alila robbers and identified as having been borrowed by Bill Dalton to lend to his brothers, the Tulare County grand jury indicted all four Daltons. Grat and Bill were seized, and the SP offered a $1,500 reward for Bob and brother Emmet Dalton, now on the scene; to this sum Hume added the customary Wells, Fargo bounty of $300 apiece. Any information on the whereabouts of the two missing Daltons was to be forwarded to the sheriff of Tulare County, the SP Railroad Detective, Bill Hickey, or to Jim Hume.

In June, 1891, as the jury was being impaneled to try Grat Dalton, Hume was laboring hard to work up a case against him. He wrote home from Tulare of his painstaking investigation: "Last night I was completely worn out but this morning am as good as new. We are having first-rate success and the robbers will certainly be caught, maybe today, and when caught we have *ample* testimony to warrant a conviction. Last night is the only night's sleep I have had. Have taken in the whole line of the railroad for 150 miles." Hume was overly optimistic; no cronies of Grat Dalton fell into his net, and by August he was off the case and in Portland, Oregon, investigating the theft of some opium in transit, by two Wells, Fargo employees.

The fourth raid on the SP occurred at Ceres, near Stockton, on the evening of September 3, 1891. Wells, Fargo messengers Reed and Charles resisted when the bandits compelled the engineer and fireman to give the express car door forty whacks with a coal pick and continued to do so even when the robbers set off a bomb. The explosion shattered the door and the floor and shook up the guards, but luckily, they were not hit by the jagged splinters that were driven deep into the opposite wall. The resulting hole was just big enough to crawl through. The robbers drove the quaking fireman, carrying a candle and match, through the hole, but Reed put a pistol in his face and drove him right back out. Undeterred, the badmen tossed in a bomb. Its wick came off, and a hand reached in and retrieved it before the Wells, Fargo men could grab it. Just as the outlaws were about to toss it in again, their attention was diverted by pistol shots. Two of the train's passengers were deadheading SP Dectectives Len Harris and J. Lawson. In the exchange of fire, the masked men wounded Harris in the head and neck, then escaped on the horses they had left tied nearby. The sheriffs of San Joaquin, Tulare, and Stanislaus counties joined in the manhunt, spurred on by the joint Wells, Fargo-Southern Pacific reward of $3,000 for the two culprits. As usual, the pursuit was fruitless.

The train robberies motivated public-spirited George Durbrow to urge Wells, Fargo to take new defensive precautions. He suggested that express cars be equipped with tubes projecting through their roofs, enabling guards to fire off skyrockets and parachute flares. These, combined with bombs for noise, and white and blue lights and roman candles, would attract enough lawmen and citizens to discourage holdups. He also recommended that trackmen be armed, and ready to rush by handcar to the brightly lit scene of a robbery. Some newspapers liked the plan; others thought it more entertaining than practical. One suggested, as an alternative to Durbrow's idea, that a searchlight and a Gatling gun be mounted in an armored car at each end of a train. If Hume had any opinion on these schemes, either he kept it to himself or the newspapers failed to mention it. However, the attitude of the editors of the *Express Gazette* was no secret. They called for remedies more stringent and surefire than pyrotechnics. An 1893 editorial, for example, suggested that train robbery be made a capital offense, saying, "Nothing short of hanging will check this growing evil."

Prevailing opinion, which regarded the Daltons as guilty, was upset by the Ceres robbery, which occurred when Grat was in jail and Bob and Emmet were in Oklahoma. (Littleton seems to have been above suspicion.) But Bill Dalton and a crony were arrested and escorted to the Modesto jail by a guard which included Jim Hume. Hume and Thacker then attended a meeting of railroad detectives and local law enforcement officials in the El Capitan Hotel in Merced. After the discussions, railroad dick J. Lawson informed the press of the consensus that the Daltons were guilty. Then he expressed an opinion that was hardly news in the Valley, "The Daltons are well acquainted with the country people here and it will be hard to convict them, if arrested." Bill Dalton protested via the columns of the Fresno *Expositor,* "The truth is, I am like Paddy Miles' boy—no matter what goes wrong, or what depredation is committed, Bill Dalton is always charged with same." Hume and the others were probably barking up the wrong tree, but it cannot be said for certain. To this day the robberies have not been solved to the satisfaction of California historians.

At first, Hume had been moderately optimistic. He wrote Lida from Modesto, "Not making any particular headway in the business but think it will be fixed upon the Dalton outfit." The next day he wrote her his revised opinion: "Bill Dalton and Riley Dean are not the men who robbed, or attempted to rob, the train on the 3d. Bob and Emmet Dalton are the fellows." A lead in Bakersfield turned out a dud and a tip on a contemplated train robbery forced Hume to miss part of Bill Dalton's trial, as he rounded up two good men to ride shotgun on the express car expected to be a target for raiders. But he was able to testify in the trial before heading East on a new case. When one of Hume's fellow detectives, named Devine, identified Bill Dalton as being 120 miles from Ceres at the time of the stickup, the case against him disintegrated. Hardly had the case been dismissed before Bill was rearrested on suspicion of a San Luis Obispo robbery. It was a lucky break because it prevented him from joining his rash brothers in the raid on two banks at the same time in Coffeyville, Kansas. The Kansans cut the Dalton gang to pieces, killing Bob and Grat and seriously wounding Emmet.

Far removed from the San Joaquin Valley, Hume was now in Pennsylvania awaiting extradition papers from California for a suspect in a theft case. He told Superintendent S. D. Brastow of the cooperation he was receiving in the East—"The officers of New Castle are splendid fellows and I think will hold him for a month, if actually necessary." Spring found Hume in Ohio, where he thought he had an open-and-shut case on Wells, Fargo employee H. D. Maize. He wrote Lida, "The Springfield Agent is a thief and stole the $549.36 that is missing." He suspended Maize and told Lida, "While I don't think he can be convicted, I will have him dismissed at all hazards and will recover the loss. Will try to secure a confession as soon as we have gathered all we can against him. . . . Tomorrow, I will give him my final Medicine Talk and if he 'falls down,' I will leave next day for Lima. He is smart and wily but I am now loaded with convincing proof of his financial embarrassments and untruthful statements and will fire them at him in that interview." He also wrote to Wells, Fargo's General Superintendent Colonel Dudley Evans in New York: "I have no misgivings as to the correctness of this opinion but I do not think the evidence of his guilt is in shape to warrant an accusation and arrest. You know how almost impossible it is to get the intricacies of such testimony in the mind of an ordinary juror and, besides, his standing in this city with businessmen and the public is generally good."

By this time, March 4, Hume had convinced the insurance company inspector and the Wells, Fargo route agent, but he faced the disagreement of Superintendent Thomas DeWitt. In fact, he confessed, "I had quite a spat with him and threatened to take my grip and leave the matter in his hands to manage in his own way." Fortunately for Maize, Hume was as honest and thorough as he was stubborn and dogmatic. He kept digging until, to his frank surprise, he uncovered evidence that vindicated DeWitt's opinion and cleared Maize. First, he found a witness who had helped Maize count, package, and forward the missing money; then he determined from a minute examination that the package had been opened, probably in Chicago, and retied, but, this time, by someone who was left-handed. Because Hume had maintained his usual reticence, he had no explaining to do as he performed his discreet about-face. He had given interviews but revealed little, and the Springfield *Gazette* paid tribute to his taciturnity by observing, "Anyone who can get information from Mr. Hume has got to have a stomach pump and chemicals."

Hume's attention was riveted on California once again by a strange, belated outbreak of stagecoach robberies involving murders. From ambush a road agent on April 30, 1892, shot and killed the driver and a woman passenger on the mud wagon running between San Andreas and Sheep Ranch and wounded Wells, Fargo Agent Mike Tovey. Many people suspected Milton Sharp because he was thought to be seeking revenge for Tovey's killing of his outlaw partner in 1880. Hume disagreed and characterized Sharp as an educated gentleman, not a bushwhacker. (Hume also recalled that Sharp had dragged an Oregon boot on one ankle for 12 miles after his Aurora jail escape and had then smashed it with a boulder—the only man Hume had ever known to escape from one of the devices.) Sharp was arrested in Red Bluff, where Hume interviewed him and came away convinced he was innocent. Sheriff Ben Thorn had abandoned the chase when Hume arrived on the scene of the murder, but the open area, devoid of cover for a retreat, plus the spraying of the vehicle with buckshot, suggested to Hume that the job was the work of an amateur who had panicked.

Not long after the state matched Hume's $300 reward and the murdered girl's uncle had added $2,000, two robbers shot and killed Amos Buchanan (Buck) Montgomery, one of

Hume's shotgun messengers, on the Redding-Shasta stage and wounded the driver and a passenger. One outlaw, wounded, was captured. He gave his name as Lee R. Howard, alias Charles Shaw, and said that his partner was Tom Horn. Hume correctly identified him, however, as Charles Ruggles and his partner as his brother John D. Ruggles. When John was wounded and captured in the Opera Restaurant in Woodland in June, he was carrying a rambling confession-cum-autobiography in which he threatened to kill every Wells, Fargo man he encountered on a stage. When the women of Redding began to feel sorry for "the poor boys" and to bring them flowers and cakes and when the defense attorney bragged that he would put the dead messenger on trial, the menfolk of the town lynched the brothers on July 24, 1892. Hume, who had at first been deceived by Charlie's innocent pose—until he learned that he had planned an abortive stage robbery, months before, with Arizona Pete—commented on the lynching: "They deserved their fate. I am very opposed to mob law and would much rather have seen these men legally punished, but their crime certainly was a most atrocious one and they were utterly undeserving of clemency." He added, parenthetically, "Wells, Fargo and Company loses $3,000 by their premature execution, for John Ruggles told me in Woodland that he had bullion to that amount buried somewhere, promising me at the same time that he would tell me later where his treasure is cached. He would probably have told it right there had I held any inducements for him to do so, but I would not make that many promises if the amount were ten times $3,000 and, so, his secret probably died with him."

Another "Dalton" holdup occurred on August 3, 1892, at Rolinda, just out of Collis (now Kerman), about 15 miles west of Fresno. One of the two masked men handed the fireman a bomb and told him to use it to cripple the engine. The new Wells, Fargo express car proved to be a tough nut to crack, dynamite charges on both doorsills only twisting the ironwork and splintering the planking. The holes made by the explosions were too small to enter, but the bomb-happy bandits tossed another missile in through one of them. Wells, Fargo Messenger George D. Roberts, whose shoes had been blown off by the first blast, and shoulder dislocated by the second, was stretched out on the car floor when the bomb, spitting and sparking, skidded across the floor. He leaped to his feet and, like a soccer player, tried to kick it outside but only sent it spinning into a corner. Roberts dived into the opposite corner and covered his head. The explosion dazed him, and he could not stop the bandits from forcing their way in. Even though two men from a threshing crew in a nearby field began to take potshots at the masked men, they took Roberts' keys away from him, after clubbing him with a pistol because he refused to surrender them. They then secured three bags of Peruvian silver coins and a bag of gold from two small safes. When they demanded the combinations of the three large safes lining the wall, Roberts told them that they were time-locked to open only in Kansas City, Chicago, and New York.

The sheriff of Fresno County started a posse on the fleeing bandits' trail toward the Coast Range. Suspicion, at first fixed on Grat Dalton and Riley Dean, then shifted to a pair of brand-new suspects, Chris Evans and John Sontag. Evans was an intelligent, well-read, and reasonably well-liked Canadian. Forty-five years old, he was a farmer and teamster who hired himself out to drive Stockton gang plows (called Yankee fiddlers, locally), Fresno scrapers, and combine harvesters, for other sod-busters. Although he had once worked for the SP, overseeing Chinese trackmen, Evans sympathized completely with the sandlappers. His sidekick, John Sontag, was a thirty-two-year-old New Englander who had been born John Contant but had taken his stepfather's surname. An ex-SP brakeman, he had been injured on the job and then thrown out of the hospital before he was well—at least, that was the way he saw it. When he had asked the company for an easier job than braking, because of his punctured lung, he was given the runaround. As he described it, "They treated me as though I was asking them to make me a present of the road and the rolling stock!" Both men detested the Southern Pacific, which was not unusual in the San Joaquin Valley, but they were more outspoken than most of the monopoly's critics.

When Thacker followed the trail of the Collis bandits almost to Visalia, where Sontag and Evans lived, and when it was learned that both men had been away from home at the time of the robbery, their movements came under close scrutiny. Detectives learned that they had hired a buggy the day before the holdup and had returned it the day after. Also, George S. Sontag, John's brother, began to talk about the robbery, giving many details. When asked to account for his minute knowledge of the affair, he claimed to have been a passenger on No. 17. Southern Pacific Railroad Detective William Smith questioned Chris Evans on August 5, 1892, but did not detain him. He then got George Sontag to go to the sheriff's office to talk to Thacker. Sontag's answers did not satisfy Hume's aide, so Smith decided to go to Chris Evans' house at the north end of Visalia to find John Sontag. He took George Witty, a desk deputy (virtually a clerk) from the sheriff's office, with him. Smith then wired Hume, "I have them." The Wells, Fargo detective, who had been working on a case in Phoenix, naturally assumed that the SP detective had arrested the Collis robbers.

As Smith and Witty tied their team to a post, they saw John Sontag enter the Evans home. Since the front and back doors were open, to let the cooling breeze sweep through, the two officers strode right into the living room without knocking. Eva Evans, Chris' sixteen-year-old daughter, looked up in surprise. Smith said that he wanted to see Sontag. Eva, who had not noticed her father's friend enter, said, "Mr. Sontag isn't here." These few honestly intended words by a young girl embroiled Hume (and Thacker, more so) in a really hot SP war.

Smith said either of two things in reply. He claimed, later, to have merely said, "You are mistaken. I just saw him come in." Just as likely, he blurted out what Eva swore he said—"You're a damned little liar!" According to some Visalians, Witty then called the girl a filthy name.

In any case, Chris Evans came to see what was going on. He entered the back door, picking up a .44 pistol as he did so. He did not examine it but slipped it into a pocket, unaware that it contained only two rounds. Sontag picked up a shotgun and went into the children's bedroom. When Smith pulled aside a portiere, he found Sontag and a shotgun staring him in the face. He went for his pistol. Eva, her father, and Sontag claimed that he fired a shot that went out the open back door. Smith claimed that his buttoned coat got in the way and he was unable to draw. Anyway, he ran outside, followed by Witty. The railroad detective cut through the Evans' tomato patch and got tangled up in the fence, made of strong redwood grape stakes. A charge of birdshot from Sontag's gun stung him in the buttocks. Evans' first pistol shot caught Witty in the shoulder. He fired again and missed, then realized the pistol was empty. Since he was still wearing a carpet slipper on a foot which he had injured with an adz in the Sierra, he gave up the chase. The usually calm Evans was enraged as he told his daughter jubilantly, "I got that son of a bitch!"

Smith and Witty returned to the Evans house with upwards of 100 men, but Chris and John had fled with the sheriff's rig. Whether the two actually had had anything to do with train robbery—or *everything* to do with it—their flight convicted them in the eyes of most San Joaquin Valley lawmen. They were also entered in Hume's criminal dossiers. Had Sontag and Evans stood fast, they would most probably have been let off easily by any jury of their peers that could have been found between Stockton and Bakersfield. But they ran for it.

When Hume arrived in Visalia, he found only George Sontag in jail. The posse had returned, unaware that Chris Evans and John Sontag had simply hidden in a haystack not far from town. That night they returned to Evans' house just as Deputy Sheriff Ben Overall surrounded it. Deputy Oscar Beaver called out, "Who's there? Make yourselves known. We have you covered!" Sontag and Evans answered with gunfire, and Beaver fell, gravely wounded. He died shortly, but his own shots had killed the outlaws' team of horses, and they had to flee on foot. Both men were lame, for Evans' adz wound still bothered him and Sontag had broken his ankle not long before. Still, they gave the posse the slip. Evans led Sontag through oak woods, rough fields, and the syrupy swamps near Yettem called the Buffalo Wallows until the exhausted posse gave up and returned to town. The fugitives holed up in a cave in Blue Mountain, breaking their fast after four days by inviting themselves to a meal at a nearby ranch. By the time a fresh posse was in the hills after them, they had secured from Eva a horse and Petaluma cart, which gave them such mobility that they could dash either to the plains or the Sierra foothills with ease.

Hume and Thacker questioned George Sontag in jail, and on August 7 the two detectives made a thorough search of Evans' barn for hidden booty. They found nothing. Hume let the younger officer lead a Wells, Fargo posse, the third in the field, while he took care of the less strenuous work of following up leads and tips. He did not fail to note that Will Smith, who had started the whole fracas, was unable to recruit men to join him when he tried to head off Sontag and Evans' escape eastward by blocking the Sierra passes. Hume read in the Fresno *Expositor* of August 10, 1892, of Smith's dismal results—"No one would volunteer to go under his leadership, as people had lost all confidence in his methods."

Ten days of searching brought only sore muscles to the men of the three posses. The Fresno paper was no more surprised at the lack of success than was Hume. The newspaper suggested that Sontag and Evans were probably being well supplied with provisions by local friends, of whom they had a large supply, in contrast with the SP, and that "the memories of the Mussel Slough tragedy are too lasting to cause old-timers to rise in arms and assist the railroad company in apprehending the desperadoes." Even Will Smith had to agree, reluctantly, when attempts to bribe valley and foothill folk to betray Evans and Sontag utterly failed. He observed, "Men have been heard to say on the streets of Visalia today that they admired his [Evans'] nerve and hoped he would escape all his pursuers. The Railroad and Wells, Fargo are as heartily detested by these men as Evans is admired. . . . The whole San Joaquin Valley contains a large number of sympathizers. The community is not to be counted on to help the officers or to convict the bandits under any circumstances."

For once, Smith was right. Hume's firm tried to counteract the wave of sympathy for the fugitives by joining the Southern Pacific in offering a reward of $10,000 for the arrest and delivery of the two men. This was a far cry from Hume's customary rewards of $300 for run-of-the-road robbers. The circular blamed Evans and Sontag for only the Pixley, Goshen, and Collis robberies, since Bill Dalton was already in the pokey for the Alila affair. In the public eye, Evans and Sontag were now "officially" branded as the Southern Pacific Bandits.

Even with the large reward offer, Hume saw the case stalemating before his eyes. He gave it a personal boost, however, when he returned to Chris Evans' home at 5 A.M. on August 30. This time, ignoring the barn, he led Thacker and Vernon Coke Wilson over the yard, probing it with long thin iron rods. He was determined to punch holes in the topsoil for a week if he had to. But at a spot where he had been told Evans' wife and daughter often went to hold private conversations, Thacker's probing rod struck something. Two canvas bags were dug up, and in them Hume found 1,700 Peruvian silver coins valued at $1,020. Because Hume had kept his hunch and the search completely secret, hostile segments of the public insinuated that he had planted the currency in Evans' yard. Hume shrugged off the innuendos and continued his relentlesss search for additional evidence.

As the date for George Sontag's trial approached, the usual courthouse square bravos began to shout, "Lynch him!" George decided that it would be safer to part company with Visalia, and started to cut his way out of jail with a file and chisel supplied him by one of his many sympathizers. Although he worked all night, he was lying exhausted on his bunk, staring at the too-small hole in the roof of his cell, when the guard brought him breakfast—and, ironically, a ball and chain to be attached to one ankle. At the trial the Wells, Fargo messenger could not identify George Sontag as one of the Collis robbers. Sontag's attorney tried to shake Hume's testimony about the stolen silver found in Evans' yard, asking why he had left Fresno when the grand jury was in session and desirous of his presence in order to make the search when he did. Hume answered, "Because I had ample time to do it at that time and I went for the purpose of restoring it, for the value of it, for the purpose of restoring it to its owner; too, the further reason of using it as testimony, if necessary."

Coldwell, Sontag's attorney, interjected—"You had waited twenty-seven days. . . ."

"Well, it was immaterial," countered Hume.

But the lawyer bored away at him. "Now then, was there any more reason for hurry or expedition upon or after the 29th of August than there was before?"

"Well," said the detective, "there was a good deal of commotion in Visalia and all men that were available for my purpose were busy and I didn't care to commence the search until I was ready to make it thorough; I didn't want to exhibit my opinion of its being there and make a partial search and go off, for somebody else to avail themselves of my opinion of the matter and [to] continue the search, or any parties interested to remove it during any interval that I might be at it. I was prepared to go there. Wilson and Burke were there. They were honorable men and I went down there and arranged with them, that night, to search the next morning, make a search of the premises thoroughly."

Coldwell could not shake Hume's story, and Jim wrote his wife that the case was almost closed. "Defendant's attorney tells our attorney that he has no hope of even a hung jury. We have a *dead* case and our attorneys say we are certain of a conviction. District Attorney [W. D.] Tupper says it is the best prepared case he has ever tried in the county." It was all circumstantial evidence, but Hume's Peruvian *soles* and Detective William Hickey's testimony of finding in Sontag's trunk clothes matching those worn by one of the Collis robbers were enough, when coupled with George Sontag's criminal record of two years in the Nebraska State Prison, for embezzlement. He was given a life term in Folsom.

Besides the local idlers who were trying to trail Evans and John Sontag, lured by Wells, Fargo and SP blood money and dreams of eternal saloon credit, there was a hardcase from Tucson with some unconventional ideas. He was Vernon C. (Vic) Wilson, the man who had helped Hume find the Peruvian coins. A former Texas Ranger and a defeated candidate for sheriff from Arizona Territory, he brought two Indian trackers with him from Yuma. The two redmen, with black hair streaming down their backs like horsetails, were taken for Apaches, but another Arizona detective working on the case with Hume, Frank Burke, said that they were only Yumas. Wilson and his picturesque associates swaggered about Visalia's streets, bragging about their impending capture of Evans and Sontag. One day, noticing Eva Evans nearby, the loudmouthed Wilson declared, "I've already got twenty-seven notches on my gun and when I get on the trail of Evans and Sontag, there'll be twenty-nine." With those words, he signed his death warrant. For, already, Eva was liaison officer for the outlaws. She fed news to them regularly and quickly sent her father word of Wilson's boast. Wilson did not intimidate Chris Evans in the least; on the contrary, Evans looked forward to meeting him.

Their confrontation occurred far sooner than Hume had anticipated. The Indians were such good trackers that at times they were only an hour behind the fugitives. But Evans was a genius at eluding pursuers, and he and his pal doubled back to Traver while Wilson and the Indians were beating the brush in the foothills to pick up the trail. The two outlaws put up in a stable and, never worried about keeping their general movements a secret, left the hostler a polite little note propped on an upturned water bucket: "We are very sorry to have disturbed you at this

261

time of night, but owing to the urgency of our business and the necessity of our progress, we cannot help it." When the Indians picked up the trail again, it was in the hills 50 miles from Traver, and Hume wondered if the note in the stable had not been planted by some friend of the fugitives to confuse Wilson, Thacker, and the others by suggesting that they had returned to the San Joaquin Valley.

Clinging to the trail now like ticks, the Indians led Wilson from an abandoned camp on Mill Flat Creek, half a mile from the Crabtree place at the north end of Davis Flat, to the little town of Dunlap in Mill Creek Valley and from there toward Evans' old stamping grounds, Sampson's Flat. Along the way Wilson profanely—and vainly—asked for information on "Christ Evans." September 13 found Wilson and his posse approaching Jim Young's clearing, where smoke from the cabin chimney reminded them that it was almost noon and time to eat. They relaxed their watchfulness when they saw E. S. R. Mainwaring, a harmless English neighbor of Young's, carrying a bucket to the spring. What the lawmen did not know was that Mainwaring had been cooking late breakfast for Evans and Sontag in the cabin. He had been sent out by them, not as a ruse but to get him out of harm's way.

When Vic Wilson was 15 feet from the stoop, Sontag yanked the door open and fired his shotgun at him. At the same time Evans stabbed a shotgun through a windowpane and fired at Andrew McGinnis. Wilson fell dead; McGinnis dropped wounded. The Indians fired but were wide of their mark. McGinnis, one of Evans' erstwhile friends, begged for his life, but when Chris turned away in disgust, McGinnis shot the outlaw, grazing his left eyebrow. Evans turned and blew McGinnis' brains out. Sontag had been hit in the upper arm, but Evans gave Deputy Alfred Witty (George Witty's brother) some buckshot and killed another posseman's horse. Dropping his shotgun, Evans swung up his Winchester, which he carried on a sling, military style, and exchanged shots with gutsy Frank (Badman) Burke, the half-breed detective who was not quite ready to call it quits. The battle was soon over. The two outlaws withdrew, over 12 miles of mountain trails, to the Downing ranch, where Sontag holed up for ten days while his arm healed. The badly whipped posse made no immediate attempt to follow them.

Pursuit was resumed by a new posse, starting from Young's cabin. But the Yumas had had a bellyful of California outlaws and had gone home. Mainwaring and other mountain folk were seized, but released. Wells, Fargo and the SP now revised their reward circulars to read "dead or alive." So many reward hunters were scrambling over the Sierra foothills and taking shots at one another by mistake that both Thacker and Burke gave up the hunt in disgust. Thacker was back in Visalia by September 23, to report to Hume. The throng of pursuers could not close with Sontag and Evans, but they did find one of their hideouts. It was a fort that might have defied howitzer fire. Boasting an entrenched rifle pit, it was sheltered by a boulder barricade pierced with loopholes for guns. The fortress, on a mountain slope under an overhanging precipice, was virtually demolished, but the site is still known as Sontag's Point on U.S. topographical maps. Some of the supplies captured there were so old that people leaped to the conclusion that Evans had hidden them there long before, thereby "proving" that he had planned the train holdups well in advance. The fortress impressed Hume as much as it did the general public, but it did not surprise him. His reaction was quoted in several newspapers—"Chris Evans is a remarkable man. He may always be expected to do the unexpected. That is what makes him dangerous.

Hume carefully followed the progress of the pursuit, noting that two men ("unidentified," of course) had bought powder and shot at lonely Sycamore Creek and had borrowed the storekeeper's cartridge-loading tools. Many such tips were worthless, but there was no doubt that Emil Tretten had fed the now-ragged and bushy-bearded pair in Squaw Valley, 10 miles southwest of Sampson's Flat. He reported that his guests had scanned the newspapers with great interest, occasionally cursing the "blood hunters" on their trail. Tretten was "neutral"; he neither informed on the fugitives nor hid the fact of their visit. When he was in Fresno, a few days later, he mentioned his having played host to the outlaws.

Winter closed in on the Sierra Nevada, thinning out the number of searchers as it thickened the snowbanks. Evans and Sontag were snug in their winter hideout under a cliff in Dry Creek's Dark Canyon, 3 miles from the Downing ranch, 1 mile above Cedar Springs and the Hudson Barton lumber mill, and about 300 feet from the road to Evans' old cabin and mining claim, Redwood Ranch. (It is now a storehouse for the Sequoia National Forest ranger station on Redwood Mountain, 9½ miles east of Badger.) The fugitives had a second line of defense in Fort Defiance, ½ mile downstream from the Downings. It was a deep cave, whose mouth was screened by a waterfall when Dry Creek belied its name during the rainy season. Evans hid food, ammunition and even a coal-oil stove behind a wall of fitted rocks which left only a narrow opening into the cave's mouth. Both retreats lay south and east of Camp Badger, near Eshom Valley, and about 15 miles from Sampson's Flat, scoured so often by posses. The relaxed outlaws sent word to Visalia by a lumberman that they had enjoyed a fine Thanksgiving Day dinner at "Camp Manzanita." In their little shack, made of boards from the Hudson Barton mill and papered inside with news stories about their flight, they had put away trout, quail, and wild honey, as well as such staples as bacon and bean soup and canned tomatoes. The outlaws not only wrote out their Thanksgiving menu and sent it to town, but, when Christmas came, they sneaked into Visalia and, incredibly, spent almost two weeks right under the noses of the law.

As winter came, Hume was far from the Sierra, on an investigation that took him to Nashville, Cincinnati, and Louisville, with a new aide, Fred Dodge. Hume was lonely, as usual, but was healthy and strong as a bear, eating eight or nine fresh eggs a day. He was sure that two missing packages of money, totaling $35,000, sent from New York to Galveston, had been looted not on Wells, Fargo's portion of their route of travel but on either the Adams Express Company section or the Southern Express Company line. He told Lida, confidentially, "These two companies are not our sort of people. That is, they would try to fix the responsibility on us even tho' they knew their employee committed the theft, if they thought we could not judicially fix it upon them. We never feel this way." After questioning employees of the two other express companies, he wrote Dudley Evans in New York, "Whoever committed this theft made his preparations knowing that he would have an opportunity to utilize them and only waited until packages containing sufficient value to satisfy his cupidity came into his possession. He knew, too, that he would have sufficient time for the work without danger of interruption or discovery. I can see no place on the route that offered such a safe opportunity as between Cincinnati and New Orleans."

To Lida, Hume wrote, "You can't imagine how completely absorbed I am in this case. I *must* make a success of it or, at least, satisfactorily fix it somewhere. I am already satisfied that the crime was *not* committed on our lines but, of course, may modify or change that opinion, hereafter, upon further investigations." He was very pleased with Thacker's replacement, Fred Dodge, saying of the newcomer from Wells, Fargo's Houston office (though a Californian, like Hume), "Dodge is a nice fellow and is the making of a bright officer. . . . I think he will be a success. We do not disagree in anything and he is delighted at having so much time with me and, of course, I think he will learn points that will be of lasting value to him in his profession."

Called to New York by Colonel Evans, Hume was back in Cincinnati a week before Christmas, reasonably certain that he had his man in Adams Messenger C. A. Hardin of the Cincinnati-Nashville run. Of the thirty-one-year-old, New Orleans-born suspect, he wrote Lida, "He gets $70 salary and keeps pretty full of whiskey, all the time." Hume's long talk with Hardin failed to crack him, and when a reporter from the Cincinnati *Commercial Gazette* asked the Californian his reasons for accusing the man, Hume replied, blandly, "I haven't accused Hardin of anything." Colonel Lew C. Weir of the Adams Express Company agreed, pointing out the fact that Hume and Dodge had investigated every man who had handled the looted packages. Because Hardin had not been in his boardinghouse, all night long, when they were looking for him, their suspicions had naturally become aroused. Hume gave the reporter ample copy, saying, "I am satisfied now that the money left New York all right. In fact, it reached Cincinnati all right and left here all right. When it left the money desk here it was just as it left the bank in New York. Undoubtedly, it was stolen en route and that, too, after it left the Cincinnati office. So much we are sure of after the most careful investigation." What Hume did not tell reporters was that he suspected Hardin because the thief had used a brass handstamp, or seal, made in Louisville—Hardin's hometown—to reseal the packages with wax after looting them and had stuffed the packages with banknote-size pieces of paper and the kind of cardboard used by photographers for packing glass negatives. Hume knew that Hardin had been a photographer before going to work for Adams Express. Finally, the description of the customer, given by the woman who had sold the brass handstamp, fitted Hardin.

The *Commercial Gazette* was impressed with Hume's new aide, describing Dodge flamboyantly as a typical Westerner, with more grit than a grizzly bear and the alertness of a panther. Hume played his own Westerner role to the hilt, too, telling his Ohio audience that Dodge was a dead shot. "He is very, very handy, and I don't think anyone could get the drop on him." Nor were Cincinnati reporters unimpressed with Dodge's chief. They contrasted Hume with the portly and dapper Colonel Weir: "A stocky, grizzled, man whose physique is of the type that a 'scrapper' would call sinewy, strolled slowly about the brilliantly lighted lobby of the Burnet House last night. His dress was loosely worn and hung about him with the free and easy air of a man from the Far West . . . with the air of the Rockies

266

about him and the tan of mountain and plain on his skin. . . . Captain James B. Hume, whose name is known and dreaded by every tough on the Pacific slope of the Rockies and by thousands of amateurs in the same line on the Atlantic side of the same great range. . . . Captain Hume doesn't look like it, but he is. His fame is as broad as the great country over which he has trailed so many stage robbers during the past 35 years."

And the reporters were as impressed with Hume's detective work as with his person. But Hume was discouraged when his carefully built case against Hardin began to crumble. When he sent him to Louisville to be identified by the woman sales clerk, she disappointed Hume. Her words "I can't say whether it is the man or not" blew his case sky-high.

At this time Hume, curiously, tried a bit of politicking, an activity he had avoided for years. From Ohio he drafted a letter to Wells, Fargo President J. J. Valentine and sent it to Lida for proofing and improvements. Hume began: "I write you upon a subject in which I feel considerable interest. Now that the Democratic Party is soon to be the authority, the office of Surveyor of the Port of San Francisco should be filled with a person of first-class detection ability, which has not been the case for 20 years or more. [Wiley J.] Tinnin was a good, honest, and conscientious man but wholly lacking in the necessary detective talent and, therefore, constant scandals emanated from his management of the position, which brought more or less odium on the Party. I think Captain Charles Aull, now Warden of the State Prison at Folsom, is possessed of more native detective ability than any man in the state and has had considerable experience in the exercise of that genius. He is admitted to be the best warden the state has ever had. He is a gentleman of unquestioned integrity and is above average as a man of general information on all current topics. He would like the position and I am satisfied that he could and would fill it with credit to himself, the satisfaction of its patrons, and the administration of the Party. He has been led to believe that you are stronger—and will

267

be more influential with President Cleveland—than any other citizen of the state and he would feel duly grateful should you exert your influence in his behalf."

But Hume's lobbying for his good friend was in vain. Aull did not get the job.

Hume was back on the coast in the spring of 1893 when Evans and Sontag went on the offensive. Hearing that the hated Will Smith was taking a stage from Visalia to Sequoia Mills, the two bandits left their Yokuts Indian friends in Eshom Valley, where they were hunting, and held up the coach on April 29 on a steep grade a mile and a half past Camp Badger. But Smith had changed his plans at the last moment and was not aboard. When a sympathetic passenger asked why they did not flee to Mexico, Sontag told him, "We are not done with this country yet." He added that they had plenty to eat, and although they had no money, neither did they need any. A little later in the year a trap laid at Evans' Visalia house almost caught them on what Hume believed was their eighth trip to visit the folks. But they managed to escape and joked about the incident when they dropped in at Sequoia Mills to have dinner with the lumberjacks there.

A little while later Evans wrote a letter from Fort Defiance to his wife, which was printed in the Fresno *Expositor*. It proved that the charades of the bounty seekers, who posed as surveyors or quail hunters—with telescopes!—did not fool him or Sontag. "One of these days, those 'quail hunters' will make the acquaintance of the buzzards, as we are thoroughly posted in regard to every stranger," wrote Chris. As for the phony surveyors, he said, "Their work is so coarse that if they told it to a mule, he would kick their brains out." He then told his Molly, "We have warned those who are our friends on the quiet to keep out of the woods as we don't want to shoot innocent people. . . . We go where we please and not one of the detectives will enter the house of any man that he knows to be friendly to us. Young's cabin is photographed on their minds." Before he took a fatherly farewell—"Kiss the babies for papa"—he mentioned Hume's assistant, as well as the San Joaquin County sheriff, "Well, Love, we will have happy times yet, in spite of friends Thacker and [Tom] Cunningham."

The progress of the Evans and Sontag case was interrupted for Hume by the third and last of the throwback cases of stage robbery in California. It was the most distressing of the three, to Hume. A lone highwayman, attempting to rob the Ione-Jackson coach on June 15, 1893, shot and killed Hume's old associate Mike Tovey. Moreover, Hume's research soon placed him and his old friend, Amador County Sheriff Ben K. Thorn, at opposite ends of a thorny argument. The murderer had stood behind a buckeye tree near the top of Morrow Grade, half a mile east of Mountain Springs House. The Wells, Fargo messenger of twenty years' service, wounded three times in earlier holdups, never had a chance. The bandit, unmasked but wearing blackface, also creased the driver on the back and wounded two horses of the six-horse team. Once again, Milton Sharp was the favored suspect, and once again, Hume would not buy this explanation, even though Charlie Aull believed that Sharp had finally revenged himself for Tovey's shooting of his confederate many years before. Sharp was picked up, on a tip from an ex-con, in a Red Bluff shoe store. He was unarmed, but there were two guns in his wagon. From his cell Sharp wrote to Hume, who had been keeping tabs on him anyway, to give him a list of names of people for whom he had worked under various aliases since going straight. Hume ran the letter in the papers, hoping to elicit any information he could to clear Sharp.

Jim Hume took Thacker and J. C. Tice to Jackson for Tovey's funeral and then studied the holdup site. Again, he was struck by what a bad choice of terrain it was. Open stubblefield lay on each side, providing no cover for a retreat. Farmers were harvesting nearby. Hume learned, though, that Tovey used to unload his shotgun and relax on this "safe" portion of the run. Perhaps the road agent had known this. Hume's usual dili-

269

gent search produced nothing, yet on July 12 Sheriff Thorn arrested for the crime William Evans—not to be confused with the SP's archenemy Chris Evans—at Cat Camp, in Calaveras County. Evans soon made a full confession, and the case seemed closed except for the formality of the sentencing. Interviewed in Oakland, Thacker was quoted as saying, "I think we have the right man. Evans has been in jail four weeks and we have all been working on him. The first we [he and Hume] heard of the confession was when we read of it in the public print."

Jonathan Thacker should not have spoken for Jim Hume. All along, doubts about William Evans' guilt had been gathering in Hume's mind, even when he had had to discard his own suspects, Ed Morrell and William Simpson, alias John Marshall. When Sheriff Thorn had telegraphed to ask him to join in hunting Evans down, Hume had met him at Burson but refused to chase Thorn's pet suspect. "I have looked into the Evans business," he had told Thorn, "and I know he is not the man. I interrogated the Rooks [a family friendly to Evans] and found that Evans had been with them on the day Tovey was killed." But his arguments had not swayed Thorn, who had a bad case of tunnel vision in respect to the case. Later Hume explained, "Thorn insisted that the Rooks were not telling the truth. . . . Ben laid great stress on the fact that Evans had gone through the county under an assumed name—Gordon, I believe. I understood that, however, for Evans was a fugitive from justice. He had burglarized a cabin and stolen a gun or some such little piece of crookedness. Evans is not much good. He is a petty larceny thief and a worthless fellow, all around. That is one of the facts that work against him in his trial."

Before the trial opened, Hume had become Evans' staunch defender. He knew that it had taken four weeks of sweating to get a confession out of him and that it was a statement anyone could have made, given a sheaf of newspapers about the case. When the suspect later repudiated his confession, District Attorney Richard C. Rust told Hume he agreed with him that Evans was not guilty. Then Rust came to see Hume in San Francisco

270

to tell him that even though he had received a subpoena as a witness for the prosecution, he need not trouble to go up to Jackson. The DA said, "Hume, I'm going to do you a favor. You need not come up to Jackson to testify in the Evans case. I will telegraph you if I want you."

This "favor" stank to high heaven. Hume could hardly believe his ears—and nose—and retorted, hotly: "You don't mean to say that you are going to prosecute the man!"

When he said that he would come up anyway, Rust demanded, "What right do you have to interfere with the officers of the Company?" He insisted on knowing whether Hume was backed by Wells, Fargo in his position on Evans.

The stubborn Hume, ready to lay his job on the line, said no, he was speaking for himself. But, he added, "I will be at the trial to see that the fellow gets a square deal. . . . I will not stand idly by and see an innocent man railroaded to the gallows."

In the courtroom Hume took a chair next to the defendant's attorney, to the obvious annoyance of the district attorney, who asked, acidly, if Hume had enrolled himself as assistant counsel for the defense. When Hume rose to explain, Judge John F. D. Davis cut him off. No one but an attorney could address the court. His Honor mildly reprimanded the DA by saying that Hume had a right to sit anywhere he chose. Although defense attorney Diovol B. Spagnoli offered to address the bench in Hume's behalf, the detective, angered, declined with thanks and stalked out of the courtroom. He refused to enter again, unless by mandate of the court.

Back in San Francisco, Hume decided to address the press since he had not been allowed to address the bench. On October 25 he gave reporters an earful, telling them, flatly, that Evans was not guilty and that his prosecution amounted to persecution. "I was in Jackson all last week. I returned yesterday. I met with such treatment that I could not, in justice to myself, remain in the courtroom. I never spoke to a witness during the trial, nor to Evans but merely suggested a few questions to Mr.

271

Spagnoli. The District Attorney raised a row about it and I left."
He told the newsmen that Evans' so-called confession had been
secured by filling him full of opium and whiskey and by intimi-
dation. A blacksmith had been brought into his cell to rivet leg
irons on the poor, confused ne'er-do-well. Then Sheriff Thorn
had used a fellow prisoner to pump him for incriminating information. When this failed, he had put Constable Masterson in
the cell, posing as a jailed woodchopper. This, too, had failed,
so Thorn, according to Hume, had forged a letter from Annie
Rooks and faked clippings from the Amador *Ledger* to convince Evans that his friends the Rooks' had betrayed him. Hume
told the reporters, "I am not taking Evans' statement for this,
at all. The Sheriff told me of these doings, himself, and seemed
very proud of them as specimens of the sharp work he had done
to get the confession. Neither am I taking Evans' statement for
the fact that he was under the influence of liquor and drugs
when he made his statement. He was supplied with all the whiskey he wanted and they also gave him opium although, up to
that time, he had never had the opium habit." Furious and
vengeful, Evans then had signed a confession, said Hume, in order to implicate the Rooks, whom he thought guilty of treachery. Thorn had made it easier by promising Evans that he would
never hang if he signed a confession.

"Sheriff Thorn is, as you know, a very popular man in that
part of the state," Hume continued. "People up that way have
so much confidence in him that they are very likely to adopt
his views. Altogether—the Sheriff's popularity, Evans' bad
character, and the fierceness of the prosecution will, I fear, result in this man's conviction of a murder I am more than certain he did not commit. I was, of course, very much surprised
when I heard that Evans had confessed the murder. When I
learned how that confession was obtained, however, I was sure
there was no truth in it."

Hume's doubts were not prompted entirely by the inconsis-
tencies of Evans' confession and the means Thorn employed to
extract it. He had noted that Evans, when driven over the Ione-

Jackson stage road, had not had the foggiest notion of where the holdup and murder had taken place. But even without this supporting evidence, Hume was sure that Evans had been prompted and coached into learning a "confession" from newspaper articles supplied him along with whiskey and opium. As he told the newspapermen: "One thing, in particular, that makes me certain of this is the statement about the burned grass at the foot of the buckeye tree which shielded the murderer when he shot the messenger. In the newspaper account of the affair, the statement was made that the road agent must have waited for some time by the tree, for he had burned the grass in order that his tracks would not show. This statement is repeated in Evans' confession. He says he burned the grass to get blacking for his face. As a matter of fact, the grass was burnt by the District Attorney and the officers of the County when they were looking for the shells from the murderer's Winchester. They told me so."

Hume, indentured to his sense of justice, could not contain his sense of outrage. "Measures have been resorted to in order to procure evidence against him that have never been employed since law and justice pretended to be interchangeable terms. Yet Evans is as surely innocent of the murder of the Wells, Fargo and Company's messenger as Grover Cleveland is." By now Hume had convinced his superiors of the correctness of his stand, and he spoke for them, as well as for himself: "You can imagine that the Company is more eager to punish Tovey's slayer than anyone else and if I believed this man to be guilty, nobody would work harder for his conviction than I. But, in this case, so convinced are we of his innocence that the Company offered to employ an expert criminal lawyer to defend him. His attorney would not permit this and there is nothing to do now but wait. If he is convicted, the case will be appealed to the Supreme Court or the facts will be brought to the Governor's attention and he will be asked to pardon Evans."

The detective reminded the reporters that Thorn, after jailing Evans' friends Mr. and Mrs. Rooks, had had to release them for lack of evidence. He reminded them that Evans had recanted his confession. He told them that Thorn had promised the Rooks' $500 if they would swear that Evans had not been at their house at the time of the holdup. But while he was testifying in absentia, the trial went on in Jackson. Witnesses placed Evans both near the scene of the crime at the time of the holdup and far away at the Rooks' place. To the DA's chagrin, a star witness for the prosecution retracted his earlier testimony against Evans, terming it a lie and admitting that Thorn had promised him $100 for it. Although Rust managed to show that Thorn was willing to pay witnesses only for "the truth," the *Chronicle* observed that "the testimony of money overtures produced a painful impression." The Rooks' reiterated the testimony of earlier witnesses, that Evans had been working in a field of their property, hoeing corn, at the time of the crime. Mrs. Rooks also mentioned that Evans' rifle was a .44 (Tovey had been shot with a .45) and when the DA tried to get the sheriff off the hook for offering her and her husband money to testify "properly," she snapped, "He *did* ask me to tell the truth but at the same time he did not mean it. I *told* him the truth—that Evans was home, June 14th and 15th."

Hume had something to say about the prosecution witnesses, particularly the stage driver, DeWitt C. Radcliff: "The driver almost positively identified Evans as the man who shot Tovey. He describes his appearance and his clothes and says that between the time the man rose by the roadside and the firing of the first shot, he took in all the details of his face, noted the color of his eyes, and recognized that the rifle was of larger calibre than .44. On the witness stand, he said this space of time was probably two seconds. The murderer's face was blackened and his hat pulled over his eyes. But in those two seconds, stage driver Radcliff says he made all those observations. I say that is impossible. There is not a man on earth who, in two seconds' time under such circumstances, could note the color of a man's eye and the calibre of his rifle."

The scrupulous Wells, Fargo detective kept hammering away at Rust and Thorn in his own trial by publicity: "That man is as innocent of the murder of Mike Tovey as I am." When a *Chronicle* reporter asked, "But if he is innocent, why are they trying so hard to convict?" Hume pondered a minute, then said: "I can't answer that. I have known Ben Thorn for thirty-three years and I believe he is a thoroughly conscientious man. ʻ. . . I think he has worked himself up to the belief that Evans is guilty and is doing everything in his power to secure a conviction. He will probably succeed. At the second interview I had with Thorn, I informed him that I was convinced of Evans' innocence. He was convinced to the contrary, and there we parted. . . . Why is he being persecuted so strongly? Evans is a worthless character and has been guilty of a number of offenses. For that reason, a good many people think it would be nothing amiss to hang him for the crime he never committed. At least, I was told that up there."

When a reporter asked him if Evans was an imbecile, as some said, Hume shook his head: "No, he is not very bright but he is perfectly responsible for his acts. He is not a very desirable person to have around, for several reasons, but he never killed Mike Tovey. His own confession—the one exacted from him in prison —ought to convince anyone that he is innocent. It carries the evidence of its own falsity. They had placed Evans in a cell, sent him forged letters and given him opium and whiskey until he made a confession of guilt. Even if this confession were not found of a worthless character, the manner in which it was obtained is enough to discredit it. After I had washed my hands of the Evans business, stories were published on the jealousy and incompetence of Hume, Thacker, and other detectives of Wells, Fargo and Company. It has been asserted that my expressed belief in Evans' innocence and the refusal of the Company to prosecute was due to a desire to save the $300 reward the Company has offered. Why, we offered to hire James H. Budd of Stockton [later, Governor of California] to assist in the defense but the attorney appointed by the court to defend Evans declined any assistance. He is a young man who thinks well of himself and was determined to manage the case his own way. . . . Mr. Spagnoli, though an able man in civil cases and loyal to his client, has had little experience in the criminal branch of the law."

Asked again if he thought that Evans would be convicted, Hume had to nod an affirmative. "I rather think so. The prosecution is strong and determined while the defense is weak. Ben Thorn is practically conducting the prosecution and he thinks he must secure a conviction. Evans is a bad character and without friends or money while Thorn has a host of friends who will take his side of the case without taking any trouble to investigate." His anger rising, Hume added, "I tell you, it is infamous. The prosecution is simply an effort to hound an innocent man to death. I am not going up there again, however. I was almost bounced out of court when I was there. I have done what I could."

Hume's prediction of William Evans' conviction came true. In just three hours, on March 18, 1894, the jurors returned a verdict of guilty, dashing Hume's last hope that disagreement would result in a hung jury.

The San Francisco press had favored Hume's view in the quarrel. Some papers, like the Stockton *Independent,* were neutral or, at least, objective. The *Independent* guessed that Hume was defending Evans not only to prevent a man from being railroaded but also to avoid wrecking the case against the *real* killer, should he be caught.

Sheriff Thorn did not attempt to rebut Hume publicly until more than six months after Jim's emotional outburst. The lawman's excuse for the long delay was that unlike Hume, he had not cared to inflame public opinion while the trial was on. The Calaveras *Weekly Citizen* of San Andreas was Ben Thorn's mouthpiece. On May 5, 1894, it ran a long, self-vindicating statement by him which purported to present the stubborn facts and to give the lie to Hume's claims. The editor headlined Thorn's apologia thus: "WELLS, FARGO & CO.'S SPECIAL AGENT

276

SHOWN UP IN HIS TRUE COLORS. EVERY STATEMENT MADE BY HUME IN THE INTERVIEW PUBLISHED IN THE SAN FRANCISCO EXAMINER OF OCT. 25, 1893 PROVEN TO BE A MALICIOUS FALSEHOOD."

Thorn stated that the proof against Evans had been as plain as the midday sun. Against it, Hume had been able to offer only imaginative brainwork, with the object of belittling and misrepresenting the officers prosecuting "the arch assassin." His motive? Mercenary (somehow). Thorn tried valiantly to explain away all of Hume's charges but had to admit to many of the actions cited by the detective. He had given Evans opium and whiskey—but only a little. Yes, he had sneaked a constable in the guise of a jailed woodchopper into Evans' cell. No, he had not hired another prisoner to spy on Evans; the fellow had taken notes voluntarily and offered them to him. He labeled a lie Hume's charge that he had promised Evans that he would never hang if he confessed. He stressed the physical evidence against Evans—largely his pipe, found near the murder site on the day *before* the atrocity.

After reproving Jim Hume for his "low, contemptible, cunning," Thorn reassured his audience that "that kind of nonsense and sophistry won't work in this enlightened age." He admitted printing false clippings to fool Evans into thinking Mrs. Lou Rooks, his friend, had made some kind of confession as an accessory to Evans' murder of Messenger Mike Tovey. Incredibly, the sheriff excused this action by stating that Evans had asked if there were such stories in the press and had requested to see them, if they existed. Asked Thorn, rhetorically, "Would any innocent man have made the request he did?" According to the sheriff, when Evans saw the falsified clippings, he gasped and said, "My God, I'm gone! The dirty bitch has given me away! She has told it all. It was a big game and they have played their hands and it will be my turn next. I will have to hang for it, but they will have to suffer with me. I will tell the truth about what has been going on there for years."

Thorn also conceded that he had forged a letter in response

to a note that Evans had sent to Frank Rooks. Supposedly from Frank's daughter Annie, it upset the prisoner so much that he cried, "It is so. The dirty son of a bitch has gone back on me. I have done it and will tell the truth about it all." The sheriff justified his clapping irons on Evans in his cell because he was a dangerous murderer who later unbolted his irons with his belt buckle and grappled with the sheriff of Amador County in an escape attempt. In answer to others of Hume's "venomous" paragraphs, Thorn denied that any newspapers had been allowed in Evans' cell. As for the prisoner's inability to identify the murder site, Thorn lamely said that on a second passage of the site, he had halted the wagon and Sheriff Gregory of Amador County had demanded of Evans if it were not the site. Evans— naturally—said yes.

Hume had accepted the testimony of Frank and Lou Rooks and their daughter that Evans had been far from the murder site at the time of the shooting. Thorn called all the Rooks' "liars." Still, he had to admit having offered Mrs. Rooks $500— but only to tell the truth and nothing but the truth.

Thorn shot all his bolts in the newspaper story, trying to blacken Hume's character with innuendo and accusation at the same time that he made lightly veiled threats of future noncooperation with Wells, Fargo's detectives in order to intimidate Hume's superiors. First, he claimed that Hume had bearded a friend of his in front of Tam's Saloon in Jackson and had boasted: "Ben Thorn shall never convict this man. I will spend a thousand dollars before he shall do it. I've got enough influence with the Supreme Court to keep him from hanging Evans or sending him to the State Prison for life. And even if they do send him for life I'll get him out inside of one year." Then Thorn suggested that Hume was a coward: "Why should Hume taunt me with my pride in the performance of duty when I did not so much as envy him of the pride he took in remaining in safety in the hotel in Visalia while Sontag and Evans were engaged in slaughtering brave Oscar Beaver at the outskirts of that place; neither can he accuse me of envying him in the pride he took in hand-ing over his two fancy six-shooters to an impudent road agent while in Arizona, a few years since." Finally, Thorn (who had tried to prevent Hume's attending the trial by wiring company president Valentine—"Will Wells, Fargo permit such a course?") brought up the matter which weighed on Hume's mind as much as Valentine's but which the former, with his characteristic—and, often, annoying—sense of righteousness, dismissed. "Wells, Fargo and Company . . . can ill afford to lose the friendship and active cooperation of the local officers through the wilful course pursued by their Special Officer. . . ."

In the long run, Hume's losing battle ended in a triumph. But it was too late to matter to the detective. The September 16, 1907, San Francisco *Call* headlined a story "INNOCENT MAN WILL GO FREE AFTER 13 YEARS" and subheaded it "Proof That Wm. Evans Was Railroaded to San Quentin." The story, embarrassing to officials, was extremely hazy, its details having apparently been suppressed. But the *Call* reported that Judge John F. D. Davis, who had sentenced Evans, now declared him innocent because "one of his prosecutors made a deathbed confession to railroading the forgotten man." Absolute, convincing proof of innocence, however, was still lacking—the kind of proof demanded by the state prison directors—even though the *Call* reported on October 20, "Liberty Looms Near Convict Wm. Evans." Hume's old aide Jonathan Thacker then intervened as a kind of proxy for Hume and resumed the fight to free Evans after more than a dozen years. Finally, on December 29, 1909, three years and five months after Hume's death, the pathetic logger and handyman and four-time loser was paroled. Evans did not live long to enjoy the freedom that Hume had known he deserved; he died, after a Los Angeles streetcar accident, on March 23, 1910.

From Amador County and William Evans, Hume turned his attention during the summer of 1893 to his friend Charlie Aull's Folsom Prison. Aull was tipped off that an attempt to spring George Sontag would be made, but he did not know how or when. Incredibly, Chris Evans and John Sontag were arranging the break from their Sierra hideout. Through Eva they got an ex-con named William Fredericks, alias Johnson, to smuggle guns into the prison rock quarry. On June 27 George Sontag saw the chalk mark on the water tower, signaling that the pistols were in place. He made his break with some pals, but three prisoners were killed in the ensuing melee and two, including Sontag, wounded and retaken. A few weeks later, from his prison hospital bed, he offered to make a confession—but only to Jim Hume and J. B. Wright, the division superintendent of the Southern Pacific Railroad. Hume and Wright went to Folsom with a professional stenographer and heard Sontag out. He confessed to having planned the Ceres holdup with his brother John, telling Hume that Evans had substituted for him when he was unable to get to California to play his part. He told the detective that he and John had held up a train at Western Union Junction near Chicago, in November, 1891, and had made an attempt on another at Kasota, Minnesota, before all three of them carried out the Collis robbery.

Hume's enemies—and he was never without them—immediately cried, "A deal!" and compared George Sontag's confession to poor William Evans'. Chris Evans flatly refused to believe that his pal's brother had peached. He called it a "julep" and a pack of lies. According to an *Examiner* correspondent who visited Chris, "He believed it was a scheme gotten up by Jim Hume to get him [George Sontag] to say something and convict himself and announced that he would add another class to his classification of criminals, for railroad detectives." Exactly what had Hume promised George Sontag? In Hume's words, he had assured the prisoner, "Anything you say to us in this interview, of the crimes in which you have been a participant, shall not be used against you. . . . Just tell us whatever you feel like saying. I am anxious to know of your connection with Chris Evans, when you first made his acquaintance, and all your criminal transactions and social relations with him and your brother, John."

In spite of young Sontag's confession, Hume saw public opinion, more and more, shifting in favor of the embattled outlaws. Only the Visalia *Daily Times* excoriated the "heartless murderers." William Randolph Hearst, then of rather liberal persuasion, was fighting the Southern Pacific with his San Francisco *Examiner*, called the "Eczema" by the pro-SP crowd. He got his star writer, Ambrose Bierce, to say some kind things about Evans and Sontag in his "Prattle" column. Warming up for a period of yellow journalizing, Hearst next ran a fake interview with the outlaws by the flamboyant poet Joaquin Miller. The big story—also labeled a hoax but never proved so—was an exclusive interview with Sontag and Evans by *Examiner* reporter Henry D. (Petey) Bigelow, which appeared on October 7, 1892. The reporter was understandably secretive about the circumstances, but Hume learned that the meeting had probably taken place in John Coffee's mountain home near Centerville, to which Evans' friend S. Clark Moore had guided the newsman. Bigelow came away not only impressed with the courage of the hunted men, but convinced of their innocence.

Both Evans and Sontag told Bigelow that they had committed no train robberies, and they pleaded self-defense for their violent actions. Said Evans, "As to the killings we have done, it seems to me it has been a pretty good riddance for the County of the so-called 'badmen.' Take Oscar Beaver. He killed sheepman Kripe near Lemoore in cold blood and, another time, he shot a fellow in the Laurel Palace Saloon in San Francisco. As for Andy McGinnis, he shot a young Negro lad who was sleeping in a boxcar at Modesto and was concerned in the whitecaps business there. I never kept track of Vic Wilson's graveyard but everybody always knew that he was terribly dangerous." Evans' hatred was strongest for railroad Detective Will Smith, but he lumped Hume's adjutant, Johnny Thacker, into the group of whom he said, "I wouldn't leave one of them alive. They deserved to be born dead." He challenged Thacker and Smith to take him.

When Bigelow heard that the SP was pressuring the governor

to call out the militia to round up Evans and Sontag, he personally protested. Hume bore some grudging respect for Sontag and Evans, but he was *not* convinced that they were innocent of the SP robberies. Interviewed in San Francisco after Bigelow's story broke, he said, "I see they claim ability to prove alibis enough to clear them. We would like to give them an opportunity to try it. There is no doubt that Evans and Sontag wrecked the train and Tupper, the District Attorney there, says we can fully establish their guilt." After reminding reporters of the Peruvian coins he had dug up in Evans' yard, Hume added, "All the circumstantial evidence strongly points to these outlaws—their flight and defensive action. . . ."

The law finally caught up with Evans and Sontag on June 11, 1893, at the battle of Stone Corral, in the Sierra Nevada foothills, some 18 miles from Chris' Visalia home. Thacker had wired U.S. Marshal George E. Gard to join in the pursuit, and he fitted up a posse of some pretty hard *hombres,* including Detective Tom Burns and Tresno Deputy Hi Rapelje. Tipped by a false friend of Evans' that he and his partner were heading for Stone Corral via Wilcox Canyon, the posse tucked itself away in the vacant Billy Bacon cabin near the corral as its leader prepared the trap. That Sunday evening the Young's cabin situation was ironically reversed. The outlaws walked up to the building completely unaware that the possemen were inside. Fred Jackson shot Evans at short range but only creased his back. The plucky outlaw crawled behind a pile of hay and manure, where Sontag joined him. They put a volley into the cabin and shattered Jackson's ankle when he crawled around in an encircling movement. But Sontag was hit in the right arm, and Evans' left arm was smashed, his right arm less badly wounded. Next, Rapelje shot Chris Evans in the face, knocking out his right eye. Another bullet shattered Sontag's shoulder and pierced his lung. The two outlaws were being cut to pieces in their flimsy cover; some 100 to 130 shots were fired in all.

An almost helpless Sontag urged his partner to make a run for it in the dark. Evans took off and, miraculously, managed to cover seven miles through the brush before holing up in the Perkins cabin in the Elderwood area of Wilcox Canyon. The posse was not too anxious to follow him closely but stood guard over Sontag all night. At daybreak the officers captured him, so far gone that he had failed in two attempts to shoot himself in the head. Then the men followed Evans' trail of blood until it vanished, as if into thin air. Soon, however, Evans sent word that he was ready to surrender, if Mrs. Perkins would get the reward. (She had agreed to use some of the money to help Evans' wife.) Fresno and Tulare county officers raced each other to the cabin to make the arrest, and Under Sheriff Fred Hall of Tulare County won. On June 13, 1893, the long manhunt ended and, with it, supposedly, the Southern Pacific war. Hume turned his attention, that summer and fall, to more humdrum cases in such cities as Bakersfield and Medford, Oregon.

As Evans, in prison, was recovering from his wounds and the amputation of his arm, he toyed with plans for breaking out. To raise money for his defense, his wife and daughter had joined the cast of a popular melodrama, *The Collis Train Robbery*. John Sontag died of his wounds in the Fresno jail on July 3, 1893, but Evans was brought to court on November 20 to stand trial, not for train robbery, but for the murder of Wilson and McGinnis at Young's cabin. On December 4 he heard the verdict—guilty. While waiting for his sentence, which he knew would be life, Evans got Eva to recruit a man to replace Sontag. She persuaded Ed Morrell, an ex-con who had been suspected by Hume of Mike Tovey's murder, to smuggle a gun into her father's cell in the Fresno jail on December 28. In jig time Evans and his new confederate were lost in the hills.

Hume had warned, earlier, "Chris Evans is a remarkable man. He may always be expected to do the unexpected. That is what makes him dangerous." How right he was. Now, thoroughly disgusted with the leaky jails of the San Joaquin Valley, Hume announced that Wells, Fargo and the SP had spent $30,-000 and three lives on the pursuit of Evans but would spend no more. The capture of Chris and Morrell would be up to Sheriff

Jay Scott of Fresno County—from whose jailer brother Evans had escaped. Asked by reporters who was to blame for Evans' escape, Hume gave a surprising answer—"the [court] stenographers. You remember that Grat Dalton was arrested for train robbery and convicted in Tulare County. The judge set the date for passing sentence and five or six of us detectives, knowing that effort might be made by the gang to liberate him, happened to be in Visalia the day sentence was passed, intending to return to San Quentin on the same train in order to be on hand if the attempt was made. Well the case was adjourned because the stenographer [court reporter] had not transcribed his notes and the sentence was postponed about four weeks. The stenographer and his assistant came down to San Francisco and got a lot of printed matter used in evidence, which was easier than reading his notes to the typewriter [typist], sent that back home and the two went off on a fishing trip to San Luis Obispo County. This gave Dalton's friends time to plot his escape and before the date set for sentence, he was out and gone and all our time and money was wasted. Now, look at the Evans case and you will find that, again, the stenographer did not have his notes written up, the time for sentence was postponed and—you know the rest."

Popular sentiment had not changed, in either valley or hill country; when the posse chasing Evans and Morrell tried to recruit volunteers in Sanger, they got not a single man. The sheriff followed the fugitives up the lumbering flume toward Hume Mills and picked up their trail at the mouth of the lower Kings Canyon. He even found their blankets and Morrell's ivory-handled British .44 bulldog revolver. Scott closed in on them at Pine Flat and was only a jump behind them when Newt Demaster rowed the fugitives over to the south bank of the Kings River, north of Centerville, the old village of Kings River. He was again on their heels when Evans gave him the slip and made a complete fool of him by doubling back to the San Joaquin Valley. He and Morrell rented a room in the Arlington Hotel in Visalia; then Morrell held up a store and the SP station in Fowler, between Fresno and Visalia, on January 11, 1894, in order to refinance their flight.

The trail of Evans and Morrell, which had temporarily grown cold, suddenly heated up when two deputies overran the pair in Slick Rock Canyon 7 miles west of Camp Badger and 15 miles from Sampson's Flat. No one was killed in the shoot-out, but the deputies did not halt their retreat until they hit Reedly, 25 miles away. Near Slick Rock, Fresno County Deputy William Henry got on their tracks and followed the pair through the snow to Evans' old hideout, Camp Manzanita, near Badger. Henry got the drop on the fugitives, fired, and grazed Evans' scalp. The bandits fled through a crevice in the rocks, and the lawmen made no attempt to follow as dusk slid down the mountainside. The next day, after taking the precaution of filling the cabin with lead, Henry searched, then burned it after finding not only the outlaws' supplies and ammunition but their blankets and coats and Evans' artificial arm. But even without warm clothing, Evans and Morrell lost their pursuers during a blizzard near Eshom Valley. While the lawmen retreated to town, the outlaws took refuge with their Yokuts Indian friends. Later they got supplies at the Downing ranch but had a rough winter, even though friends like Mainwaring took them in for short periods.

Hume realized that it would take more than blizzards and missing arms to whip Chris Evans. But where honest efforts failed, treachery succeeded. Someone, perhaps the cripple J. V. Brighton, who now rented the Evans' home and cared for Chris' children while Molly and Eva were appearing in *The Collis Train Robbery*, leaked a message to Evans that one of his younger children was ill. This was followed by another, more urgent note, which suggested that the child was near death. No one was ever low enough to claim credit for this stratagem, but the Los Angeles *Times* attributed it to "Detective Brighton," while the San Francisco *Chronicle* identified Brighton as a decoy hired by U.S. Marshal George Gard. Eva, however, always blamed her uncle, Perry Byrd, whom she also accused of betraying Sontag and her father into the Stone Corral trap.

285

Evans came to visit his child on February 19, 1894, and at the proper time Sheriff Kay surrounded the house. He then paid a poor boy of the town $1 to take a message in to Evans. After a brief exchange of notes Evans and Morrell came out, saying, "Our word is good. We surrender to you. There are our guns."

They were locked in the same cell from which Grat Dalton had escaped, while the usual lynching threats were heard in the Visalia saloons. Kay rushed them to the Fresno jail for safety, ahead of a mob that abandoned pursuit only a few miles out of Visalia. At 1:30 A.M. on February 20, Evans arrived in Fresno, and at 10 A.M. he heard his sentence—life imprisonment for the murder of Vernon Coke Wilson. Later Morrell was given an equal sentence, although he was guilty only of highway robbery. Judge M. K. Harris was so nervous that he first intoned to Evans, "The judgment of this court is that you, Christopher Columbus be confined in the State's prison. . . ." Even Evans had to laugh at the slip.

The Sontag and Evans war against the SP was finally over, although Hiram Johnson, another foe of the Octopus, did not parole Chris Evans until 1911. He died on February 2, 1917, already a legendary figure in California history. Morrell served nine years before being pardoned. He became a lecturer and writer in behalf of prison reform, and the prototype of Jack London's protagonist in *The Star Rover*.

Grudgingly, Hume came to respect Evans and even Morrell, but particularly John Sontag. When he had interviewed George Sontag after his Folsom break attempt, Hume had voiced his judgment of John: "I guess your brother was a pretty good 'stayer,' wasn't he?" When George had answered, "I guess he would defend himself as well as he could. I don't suppose he would quit like a cur," Hume had volunteered, "I have never known a man to be wounded so badly and in the physical condition that he was [in], at Stone Corral, and never utter a word or sound in regard to his pains. It struck me that he was a most heroic sort of a man—one of extraordinary nerve."

CHAPTER XI

———— ✦ ————

END OF THE TRAIL

A S 1890 ushered in the last decade of the nineteenth century, Hume and Thacker were in Texas on the Bangs express robbery case and several Wells, Fargo embezzlements. Because Thacker was suffering acutely from rheumatism, Hume sent him home, thereby extending his own "exile" in the Southwest, although he was dreadfully tired and complained to Lida that "these midnight arrivals and departures break me all up." Of Thacker, he said, "He is a first-rate worker and is guided in all his doings by duty, and does it cheerfully. He is a little over-vain, but I like him and when he is convinced that his theories are wrong, quits quite peacefully." By rights, Hume thought, he or Thacker should have spent six months in Texas. He wrote home, "I think *now* the management will see the necessity of having a Special Officer in this region. . . ." (They did, finally, and posted Fred Dodge to a regional agency, in Houston.) "The service in Texas is in a terrible, demoralized condition. The $7,000 lost at Beaumont; the $13,000 loss; the $1,350 loss; and several other small losses have been committed by our own employees and the chance to discover the thieves and recover the money is slim. To get testimony to warrant a conviction is the trouble and, even then, we might not be able to recover the money." Hume found that even Superintendent Andrew Christeson of the Southern Division was disheartened. "He is a clever man and I like him but he expects too much from me. But we get along together nicely." Hume was receiving excellent cooperation from Dallas lawmen and others, as he wrote Lida: "I never in my life, since my connection with Wells, Fargo and Company, have been treated better than while here. All the bank officials and all businessmen with whom I come in contact have treated me splendidly. There are a dozen banks in town and I have become acquainted with the managers of nearly all of them. The two other express companies, too, treat me in a like polite manner. . . . A large percentage of the population of this city are Northern people and I get along with them better than with Southern men."

Hume was pretty sure that he had picked up leads on the right men in the Bangs, Texas, robbery and the other cases. "I will not take the time to give you, in detail, the reasons for these opinions," he told Lida, "but you know that I am almost always right in my opinions." He was as disgusted by the carelessness of Dallas' honest Wells, Fargo employees as he was by the thieving of its dishonest workers. "If Nichols, the Cashier, had been at his post on time that morning, no loss would have occurred," he growled to his wife. But he reserved his severest criticism for Dallas Agent E. D. Peevey, who had left a box with $13,000 in it on the floor; it was stolen in his absence. "The head of the office at 12:30 blacks his shoes, takes his umbrella, and starts for dinner. . . . He had more regard for his belly than he had for the safety of Wells, Fargo treasure and I can see no reason why he should not be held for the whole amount." Hume discarded suspects, one by one, until only the porter, Solomon, was left. "No outsider stole the box in question. Sol could have stolen it without the knowledge or cooperation of any other employee; no other employee could have stolen it without the knowledge and cooperation of some fellow employee. If it should be established that he is innocent, I would be completely at sea and without a resemblance of an opinion as to who the thief is. . . ."

Sol confessed to taking the box, but he insisted that he had not opened it and refused to take officers to it until they guaranteed him that his indictment would be dismissed. The prosecuting attorney finally promised this to Sol's attorney (hired, ironically, by Hume for Wells, Fargo). Hume left the case to the Dallas officials and proceeded to Black Hawk, Mississippi, to secure evidence on his prime suspect in the Beaumont theft. For once, a train trip proved to be a tonic for him. The coaches en route to New Orleans were full of jolly Mardi Gras celebrants; the weather was delightful; the markets were full of fresh vegetables, the oaks in leaf, and the locusts in full bloom.

Later trips that year were not so pleasant, although Hume liked Denver in May—"I found myself in a city of 130,000 inhabitants, and as pretty as a picture"—for he got several colds, and his gouty foot troubled him so much that he had to wear a soft slipper instead of a shoe. That fall he developed a sore lip and had to give up chewing tobacco. From Chicago, where he was working on a case with Bill Pinkerton of the famed Pinkerton Detective Agency, he wrote Lida in September, "Haven't had a chaw since Ogden. . . . Pretty severe struggle but I guess I'll make it. You know, when I quit chewing before, I smoked *incessantly, so that* was no effort at all." By early October he could write, "Lip entirely well. But the struggle unfits me for business." This was not entirely true, for he also wrote Lida, "You would see in the papers this morning (October 16, 1890) that I got my man." Hume was referring to *the* big case of 1890, as far as he was concerned, and one of the major cases of his career—the arrest of Charles H. Thorne.

On Wednesday afternoon, October 15, 1890, on Chicago's West Side, Hume settled an old score when he, with the help of Pinkerton detectives, caught San Quentin lifer and escapee Thorne and his sidekick, George H. Shinn, alias Joe Thompson. Thorne, particularly, was an old "friend"—Hume had worked on the November, 1879, Cummings murder case that had sent him to the pen. Thorne, who had been using the aliases Charles Dorsey, Charles Moore, and George H. Lee, was hiding out in

Chicago as a rug cleaner—and, Hume was sure, a burglar. He also thought that Thorne and Shinn had been in on several recent Pacific Coast stage robberies and perhaps the train robbery at Pixley, California. Reporters for the Chicago *Inter-Ocean* paid tribute to the way "an important double arrest was very skillfully and quietly effected" by Hume, described by them as "a white haired, kindly-faced old gentleman, as far removed in appearance from the traditional detective as can well be imagined." Although Hume insisted, "I hate detective stories like poison, and this is not much of a story, anyhow. . . ," the newsmen let him tell it his way. They just slapped a little copy of their own around Hume's account and ran it, verbatim, in the *Inter-Ocean*. In so doing, they gave Hume the opportunity to clarify the details of Thorne's San Quentin escape of 1887 and also to explain the curious circumstances that had allowed Thorne, alias Dorsey, to receive only a life sentence when he had actually shot Cummings to death, while his accomplice, Patterson, an accessory to the murder, had been hanged.

"These men made their escape from San Quentin nearly three years ago. It was not a tunnel scheme or anything of that kind, it was just a sneak. Dorsey had the reputation, deservedly, of being a bad man, the worst man of all the 1,200 in that prison; but Shinn, having served about half his time and by good conduct having acquired the confidence of the officials, was granted all the privileges of a trusty. The day of the escape was very stormy. Shinn was driving a cart and had to go outside the prison walls but not outside of the line of guards. It was a duty to which he was habitually assigned. On account of the rain and storm, it was necessary to cover the wagon with a tarpaulin. By previous arrangement, no doubt, Dorsey crept under the tarpaulin and thus passed out of the gate. Taking advantage of the awful weather, Shinn drove to an obscure corner and there Dorsey and he sneaked off. By and by, the wagon came back and the escape [by rowboat, across San Pablo Bay to the Contra Costa] was discovered."

As for the murderer's sentence, Hume explained, "It transpired on the trial, that Dorsey had been one of Quantrill's men. One man on the jury was an ardent admirer of Quantrill, his men and their deeds, and resolved that Dorsey should not hang. He readily agreed to find Patterson guilty but stoutly stood out for Dorsey's life. One by one, he brought the other eleven over for, otherwise, he threatened to 'hang' the jury by voting to acquit both men. So Dorsey got a life sentence. He is and was a bad man. Twenty-five years ago I sent him to the penitentiary and he had served two terms for stage robbing before he killed Cummings. . . . Shinn was a train wrecker. He and others wrecked a train at Cape Horn Mills, Placer County, California, Aug. 31, 1881. His object was robbery. They became panic-stricken and stampeded without even attempting to take advantage of their crime."

Hume explained how he had traced Thorne and Shinn to the Windy City: "There have been a lot of stage robberies and, each time, I would hear of two men who answered perfectly to Shinn and Dorsey [Thorne]. But we could never find them. I theorized that they were making Chicago their headquarters, and that their plan was to make a couple of robberies and then get back to this city and, with their women, keep quiet for a while, then have a good time and then go off on another stage robbing expedition. About two weeks ago I knew that my men were here. I have been very cautious all that time, for they both knew me well. They have reason for remembrance; I sent both to prison. So I enlisted the services of Billy Pinkerton. I employed the best men he had. He was very courteous, I wish to say. I engineered the campaign and today I swore out the warrants. At 4:30 o'clock we nabbed one of them on Jackson Street in a rear house where we had him located and, an hour later, Dorsey was arrested on Cooper Street. There was nothing exciting in the whole thing. It is a simple, everyday, arrest. Tomorrow they go before a magistrate and, in a week, I expect to have them over the road."

Here Hume paused, to reminisce a moment: "The exciting days were those twenty-five years ago in El Dorado County.

Those were the days when that county cast a bigger vote than the city and county of San Francisco. When I left the Sheriff's office there I left a scaffold on which sixteen men were hung, not all at once but two at a time, occasionally. Those were exciting days, sure enough."

Hume helped escort the two criminals to San Quentin, then had Shinn transferred to Folsom, away from the more intelligent and dangerous Thorne. He questioned Shinn and got him to confess that he and his partner had returned to California from Chicago and pulled off many robberies, including three of the puzzling rash of belated stage holdups that had taken so much of Hume's attention. They had a hideout in the brush near Perkins, on the American River levee four miles from Sacramento, to which they retreated between crimes. Shinn's confession wrapped up a case on which Hume had been working steadily for three years.

Four years later, in April, 1894, Hume was in Chicago on the Harding case, which the Adams Express Company wanted to hush up to avoid embarrassment. Hume was sure that their employee, Harding, would be convicted *if* ever brought to trial. The Adams Express Company was more interested in a civil than a criminal trial or, at least, in recovering some of its loss. Win, lose, or draw, Hume had to inform Wells, Fargo President Valentine of the good work of his aide—"Captain Dodge has done terrible good work in this case and is highly commended by the attorneys and the Adams people, and the handling of the case will virtually be in his hands up to the time of trial." By May 2 Hume had cleared up a Buffalo, New York, case of office theft and was writing home, "I *know* I am right in this opinion notwithstanding the thief denies the accusation. He has just been bounced and will not toy long with the treasure of Wells, Fargo & Co."

July proved to be an even more trying month than May for Jim Hume as the papers got wind of a story, which they ran on the eighth, claiming that the Wells, Fargo messenger between Sacramento and Redding, named Paul Hume, who had absconded with a package containing $3,500, was Jim's nephew. The Company was mum, but the press quoted a Sacramento policeman as saying that young Hume was heading East. "He said he was in trouble and intimated that a woman in Redding was responsible for his downfall." Wisely, Jim Hume made no comment, and the press was unable to make a running feature of the incident as it had done when Hume had taken anonymous letter writers to task. Paul Hume, it turned out, had gone west, not east. He was picked up in Brisbane, Australia, and returned to San Francisco where he told Wells, Fargo officials and the press that he was twenty-two years old and the son of a well-to-do family in Illinois.

In October Hume arrived in Cleveland one Saturday at 9 A.M., and by 6 P.M. he had solved a theft and obtained a confession; by 4:25 A.M the next day he was on a train to Lima for a visit with his relatives. His brief Indiana vacation was ruined when he had to investigate the theft of $1,350 in the Atchison, Kansas, office of his firm. He was back in California in plenty of time for an affair that came to be called the case of Carl the Tramp. It began on October 11, 1894, when a trackwalker was relieved by bandits of his lantern and track torpedoes near Davisville (now Davis), just west of Sacramento. With the light and the signal cartridges, the outlaws stopped a train, uncoupled the express car, and towed it three miles away with the engine. The general area of the holdup was Sheep Camp. Brandishing Winchesters and pistols, the bandits forced the fireman and engineer to carry the 212-pound safe into the engine. Then they opened the throttle and sped off, leaving the locomotive crew behind. Two miles short of the capital, they stopped, took off the loot, reversed the engine, and sent it chugging back westward until it slammed into the stranded train. Meantime, the robbers vanished.

James Hume was assigned the case but had to confess to Lida, on the fourteenth, "We are making no headway in this case and may not for a long time. . . . [But] they ran the engine into

Washington [now Broderick] before reversing her, and I think the money is in that town." The Pacific Coast manager of Wells, Fargo wired Hume authorization to spend as much money as he needed to employ men or to buy information, but still Hume could not solve the puzzle. He kept at it doggedly, and wrote Lida, "We are making no headway yet but are clearing up the thousand and one rumors afloat. I think we will get at the meat in the coconut after awhile" and "Another day passed and no clew obtained. Simply been exploding clews and the air is full of them." On October 22, still without a promising lead, Hume was not giving up. He wrote his wife, "For two miles between the scene of the robbery and Sacramento there is a strip of water on each side of the tracks where the dirt was taken to build the roadbed. It is not unlikely that the villains tost [sic] their Winchesters from the engine into this water. Tomorrow morning at 7 I will go out with four men to search this whole stretch of water for the guns. If found, they may furnish a clew. 'T'will take all day to make the search."

If he was making no headway in the Sheep Camp or Davisville robbery, at least the mystery of the Roscoe holdup near Los Angeles was being cleared up. Two suspects, Thompson and Johnson, had been pinpointed and the latter placed under arrest. Since two innocent men had died in the holdup, Hume urged the Wells, Fargo assistant superintendent in Los Angeles to press the district attorney to call into session a special grand jury to take testimony. Johnson could not be held long without a preliminary examination, but if he were brought before a grand jury, both he and the absent Thompson could be included in the same indictment and put on ice. "It was an atrocious, wilful, murder," Hume reminded his colleague, "and I think the citizens and taxpayers of Los Angeles will not object to a little expense to bring the assassins to justice. They should receive the proper penalty for their crimes, not only that they should be properly punished but as a warning to other men engaged in like enterprises."

Hume was not really discouraged by his lack of progress in the Davisville case and he wrote Lida from Sacramento, "It was the nicest job that I have ever known in that kind of business in America and we are of the opinion that the parties guilty are almost within the sound of our voice now. This, however, is for your own information and not for the public. . . . We'll have to wait for the robbers to furnish testimony by the use of money, or departure from this region." Detective Thacker was convinced that the two Duncan brothers had pulled off the job, but Hume had already investigated them and given them a clean bill of health. At this point the Wells, Fargo detective was nettled by the receipt of a clumsily lettered postcard, designed to annoy him in the same fashion as the anonymous letters to the editor that had criticized his prowess as an investigator. It was sent, supposedly, from the Quimby House, in Portland, Oregon, and addressed to "Mr. Detective Hume." It read: "Dear Billy: It's awful the way youse fellows don't katch those awful Davisville train robbers. Whatever are you fellows a'doin', anyway? I'm tempted 2 think youse ain't doin' anything. What gross derelection of duty you are guilty of. You should be bounced. Is it true, as the *Argus* says, that you never catch a train robber? Yea, it would seem so. Why don't you rake the tule lands? Bestir yourselves!" It was signed "Fly-by-Night."

Hume *was* bestirring himself. He had company President Valentine get out a confidential letter to bankers, to put them on the lookout for the gold the robbers had taken, which they would surely try to convert to more easily carried currency. Valentine passed Hume's ideas on to the bankers: "We believe that the money was secreted in Washington near where the engine was stopped. . . . We think it probable that the men who secured the treasure will take such quantities of it, from time to time, as they are able to carry without arousing suspicion and endeavor to exchange it for currency or certificates of deposit." Hume's next move, in March, was to recommend to Valentine either that guards be added to the eastbound express trains or that treasure, at least, be shipped on the morning train out of San Francisco so that it would get all the way to Elko, Nevada, during daylight.

The break in the case was long in coming, for not until July, 1895, was robber Jack Brady caught under a bridge 17 miles from Sacramento. He confessed to Thacker, and Hume wrote Lida, "I am pretty well satisfied that Browning and Brady did the Sheep Camp job." Hume now had all the pieces—seemingly. Brady and Samuel Browning had stopped the train, taken the money, and hidden it in the tules near the Sacramento River. But when Brady guided Thacker and other officers to the site of the cached bags of coin and paper money, he could not find them. Hume wrote to Lida, "He was taken out to the region where he thinks he buried the money but failed to fix the place. He says he has been there looking for it [before]. . . . Thacker, with 6 or 7 men, has been hunting for the money all day without success. They found places where Brady says he has been digging for it. . . . A dozen men will resume the search tomorrow. The locality to be guarded tonight."

The next day, July 23, 1895, Thacker widened the area of search and turned up, instead of moneybags, rusty tin cans filled with coins! These tins yielded about $8,000. But where was the rest? It was obvious that the puzzled Brady was telling the truth; he had not dug it up. Hume was sure that someone had hijacked the hoard, taking as much of the original $52,000 as he could carry off. He played a hunch—that the hijacker had been a hobo—and had agents question the bums in all the jungles along the river and railroad right-of-way. His first clue came to him not from some railroad embankment or levee but the Sacramento jail. A bindle stiff there reported the sudden disappearance of a hobo friend, known only as Carl. The next break for Hume came on February 7, 1896, when a man came to his office in San Francisco to tell him that a pal of his had met a rich fellow named Carl Herman at the racetrack. When drunk, Herman had mumbled something about digging up a lot of money near Sacramento. The stranger told Hume, "I remembered reading once about a train robbery that I think you were interested in and I just got to wondering. . . ." At a Howard Street saloon Hume persuaded the immaculately dressed Mr. Herman to accompany him to his office. There the gentleman with the diamond pin in his tie broke down and confessed that he was John Harmens and that he had been a hobo, camping near the Sacramento River one night, when he heard men burying something nearby. He had dug up the money and had reburied in tin cans, at another spot, what he could not cram into his blanket roll. He had hopped a freight to San Francisco and had landed on skid row, but by buying fine clothes and throwing money around as if it were going out of fashion, he had raised his status to that of gentleman. He told his new friends that he had inherited $50,000 from an uncle in Germany. He had gone through his wealth at a good clip, and when he showed Hume his bankbook, he had a balance of only a little more than $2,-000. There had also been a woman, May de Vaughn. Harmens was given three years in Folsom for stealing money from the robbers. His final words to the court showed how little guilt he felt: "I lived like a prince. The only thing I regret is that they didn't leave me alone long enough to spend it all."

In the 1890's Hume had to let his schedule of activity taper off. He deferred to Thacker and Dodge and a new man, John White. But he personally investigated a stage robbery at lonely Havilah in the rugged Tehachapi Mountains north of Los Angeles and commented to Lida that it was a wonder stages had not been robbed there before. "Havilah is 26 miles from Caliente and only one resident on the road. To send money over it is like throwing it away." He sympathized with Thacker in 1896, when the latter was embarrassed by a case like the Paul Hume affair of 1894. On September 20 Sonora's Wells, Fargo agent, George L. Banks, son of a shotgun messenger, and Thacker's nephew, disappeared. When it was learned that he had sailed for the Orient, the story broke. According to the *Chronicle,* Banks had been "living a fast life in Sonora during the past eighteen months, spending a great deal of money and associating with women of uncertain reputation." He was accused of neglecting his wife and child and of giving his wife a severe beating before they separated. His accounts were found to be short, though by

297

only $1,500. Banks was eventually arrested in Portland, Oregon. Again, Hume kept his mouth shut to avoid further embarrassment for Thacker.

In the spring of 1897 Hume, suffering severe pains in one shoulder, his neck, and behind his left ear, was laid up in the Yosemite Hotel in Stockton, after a painracked train ride, on which he was accompanied by his twelve-year-old son, Sam. Neither the belladonna prescribed by a doctor nor the pain-killers Sam dosed him with relieved the excruciating stabs of pain, and Hume, desperate, grabbed at folk medicine, sending Sam out for garlic when a friend said it was supposed to cure pain. The youngster wrote his mother, "Jim ate some and now he perfumes the whole room. Dr. Clarke said it would not hurt him, if it did no good." However, as Hume realized, rest seemed to be the best answer to his attack. In his letter of April 26 to Lida—dictated to Sam—he noted, "I believe that absolute quiet is the best remedy for my trouble. . . . I have had no pain in my neck since Saturday afternoon. I am eating garlic pretty freely and that may be helping me." Sam was a splendid nurse; patient and attentive, he not only read the newspapers to his father and wrote his letters, but was up several times a night, checking on Jim's comfort.

In May Jim was moved to the spa of Paso Robles, south of San Francisco. Practically an invalid when he arrived, he rested, took the baths and waters, and was soon off his "little pills" (pain-killers) and playing spirited games of six-handed euchre and whist, the latter with a "German woman with horrible teeth." Walking no longer caused him pain, and he wrote his wife, "I am improving a little every day, I think. I am sick of the place. It is so dull and lonesome. Don't fail to write *every* day. I don't know how I could endure the days if it were not for the certainty of hearing from you." Dr. T. L. Flood of Meadville, Pennsylvania, editor of the *Chautauqua,* was also staying at the spa and tried to get Hume to write an article for his magazine, but the detective was not up to it. However, he did try to keep posted on Wells, Fargo cases even while in the sanitarium.

Officers wrote him to let him know where Thacker was working. Hume recovered his health and returned to his new office, Room 3 of the Wells, Fargo building, during June, 1897. Although he did not have the strength that characterized his most active years, he got back in harness and was in Chicago in November and in Denver in December. Happily, the hours of lurching along in railroad coaches no longer troubled him, and he took time to visit his kin in Indiana in the summers of both 1897 and 1898. He still held the position of chief special officer, and when the messenger on Train No. 2, held up at Grants, New Mexico, in November, 1897, filed his report, it was forwarded to Hume from the Southwest Division so that he might organize the investigation.

As late as 1901 Hume was still making some road trips, but they tended to be shorter than before—to Sacramento and Auburn, rather than to Tucson or to Chicago. Discharged felons still made a beeline from San Quentin's gate to his office, and he still received letters from old cons who were "inside." They remembered him as a square shooter and sought his help in various matters. One such felon was William Smith, who protested having been tried twice for the same crime—holding up that much-abused Sonora to Milton stage. "All those who know about my case are mostly all dead now, except you, Mr. Hume and Mr. Thorn, and therefore, I beg you to be so kind [as] to use your good influence with the U.S. District Attorney and the Judge to pardon or commit [commute] my sentence." Hume always said, laughingly, that nowhere was his personal standing higher than among the residents of San Quentin and Folsom.

Hume had slowed down so markedly by 1903 that although he kept his title as chief special officer, Thacker had virtually replaced him and John J. White had succeeded Thacker as chief assistant. But from his home, at the age of seventy-six, Hume was working on the case of an absconding Wells, Fargo agent of Conejo, California. After six months of steadily failing health, James B. Hume died on May 18, 1904, at the age of seventy-seven, at his 3017 Wheeler Street home in Berkeley's Peralta area—"the only spot on earth that has any attraction for me," he had written Lida from Chicago, a dozen years earlier. After services at the First Presbyterian Church, his body was taken to the Oakland Crematory. Even in his sickbed, to which he was confined for the last month of his life, Jim Hume kept busy, compiling his memoirs (never completed) and giving advice to the younger men who were now playing his old role as Wells, Fargo detective. These officers told newspaper reporters that they had been able to lay the Copley train robbery at the foot of the Gates boys, George and Edwin Vernon and James Arnett, only because of Hume's suggestions.

The San Francisco *Chronicle* obituary of May 20, 1904, paid tribute to James Hume's doggedness as a detective: "This country has produced few men who have made such a remarkable record in the persistent and successful pursuit of that class of robbers who prey specially on the express and transportation companies. . . . He was instrumental in running down some of the worst criminals the country ever produced. It has been the policy of the express company never to abandon or relax the pursuit of anyone who has committed a criminal offense against it. In some instances, the pursuit has extended over a series of years and been carried abroad to remote countries. The policy has proved to be a wise one, for it has acted as a deterrent as well as a punishment of crime. . . . Whenever Hume started on the trail of an offender against the corporation in whose service he was employed, the pursuit was never given up until his capture was effected. For more than a generation his name has been a terror to stage and train robbers. They learned to know him as a keen, intelligent, officer who was as untiring and relentless as the United States Government in following and punishing offenders."

300

SOURCES

There have been no prior biographies of James B. Hume and there are few books or parts of books in existence that were of any real help to me in researching and narrating the events of Hume's life. Various books about the gold rush and the Mother Lode counties of California were helpful in providing background for Hume's life as a miner and law officer in the Sierra foothills during the 1850's and 1860's. The best of these include the rather rare work by Paolo Sioli, *Historical Souvenir of El Dorado County* (1883) and Charles E. Upton's *Pioneers of El Dorado* (1906).

Again, there are no books—and, in fact, surprisingly few existing documents or even newspaper stories—that cover either the embarrassing jailbreak of 1871 from the Nevada State Prison or Hume's subsequent role as assistant warden in restoring morale and security to the institution.

For information on stagecoach holdups, the best general work is Joseph Henry Jackson's *Bad Company* (1949). Also useful and interesting are Eugene B. Block's *Great Stagecoach Robbers in the West* (1962), Neill C. Wilson's *Treasure Express* (1936) and Ralph Moody's *Stagecoach West* (1967). I found Edward Hungerford's *Wells, Fargo: Advancing the American Frontier* (1949) inferior to Lucius Beebe and Charles Clegg's *U.S. West: The Saga of Wells, Fargo* (1949).

301

Readers desiring more detail on the robberies of Wells, Fargo railroad express cars would do well to read Eugene B. Block's *Great Train Robberies of the West* (1959), C. B. Glasscock's *Bandits of the Southern Pacific* (1929), Wallace Smith's *Prodigal Sons* (1951), and Neill C. Wilson and Frank J. Taylor's *Southern Pacific* (1952). Two trusty old friends of anyone seriously studying the long history of crime in the American West are Thomas S. Duke's *Celebrated Criminal Cases of America* (1910), and Pete Fanning's *Great Crimes of the West* (1929).

This biography, however, was written almost entirely from primary sources, including California and Nevada newspapers of James Hume's day in Allan Ottley's California Section, State Library, Sacramento; the Bancroft Library, University of California, Berkeley; and the Henry E. Huntington Library, San Marino, California. In the latter, too, are runs of express trade journals and the excellent 2,000-piece Hosmer B. Parsons Collection of Wells, Fargo manuscripts, documents, etc. The journals proved useful to this study; the collection happened to throw little useful light on the subject of this biography but is recommended to future researchers and writers of Wells, Fargoana.

Overwhelmingly, *the* source for virtually all information in this biography was Irene Simpson's History Room, Wells, Fargo Bank, San Francisco—chiefly James B. Hume's own letters and telegrams (by the hundreds) and his voluminous scrapbooks of newspaper clippings and photographs.

Other institutions which provided valuable documents of one kind or another include: the aforementioned California State Library, Bancroft Library, and Huntington Library; National Archives; California State Archives; Jefferson County (New York) Historical Society; the Illinois State Historical Society; the Arizona Pioneers Historical Society; Nevada State Archives; Nevada Historical Society; California Historical Society; Nevada State Library; Indiana Historical Society; Lagrange County (Indiana) Recorder's Office; Delaware County (New York) Historian's Office; New York Historical Society; Indiana State Library; University of the State of New York; and the Southwest Museum, Los Angeles.

INDEX

319